BRITAIN BETRAYED!
SLASH AND BURN

DELUSIONAL

DYSFUNCTIONAL

DISHONEST

DEGENERATE

SUE WOOD

THE CONSERVATIVE GOVERNMENT 2022-2023

I dedicate this book in loving memory

to

Ros, Bill, Viv and Regine.

*A senior teacher, an NHS consultant, a
headmaster and a barrister.*

My sister, brother, brother-in-law and daughter-in-law.

Your wonderful strong voices reverberate throughout this book.

CONTENTS

CONTENTS

PREFACE

The worst thing that could possibly happen to this country has just happened.

Four weeks ago, on 5th September 2022, just over 80,000 members of the Conservative Party voted for Liz Truss to be Prime Minister. These are not elected politicians and they have absolutely no mandate from the general public. The majority are white, elderly, reasonably well-off and politically to the right of centre.

On page 543 of my book *Behind the Headlines* I wrote about all the contenders for the job of PM and of Liz Truss I write: "mad, bad and dangerous to know. Thinks of herself as the new Margaret Thatcher. She is being supported by Jacob Rees-Mogg and ....wait for it.... Nadine Dorries. 'She is probably a stronger Brexiteer than both of us' says Nadine."

Nothing I have observed over the previous four weeks has caused me to change my mind. However I had decided not to write a third book because unlike Boris, who still, believe it or not, has his admirers, the incompetence, ideology, prejudice, and the fact that Liz Truss is so completely out of her depth, is plain for all to see.

But then I read an article by Pippa Crerar the Political editor of *The Guardian* about a free-market think tank called 'Free Market Forum' which is an offshoot of the IEA (Institute of Economic Affairs) which has close links to Liz Truss and her Chancellor Kwasi Kwarteng. It makes me so angry that I have to write about it.

I think that you need to know about it, and it accounts for the subtitle of this book.

Here are some of its 'slash and burn' suggestions. They recommend the scrapping of free childcare hours, the releasing of green belt land for housing, abolishing corporation tax, and dropping teacher training qualifications for graduates who want to teach.

I promise you it gets worse. They also suggest that there should be remote learning so parents can pick and choose the best teachers (what? how?) and they want to amend the Equalities Act so that white working-class boys are better protected (racist and sexist).

But they are not finished yet. They think it would be a good idea to restore the link between tax and household income so that a married woman's income could be seen as part of her husband's (misogynistic and illegal). As someone said "I'll divorce my husband first".

There is a lot of detail about these ideas in this article but I will just pick out the two which were the decisive factor in my starting this book.

Annabel Denham argued that the 15 hours a week free childcare costs the state around £6 billion a year but "there isn't much to show for it" and adult-to-child ratios are "unnecessary and damaging" and, she says, that early years assessments should be dropped.

How ignorant.

The early years are by far the most important in a child's development.

And Cabinet Officer Brendan Clarke-Smith, when talking about the tax system and married women, says, "Of course attitudes towards women's careers have changed...."

You bet they have mate. I have never heard such retrograde ideas in my life. I hope that by now you are as angry as I am.

This is why I have to turn this into a trilogy. There is already talk amongst Conservative MPs about how to oust Liz Truss. And if there were a general election today Labour would win 498 seats - a gain of 296. The Tories, meanwhile, would slide to just 61 seats, giving Labour a majority of 346 and virtually wiping out the Conservatives.

So, come on everyone, let the fireworks begin.

****

JUST FOUR WEEKS

On the 5th September 2022 Liz Truss became Prime Minister. Did I give her 6 months?

Today, **8th October**, Conservative ministers are saying she will be out by Christmas. These last four weeks have been chaotic.

On Tuesday **6th September** Boris Johnson went to Balmoral to tender his resignation with Her Majesty the Queen. Liz Truss also went to Balmoral to accept the invitation from the Queen to form a government.

In her first PMQs the following day she promised to tackle energy costs and said that "What we need to do is increase our energy supplies long term." She went on to say "That is why we will open up more supply in the North Sea... that is why we will build more nuclear power stations... that is why we will get on with delivering the supply as well as helping people through the winter."

She also appointed her new cabinet. I think people were hoping that she would reach out to all sections of the party. But no. She appointed only those who had supported her bid for the leadership.

Her good friend and ally Kwasi Kwarteng is her Chancellor. Not too sure about him.

Therese Coffey is the new Health Secretary. I **am** sure about her. I think she will be completely inadequate.

Suella Braverman is the new Home Secretary. I cannot begin to tell you how shocked and frightened this woman makes me feel.

Jacob Rees-Mogg our previous Brexit opportunity minister is now the Business secretary. He never found any Brexit opportunities.

Nadhim Zahawi is the new Equalities Minister. He was education secretary, then chancellor and now this, all in the space of a few months.

There are others of course who will no doubt come up for discussion as we progress but that is enough for now to let you see the general calibre of the new cabinet. Believe me it is not looking good.

Then on Thursday 8th September we hear that, at the age of 96, the Queen has died and the whole country goes into official mourning, which of course meant that Parliament isn't sitting and we all came to terms with the fact that we had a new Prime Minister and a new Monarch.

****

But we then go into the Conference Season so parliament continues to be in recess. The Lib Dems abandon their conference completely due to the Queen's funeral on the **19th September** but just before the Labour Party Conference we get a 'fiscal event' from the Chancellor on **Friday 23rd September.**

He doesn't call it a budget because he would then have had to ask for, and publish, a forecast from the 'Office of Budget Responsibility' and it is their duty to examine and report on the sustainability of the public finances.

Now why was this do you think?

Could it have something to do with the fact that following this announcement the value of the pound plummeted and interest rates spiked so causing complete economic chaos?

But the Chancellor was very up-beat about it all and he said that "we won't apologise" for focusing on economic growth. This statement will provide the "biggest package in generations" of tax cuts to send a clear signal that economic growth is the government's priority.

He also says next year's increase in corporation tax from 19% to 25% will be cancelled. It will remain at 19%. "We will have the lowest rate of corporation tax in the G20."

The basic rate of income tax will be reduced by 1p to 19p.

We hear that things only calmed down a bit after the Bank of England made £65 billion available to bail out the pensions industry.

By contrast, the cost of government borrowing in America and the EU remained relatively flat while Britain's financial markets went into meltdown.

Well if all of that had been forecast I don't think the Chancellor would have gone ahead with it. Would he?

There is a huge backlash over the bit that reduces tax for billionaires. The top rate of tax which is 45p in the pound has been reduced to 40p in the pound. At the same time mortgage rates for homeowners go up, with the average cost of a two-year fixed rate deal reaching 6% for the first time since 2008. **So many first-time buyers who were just getting onto the property ladder had their mortgages snatched away from them**. It is heart-breaking.

Defending the top rate reduction Liz Truss, in a television interview, says she will not back down on this in spite of the criticism. She wants to make Britain a country where people will want to come to invest. Sorry Liz, I'm no economist but I really don't think this is the right way to go about it. She also says that she doesn't mind being unpopular. Well that is very lucky because the very next day she says "actually I have listened. I get it. The Chancellor (whose idea it was!) will reverse this decision."

So this is an absolute gift to the Labour Party who are already gathering in Manchester for their conference! **The first U–turn after only 19 days!**

****

The Labour Conference runs from the 25th to the 28th September and is followed by the Conservative Conference which runs from the 2nd to the 5th of October and is in Birmingham.

What a contrast. Just three years ago Labour had their worst defeat in a general election in 84 years. As well as losing 59 seats, the second-highest loss by any opposition for a century, the party lost votes in every part of the country, with the most significant swings being in north-east England, the West Midlands, Yorkshire and Humberside and the east Midlands. It was catastrophic. At that time the Labour party was extremely left-wing with Jeremy Corbyn as the leader.

Today, under the leadership of Sir Keir Starmer they are a government in waiting. If there were a general election today the polls give the Labour party an outright majority and the Tories would suffer a complete wipe-out in Scotland.

Their conference, which began with the singing of the National Anthem, was dignified, united and serious. Their policies were well thought-out, costed and a welcome relief.

****

The Conservative conference on the other hand was chaotic and divisive and will have done nothing to allay their fears and concern regarding their new leader.

It didn't start well when the Chairman of the Young Conservatives said that **"Birmingham is a dump."** But during the conference ministers did not exactly help her cause.

Truss plans to increase benefits in line with earnings rather than inflation. This would mean breaking a manifesto promise made by Johnson, and the following ministers are already breaking rank. It has been described by **Michael Gove** as wrong and difficult to justify. It would actually push 200,000 more children into poverty.

So **Suella Braverman** accuses Gove of organising a coup against Liz Truss!

Jacob Rees-Mogg criticises Gove as well and calls him "a bit wet" for only doing 9 fringe events when he used to do "13 or something."

And **Penny Mordaunt** also spoke up saying that benefits should be in line with inflation.

Then **Nadine Dorries** criticises the PM for lurching strongly to the right and ditching all her hard work on the online safety bill.

And **Rishi Sunak, Sajid Javid, David Davis and Mel Stride** all boycotted the conference altogether.

Many of these were her supporters! Not looking good.

The conference ended with Truss's speech which they were all hoping would try to unite the party. Halfway through it was interrupted by Greenpeace supporters. This is not surprising as Truss and her colleagues plan to re-introduce fracking, give licenses to companies for North Sea drilling for oil and gas and they are reneging on climate change targets and on environmental protections.

She then gives us her three word slogan which appears to be mandatory for Tory prime ministers. Here it is: "Growth, Growth, Growth". It sounds completely vacuous to me but I am presuming that means growth for the economy. However I do not know how the economy can grow when we have strikes, strikes, strikes. We hear that the ballots for doctors and nurses strikes are going ahead, midwives are also balloting, as is the London ambulance service. Barristers, train drivers and workers are still on strike and the docks at Felixstowe are still feeling the impact of the 8 day strike which ended 5 days ago.

Truss then started talking about the **"Anti-growth coalition"**.

What on earth is that?

Well we soon found out. She gave us a list of all those she accuses of being anti-growth and they include:

- Labour
- Lib Dems
- SNP
- Unions
- Vested interests dressed up as think tanks
- Talking heads
- Brexit "deniers"
- Extinction Rebellion

And also people who "prefer protesting to doing", as they "taxi from north London townhouses to the BBC studios to dismiss anyone challenging the status quo". Oh dear, poor North London is a favourite bashing ground for unhappy Tories.

Well I think that is most of us actually and I object to being put into a non-existent group by an incompetent and ignorant Prime Minister.

But yes I am anti-growth when it comes to some instances.

I am anti the growing NHS waiting list, the growing backlog of crown court cases, the growing number of teachers and teaching assistants resigning, the growing number of hungry children in our schools, the growing number of people being pushed into poverty, the growing number of collapsing businesses due to Brexit, the growing number of children's nurseries closing due to lack of funding, and the growing number of women who are forced to give up work because of unaffordable childcare.

Some are saying it was the worst conference they have ever attended and polls state that Truss has the lowest rating of any Prime Minister ever. That includes Johnson and May at their lowest which is a really low bar.

****

So I think everyone agrees that the first 4 weeks of a new Prime Minister has been disastrous. But just wait until they read the Sunday papers.

****

WHAT THE PAPERS SAY

Well today we read in the papers that even Tory backbenches are saying Liz Truss will be gone by Christmas.

Where to start?

Well let's start with **Grant Shapps**. In an article in *The Sunday Times* by Tim Shipman Chief Political Commentator, we read that Shapps has bought a new phone called the Samsun Galaxy Fold. Apparently he was very excited by this phone and was showing it to colleagues at the Conference.

Stay with me here.

It opens up to create a double sized screen on to which he can put a spreadsheet where he is recording the views of Tory MPs about Truss and her plans and it is not looking good for the PM! He is already being touted as a caretaker Prime Minister for goodness sake. He criticises the way Truss is creating enemies and says that she has alienated a group called the G-group which consists of about 20 right wing Conservatives. There are so many groups within the Conservative party it is really hard to keep up. But she sacked Peter Bone who is a member of this group. Peter Bone was made deputy leader of the Commons by Johnson, he voted for Truss, and he joined her transition team. She hasn't reached out to anyone who did not support her in her bid for the leadership which is extremely stupid, but to sack those who did support her is incomprehensible.

****

Then we read in *The Observer* in an article by Helena Horton, Toby Helm and Michel Savage that senior party figures such as William Hague have joined forces with the National Trust, the RSPB, the Angling Trust, and Wildlife Trust in criticising what they see as environmental vandalism. Wow, that is some partnership. Apparently these nature charities were also on Truss's anti-growth list. George Eustace is angry at the way his former policies are being dismantled. These groups are now mobilising their members against Conservative policies. And believe me, they have millions of members.

The Truss government has also prompted anger from farmers by deciding to review the Environment Land Management Scheme.

Then of course they are planning further cuts to public services. But in *The Observer* today Andrew Rawnsley quotes a senior Tory on the right of his party who says **"There are not many bleeding stumps left to cut off. I'm not going to vote for a cut to universal credit, I'm not going to vote for a cut to the NHS, I'm not going to vote for a cut to education, I'm not going to vote for a cut to defence."**

****

Rees-Mogg is having an argument with Truss about the energy crisis. He has put together a £15 million report which will advise people what to do in order to save energy costs and to prepare for blackouts this winter. However Truss says don't be ridiculous, or words to that effect, we are not a nanny state, people can work out what to do for themselves. Well of course some people can but Mogg is not happy and people are saying that actually offering advice is the minimum the government should be doing. People expect leadership from ministers and if that is not forth-coming then it implies that the government is not really taking the issue seriously.

****

And the Chancellor, Kwasi Kwarteng is in trouble. The head of the civil service is facing calls to order an investigation into whether

he breached the ministerial code when he attended a champagne reception with hedge fund managers on the evening of his mini-budget.

Well whether he did or whether he didn't, to my mind he breached the moral code. To go off to sip champagne having just caused hundreds of first time buyers to have their mortgages snatched away, is the epitome of arrogant elitism to me. It is despicable.

****

But not quite as despicable as this. We have to mention Suella Braverman. She gave an interview to *The Express* and was asked about immigration. She replied by saying, **"I would love to have a front page of *The Telegraph* with a plane taking off to Rwanda. That's my dream, it's my obsession."** As she said this she waved her arm in the air to imply an aeroplane taking off.

We all thought Priti Patel was inhumane but Braverman takes inhumanity to a whole new level. Are there going to be Ukrainian refugees on this imaginary flight of hers? No I don't think so. So this remark is inflammatory, racist, inhumane, and, as she well knows, would be illegal.

****

But it is hardly surprising that a headline in *The Times* is saying "Truss turns on the charm". I don't think so. Far be it for me to challenge a *Times* headline, but I think it should read "Truss begins to panic."

But actually the best headline is, as we would expect, is from Andrew Rawnsley when he writes: **"Johnson was slow-poisoning arsenic for the Conservatives. Liz Truss is instant cyanide."**

Tomorrow they all return to Westminster.

What could possibly go wrong?

PARLIAMENT RECONVENES

Well I have three items to write about before I have breakfast. It is rather disheartening as they are all things I have mentioned in my previous books. Disheartening, but as you will have heard me say in my other books over and over again, not surprising.

11TH OCTOBER

Do you remember the **Festival of Brexit**? No? Well it cost £120 million of tax payers' money so it is important that you know what has happened to it all.

It was first suggested by Theresa May in 2018 as she had the idea of a carnival of "British creativity and innovation, culture and heritage" that would echo the Festival of Britain in 1951 and the Great Exhibition of 1851. This one was going to celebrate Britain's departure from the EU. Hmmm, that gives us a bit of a clue.

Well after Jacob Rees-Mogg had tried to publicise it they decided to depoliticise it and renamed it "Unboxed: Creativity in the UK". Heard of it yet? Well I wrote about it all in *Behind the Headlines* and I am not at all surprised that it is back in the news.

This morning, we hear that it is being investigated by the National Audit Office because MPs are alarmed by its "exorbitant" costs. It was supposed to have entertained 66 million people this year but by the end of August only 238,000 had attended events. I'm surprised it was that many actually. The Audit Office has said that the money has been "frittered away".

What a ridiculous idea to try to celebrate the most controversial and politically damaging decision ever, with a festival that has hardly registered with the public. I am delighted to hear that it is under proper investigation now.

****

Then on the radio this morning we hear Jamie Oliver. I cannot tell you how upset I am that the issue of free meals to children in school in England is still not resolved. I first wrote about this on June 15th 2020 in *Beneath the Bluster.*

Jamie Oliver was speaking in his usual impassioned and articulate way and saying that all children in households on universal credit should be given free school meals. Wales, Scotland and N. Ireland are all planning to extend free meals in schools and as Oliver said, England is by far the meanest. Currently any family which has earnings from work of more than £7,400 a year is ineligible, and not all recipients of universal credit can get free meals.

We hear of children in tears, misbehaving, and stealing food at school because they are hungry. I find it heart-breaking.

And then Therese Coffey comes on air and my mood turns to anger.

Her answer to nearly every question is "I can't answer that", "I am unware of that", "oh that was a long time ago", and again "I am unaware of that".

She is the Deputy Prime Minister for goodness sake and when pushed further and asked to just say in principle what she believed she said, "This is the joy of being in government that we work together as a team, it's not a case of having all sorts of individual personal views." She declined to endorse a call from Jamie Oliver to increase the number of children eligible for free school meals. She has no principles.

On other issues Jamie Oliver criticises the fact that she is not going to scrap the 'buy one get one free' principle which Oliver was saying is essential to the nations' health. When short of money people will go for this sort of offer which is nearly always on junk food.

Then I hear that she has refused to support a new smoking reduction plan for England saying it is not something she is focused on. Again she said she was not "aware" of the plan.

And just listen to this. **In the past she has actually voted against anti-smoking measures.** These included the ban on smoking in enclosed spaces, the outlawing of smoking in cars carrying children and forcing manufacturers to sell cigarettes in plain packages.

Then she is asked about the fact that nurses are balloting for strike action. Is she concerned about this? Well the answer is no, not in the slightest. Daniel Keane of *The Evening Standard* reports that Coffey said, "The Government has intervened in a number of different ways to help with the cost of living. There was already a package focused on helping people on low incomes and we've enhanced it with the energy price guarantee. I feel we have acted, and NHS staff have already been offered an annual pay rise of £1,400. We have accepted the recommendation of the pay review body."

Yes she knows nurses are leaving but that is their choice she says and there are open routes for nurses to come into this country.

24% of nurses left the profession last year alone. It is morally reprehensible that we expect our hospitals to poach medical staff from other countries who are in need of those trained medical staff. We choose not to train up enough doctors and we choose not to pay nurses a sustainable salary.

This is the woman who is in charge of the NHS.

I think I have run out of words.

****

Well actually I have discovered a few more words which is just as well as I am trying to write a book. And this is extremely concerning.

Simon Clarke, the levelling-up secretary, has written to Liz Truss with proposals designed to boost house-building and drive economic growth and yes, I think you should be worried.

There are plans to exempt developers from having to build affordable homes, to scrap environmental protections, and to allow people to add extensions without permission. Also ministers are discussing shelving legislation drawn up by Michael Gove's predecessor to ban no-fault evictions. It will certainly be delayed as it is not a priority by the new administration.

Simon Clarke is determined to end a moratorium designed to protect the health and bio-diversity of wetlands, by allowing the construction of 100,000 homes in parts of Norfolk, Hampshire, Devon and the northeast.

I said you should be worried.

But wait, I see Therese Coffey's name again. When asked about these plans she said ....wait for it............ "I am not aware of these plans." What? *The Times* is aware of them, I am aware of them, where are you? She should be sacked.

****

We are now hearing of one or two (and maybe more) disagreements between Truss and her colleagues.

We will start with Suella Braverman. A trade deal is being negotiated with India at the moment and will be one of the flagships of Global Britain. She hopes to have it finalised by 24th October although this is apparently a bit optimistic. Anyway Truss would like the Home Office to issue more visas to Indians so they are able to come over here to help us out with our shrunken labour force.

Now why is that again? Oh yes, I know, and of course so do you.

Well our new Home Secretary told the *Spectator* magazine that she had concerns about the trade deal. "I do have some reservations," she said. "Look at migration in this country ----- the largest group of people who overstay are Indian migrants."

Wow! That didn't go down well with India and they say that "the relationship has taken a step back." Actually a UK government source who had spoken to Indian officials involved in the trade deal put it a bit more succinctly when he said **"They were apoplectic. Mad doesn't even come close to describing how angry they are."**

Hmm I think the 24th October is looking extremely optimistic.

****

And the Prime Minister had been forced to delay the start of her blitz of pro-growth reforms after failing to agree a deregulation plan with Jacob Rees-Mogg. Planning reforms have also been pushed back. She was also going to be introducing changes to workers' rights but has had to delay that as well. This is because she was unable to agree to the more radical ideas put forward by Rees- Mogg and couldn't find alternative polices that would boost growth.

Then again she is planning to set out plans revealed to *The Times* last week which will have far-reaching curbs on the rights of public sector workers to strike.

And I think you should know this.

The programme of reform announcements had been nicknamed "Operation Rolling Thunder" by some officials. This is a reference to the US bombardment of Vietnam.

But now they just call it "**Operation Shitstorm**".

No ambiguity there then.

****

A few more U-turns.

Kwasi Kwarteng will bring forward the next mini budget or fiscal event from the 23rd November to the 31st October.

Rees-Mogg **WILL** be presenting the nation with advice about energy conservation.

Liz Truss will **NOT** be proceeding with no-fault evictions.

And Liz Truss will **NOT** be cutting public spending.

We heard these last two at PMQs.

I promise you this is just the start.

****

THE SHELF LIFE OF A LETTUCE

So how is the economy?

Well let's start with *The Economist*. They certainly do not mince their words. In their editorial about Liz Truss they called her "the iceberg lady", claiming she has "the shelf-life of a lettuce". They say "she is already a historical figure as however long she remains in power she will be remembered as the prime minister whose grip on power was the shortest in British political history. She blew up her own government with a package of unfunded tax cuts and energy priced guarantees on September 23rd." They go on to say that "Take away the ten days of mourning after the death of the Queen and she had seven days in control. **That is the shelf life of a lettuce.**"

Yes, well we can't argue with that.

****

12TH OCTOBER

It is all looking absolutely disastrous.

The Bank of England warns today, that its emergency intervention in the UK's debt markets will come to an end on Friday. They are telling pension funds that they have three days to prepare for this intervention to end. Many pension funds are big holders of UK government debt and indexed-linked bonds and already face a "cliff edge". This has caused a further slump in the pound.

The International Monetary Fund warned that while tax cuts would boost growth, in the short term it will mean that the UK will face higher inflation for longer.

The Office for National Statistics has just published growth figures. Britain's economy fell by 0.3% between July and August, down from the downwardly revised growth of 0.1 per cent the previous month. Experts had been expecting economic growth to flat-line in August.

And Jacob Rees-Mogg, the business secretary, has launched plans for a cap on revenues of low-carbon electricity generators. This, by any other name, is the same as a temporary windfall tax. **So a U-turn and a borrowing of Labour's plan.**

Kevin Hollinrake, a Tory MP and a member of the Treasury Select Committee, has suggested Kwasi Kwarteng should perform further tax U-turns on his mini-Budget.

He told the BBC: "I think it's better to have looked at this more carefully in the context of what's happened over the last few weeks and say 'I think we've got some of this wrong and these tax cuts need to be introduced over time'.

I think we've got some of this wrong'! For goodness sake, there is absolutely nothing whatsoever that you have got right.

Rachel Reeves, shadow chancellor, says that "Conservative economic policy has caused mayhem with financial markets, pushed up mortgage costs, and pension funds are in peril. **It's wiped out £300 billion from the UK's stock and bond markets. All directly caused by the choices of this government."** She describes ministers as "pyromaniacs" who have set fire to the UK economy. And there was a report in *The Independent* overnight which claimed Downing Street was re-examining the measures unveiled in Kwasi Kwarteng's mini-Budget. No 10 has now denied that is the case.

Then we get some reassuring words from the Health Secretary when she says, "I'm absolutely confident pensions are safe."

Hang on. Wait a minute. That is Therese Coffey. See above.

****

PMQs

Well the good news is that we don't have to listen to the bluff and bluster of Boris Johnson anymore.

The bad news is that we have to try to listen to the robotic delivery of Liz Truss. She speaks as though she is reading an autocue and basically she gave the same reply to every question.

This was "We are making sure that we protect our economy at this very difficult time internationally"

And sometimes "The way that we will get our country growing is through more jobs, more growth, more opportunities."

And occasionally "What our Budget has delivered is security for families for the next two winters. It has made sure that we are going to see higher economic growth, lower inflation and more opportunities."

This was what she said to questions about rising mortgage rates, crumbling hospital ceilings, nurses pay, cost of living and energy bills. When she once started an answer with "I am genuinely unclear..............." she got no further because both sides of the Commons were in uproar.

There were stony faces on the Tory side and several had their heads in their hands. Penny Mordaunt sitting next to her looked grim.

And in answer to the last question she said, "The last thing we need is a General Election,"

Too right mate. You will be annihilated.

****

And Truss goes in to a 1922 committee meeting this evening. There is some desk banging apparently but we think it could be their heads.

The remarks from Tory MPs as they leave are very enlightening.

"It was the worst meeting I have ever been to."

"The mood was funereal"

"There's nothing between the ears."

"An outpouring of despair"

"If the 22 changed the rules we would hit the confidence vote in a couple of hours"

"A febrile atmosphere"

"She's toast"

And Jon Sopel of the BBC said that a former Cabinet Minister said, Liz Truss "has unleashed hell on this country".

Sopel says "the incredulity, the cold fury, is like nothing I've seen in a decade of covering UK politics."

Well I have never heard anything like this before.

We will see what tomorrow brings.

****

13TH OCTOBER

It brings the most fast-moving and catastrophic day of this Conservative government and, as I keep saying, this is from a very low bar.

They start by blaming everyone else but themselves. James Cleverly (our Foreign Secretary) was doing the media rounds this morning and he blamed the Bank of England, the OBR, the IMF, Labour, the war in Ukraine and I think even the death of the Queen was in there somewhere.

He also said very firmly that, "there will be no further mini-budget U-turns" and "changing the leadership would be a disastrously bad idea."

What was that again? Is this really being discussed already, after just over a month in the job?

Well yes it looks as though they are, because later this morning we see this.

A former MP has said that Liz Truss is facing a Tory rebel plot against her as Prime Minister. And *'Conservative Home'* editor Paul Goodman has said some Tory backbenchers are considering pushing for Rishi Sunak or Penny Mordaunt to replace the Prime Minister.

Her approval rating stands at minus 47 with only 16% of voters approving of her in the job as PM.

Goodness, who on earth are they?

Some other comments make interesting reading. James Cleverly states that Liz Truss is doing exactly what she said she was going to do.

Nick Ferrari of LBC says **"I don't recall her saying she is going to tank the economy. I must have been out that day"**.

But then in an interview on Channel 4 the Editor of *The Financial Times* in New York, when asked if she agreed with Rees-Mogg when he said the collapse in the markets had nothing to do with the mini-budget but was the fault of the Bank of England, she replied **"Well to use a non-technical term "That's pretty much bollocks".**

I should add that her eloquence in the rest of the interview was exceptional.

That is just this morning.

****

This afternoon we hear that a BBC political editor was told by a former Cabinet Minister to "Brace for the mother of all U-turns on the mini budget today. A friendly person in the know is advising us to steer clear of the media today to avoid the explosion. We wouldn't want to look silly by tomorrow".

Hmmm, well you are all looking extremely silly already actually, but we have learned never to say it can't get any worse.

****

By the way where is the Chancellor? He is in Washington at a meeting of the IMF. Missed PMQs yesterday but was caught up with today and in an interview he said categorically that there would be no U-turns and he certainly wasn't going anywhere.

Question: "Will you and Liz Truss still be in office next month?"

Answer: "Oh yes."

Hmmm, I don't think he is quite reading the room here.

****

Good news!!

Judicial review.

I have just received an email from the 'Good Law Project' team which says: "We are pleased to announce that the Government has confirmed, in a letter to the Court and the parties involved in our case with 'Friends of the Earth' and 'ClientEarth', that it will not pursue an appeal against the High Court ruling that its Net Zero strategy is unlawful.

In a landmark victory in July, the High Court agreed with us that the Government's strategy failed to show how the UK's legally binding carbon budgets will be met."

Jo Maugham, Director of 'Good Law Project' said: "So the Government has been forced to accept that its flagship climate strategy is unlawful. Another embarrassing climb-down.

Rather than threatening communities with fracking, Liz Truss and Jacob-Rees Mogg should focus their efforts on improving the strategy so they meet the UK's legally-binding climate targets and move away from expensive fossil fuels to deliver on affordable energy.

'Good Law Project' is thrilled to have worked alongside our friends at 'ClientEarth' and 'Friends of the Earth' to deliver this landmark victory."

I mention this in my previous books and it is so rewarding to see it being successfully resolved.

And the judicial review challenge to the Rwanda scheme is set to continue.

****

Wait a minute. **It is 9.30 pm and we have just heard from the Chancellor again.** Asked once more about his budget and in particular the corporation tax he is saying, "Let's see." It is strongly anticipated that there will be a U-turn after all. He has rushed to catch the last plane out tonight and so is flying back a day earlier than planned from Washington, arriving in London tomorrow morning.

Well tomorrow is another day in this unrelenting and chaotic drama.

****

14TH OCTOBER

And the headline in *The Times* today is:

"Tories plot Sunak and Mordaunt Leadership."

Yes, after five weeks in the job Truss's days look numbered.

What a ridiculous way to choose a Prime Minister and it must never happen this way again. About "20 to 30" senior backbenchers and former ministers are trying to find a way to tell her to quit.

Kwarteng's days also seem to be numbered and if he goes then she goes too. It is looking increasingly likely that his so-called mini-budget will have to be reversed.

As James Forsyth writes in *The Times* Truss is trapped in a vicious circle.

She needs to speak to three different audiences: her MPs, the public and the markets. Well at the moment it would appear that all of those want her gone so she certainly has her work cut out.

After just five weeks.

Or have I said that before?

William Hague on the radio this morning said he has never seen anything like it. None of us have.

****

So while we wait for further news we look to see what is happening elsewhere.

The NHS

There is now a record seven million patients on the waiting list.

A&E departments and ambulance services are worse than they have ever been.

There is a severe blood shortage partly due to the lack of "donor carers" who work alongside trained nurses when taking blood.

****

Then there is the "**Mysterious case of the disappearing workers**". This is the headline in an article written by Emma Duncan of *The Times*.

She points out that no other rich country has seen such a rise in economic inactivity. Apparently the number of working-age adults who are neither in a job or actively looking for one is about nine million. And the reason? It is quite shocking. It is the failure of the health service to treat people who are ill, promptly and efficiently. It is because the over 50s who are mostly the ones off work, are suffering long-term illnesses or are looking after family members who are sick. She finished her excellent article saying, "If it (the government) puts some work into reforming the state of the health service, people may be willing and able to supply more of their labour."

****

There is a letter about anti-smoking also in *The Times* this morning urging the government to press forward with further reforms without delay. It is from eight top health officials and, as they say, smoking causes more than 500,000 hospital admissions a year and people who smoke spend longer in hospital with poorer outcomes and need social care on average ten years earlier than those who don't smoke. Well we all know that but there is no way that our Health Secretary can improve things if she is not prepared to concentrate on this. We have already seen how lacklustre she is and her neglect of the problems facing the NHS is criminally negligent. She needs to be replaced without delay.

****

Education

There is a report on *The Times Education Committee* today and an excellent editorial. This has been discussed in the Lords. They recommend a 15 year plan for our education system based on the recommendations of the report.

Lord Baker of Dorking, Kenneth Baker the former education secretary, said that Michael Gove's radical reforms that were supposed to drive up standards by ensuring that poorer pupils took more academic subjects had "totally failed." He added, "That is the indictment of Conservative education policy for the last 12 years".

****

The trade deal with India.

Well at the moment this is not happening and has been "put on hold". Apparently India wanted more concessions from the UK. However it has all gone pear-shaped and Liz Truss is being accused of pushing too hard to get a deal at any price which has really threatened the deal. She used to regularly phone the Indian Minister of commerce and industry and he got really fed up with her. He was trying to negotiate with the team at the Department of International trade.

A spokesman said "She wants a deal at any cost, she just wants a signing ceremony." Oh yes we can believe that, with at last three photographers in place. "But" he says "she's utterly scuppered the potential to get anything worthwhile for the UK. **This deal died in Downing Street with Liz Truss as the executioner."**

Wow. Strong words indeed. Britain not looking very **global** just now.

****

Breaking News

11.30am. It has just been announced that Liz Truss will hold a press conference later today, without her chancellor, when it is widely expected she will reverse her planned corporation tax cut.

Talks have been taking place about announcing a U-turn before the weekend in a bid to avoid fresh market panic when the Bank of England ends its bond-purchasing scheme today.

So Kwarteng was correct when he said "Let's see."

Yes. We **will** see!

****

Number 10 are denying reports that the Chancellor is about to be sacked.

****

1pm

Chancellor has been sacked.

Jeremy Hunt has been appointed the new Chancellor.

****

2.30pm

Liz Truss gives a press conference in the little used press room, (which cost the taxpayer £2.6 million). It is the usual bland talk about wanting a high skilled, high wage economy. But yes she does reverse the corporation tax.

There are just four questions allowed from the press. The last one is "Aren't you going to apologise?" and she abruptly cuts it short and makes a hurried exit. Many journalists were waiting to ask further questions. The press conference lasted 8 minutes 21 seconds. But to the question "are you going to resign?" she says the country needs her to stay on and give the country some economic stability.

During her speech the FTSE 100 had been up well over 100 points, but by 3.15pm the FTSE was up just 30 points at 6,880.

The pound also took a hit and gilt yields rose.

Everyone is jumping up and down and saying that she has to go. It is one almighty mess and she cannot survive.

Conservative MPs are saying she has trashed years of their hard work to make their party economically sound and trustworthy.

Well the lettuce is still looking healthy. Not sure the same can be said about Truss.

****

JUST ONE WEEKEND

15TH AND 16TH OCTOBER

So Jeremy Hunt has walked into Downing Street and become Prime Minister in all but name. He has ripped up the mini-budget in its entirety, he is on all the air waves this morning and Liz Truss is nowhere to be seen.

Everyone is so angry and the press conference was the last straw. Some of the remarks by her back benchers are not repeatable in this book. They really are a bit weird.

These are a few of the mildest ones:

"She is standing on a precipice."

"We want her out and we want her out now."

"I don't care how she goes but she has to go tonight. I will strap a rocket on her back and fire her into the Westminster sky myself if I have to."

And I promise you they just get worse from here on. **This is one thing the Conservative party are really good at. Getting the knives out and destroying someone they previously supported.**

I actually think that some of their remarks were quite nasty. No-one wants Liz Truss to go more than I do but I felt they were cruel with a hint of misogyny. I don't think they would have referred to a man quite like that.

But I think this is a very true statement: "**She is in the departure lounge now and she knows that,**" said a former minister. "**It is a case now of whether she takes part in the process and goes to some extent on her own terms, or whether she tries to resist and is forced out.**"

****

Then just listen to this. The other interesting thing that is happening is that BREXIT is being spoken about. Even *The Daily Telegraph* has a headline saying:

PROJECT FEAR WAS RIGHT ALL ALONG

They say that "**The revolution in the British economy promised by Leave campaigners six years ago finally seemed to go the way of all revolutionary movements this week. It ended eating itself.**" They finish by saying "**if Brexit had been done differently it might have succeeded but it was not. We'll be paying the consequences in reduced standing and prosperity for years if not decades to come.**"

I am in shock. This is *The Telegraph*. I think I need to go for a lie-down.

But no ....wait a minute. I then see the most brilliant article in *The Guardian* by Jonathan Freedland.

His headline is:

"The markets have taken back control: so much for Truss's Brexit delusion of sovereignty."

He goes on to say that "this is the biggest humiliation of Britain since Suez, a reminder that no government can ignore reality."

It is a long and pertinent article and I have to repeat myself......it is brilliant. As he writes about Truss he says:

"She is finished, a hollow husk of a prime minister." But he goes on to say that it is so much more than that.

"The Brexit bubble has burst" he says. This is music to my ears.

"Until Brexit, politicians only rarely got away with defying the empirical facts or elementary logic. But in 2016 they pretended that a country could weaken its trading ties to its nearest neighbours and get richer, which is like saying you can step in a bath of ice and get warmer".

We can all understand that.

He also criticises the way in which Truss and Kwarteng ignored the OBR.

" You cannot simply bypass the official spending scrutineer, the Office for Budget Responsibility, without the markets concluding that you've become unpredictable and, therefore unreliable, a bad risk."

"As Remainers were mocked for pointing out six long years ago, there is no such thing as unfettered sovereignty in the 21st century: every country has to accommodate its neighbours; the global economy, reality and the Truss-Kwarteng mini-budget was the result: the Suez of economic policy, a disastrous act of imagined imperial sovereignty."

At last. The reality of Brexit is beginning to strike home and if there were a referendum today I believe we would vote to re-join. Young people who were too young to vote six years ago are very much in favour of re-joining. If Trussonomics have resulted in this then these brief moments of a prime minister called Truss will have not been in vain!

And James Kirkup, director of the 'Social Market Foundation,' writes "We've just seen what happens when policy is based on fairy-tales not facts." And he says that "At the Tory conference I heard the chief executive of one of Britain's biggest companies tell Truss evangelists 'You don't have a plan for growth because you don't have a plan for immigration. So I'm moving work to the countries where I can find the workers I need to do that work.' "

What a disgraceful state of affairs. I send a tweet which says, "I think that Sir Keir Starmer can say with conviction that he will seek to re-join the customs union and the single market. It is time to be bold and to stand up for what you sincerely believe to be the best for the country."

Trouble is I don't think he read it.

******

Three scraps of other news that you might have missed.

Head teachers are threatening to walk out. They are being balloted for strike action which could take place after Christmas and would lead to the closure of all schools. This is the first time in 125 years. Obviously this cannot be allowed to happen as the entire country would then grind to a halt. But is anyone talking about this? Does anyone even know the name of our Education Secretary?

Well by the time you read this book, for the sake of all our children and teachers, I sincerely hope it is Bridget Phillipson.

However I now know because I make it my business to know so that I can hold him to account. It is Kit Malthouse who is apparently, "thrilled and really excited by the prospect of being Education Secretary."

Well that is good and I hope he is planning a meeting with head-teachers this very minute.

Time will tell how much of his excitement transfers to our education system.

******

Food banks are running out of food.

****

And I am really very sorry but I have to talk about our Health Secretary once more.

Her name you may remember is **Therese Coffey**. She is hoping to be able to allow pharmacists to sell antibiotics over the counter without any consultation with a GP. Doctors are horrified at this and are saying that this could cause catastrophic consequences of medicine–resistant superbugs caused by overuse.

But as if that wasn't bad enough just listen to this and despair.

She has also admitted giving friends and family her prescribed antibiotics when they felt unwell. Everyone knows that you shouldn't do that. Rachel Clarke, a hospital doctor, has called it 'staggeringly irresponsible' and 'utter recklessness'.

This is actually looking serious. All over Twitter I read that there should actually be a criminal investigation into these remarks and her existing position as Health Secretary is unsustainable.

This is our Deputy Prime Minister as well as our Health Secretary. Where has she come from?

****

But back to the main story at the moment which is dwarfing these vitally important ones.

The Sunday papers are all over the Truss debacle as you would expect.

The Observer: Tories in talks to oust Truss

The Sunday Times: Jeremy Hunt takes full control as plotters circle wounded PM

The Sunday Telegraph: Hunt delays 1p tax cuts as bank backs Chancellor.

The Independent: Hunt rips up PM's plans

The Sunday Express: Revealed: secret plot to oust PM

The Mirror: Tories want Big Ben for PM. This refers to the Defence Secretary Ben Wallace. They think he could be a unifying candidate! Few have even heard of him.

And they should also be scared of this one from:

The Sunday People: A million workers set to strike

So no sign of the PM yet but it is absolutely obvious that she will not survive the week.

Now those of you who have read my previous books will know that I am not the best person to forecast the demise of PMs as it took me a while to get Johnson right but as people are saying, if her whole ideology is up the creek then why is she still there?

And I honestly cannot see her standing up at PMQs on Wednesday. I think she will be indisposed. Which begs the question who will take questions in her place?

Oh no! Oh please no! The Deputy Prime Minister? I leave you with that thought whilst I break for coffee. (A clue there in case you had forgotten her name. Sorry!)

****

Well Mr. Hunt is telling everyone to get behind the PM as the last thing the country needs is another new leader. Hmmm. I think they are behind her actually but not in a good way. But Mr. Hunt might not have had time to read the papers yet.

He is meeting Liz Truss at Chequers this afternoon and he says she is in full agreement with the Treasury. I don't think she has a choice. There will be a large fiscal event on the 31st October. Can the markets wait until then? The OBR is saying that the economic outlook is extremely dire.

The editorial in *The Observer* says that no future Chancellor will ever again try to repeat what Truss and Kwarteng did. "The collective authors – the gaggle of right wing Brexiteer Tory politicians centred on the ERG, the right-wing think tanks, notably the 'Institute of Economic Affairs', the 'Adam Smith institute' and the right-wing media cheerleaders have been found out and humiliated".

As they say, **Liz Truss is now a Prime Minister with "no policy, no purpose and no mandate."** They and others are calling for a re-alignment with the single market and the customs union of the EU. "We need a general election because, whatever the Tories might think, this is not about preserving the Conservative government. It is about giving the country what it needs which is "stability, good governance and solutions."

There are all sorts of meetings planned for tomorrow. A BBC commentator says this is all very fast-moving. You can certainly say that again. We wait to see what tomorrow brings.

****

CHAOS AND CONFUSION

17TH OCTOBER

Oh my word it is now tomorrow! The world has imploded. Well the UK has anyway.

Jeremy Hunt cleared it with the Speaker for him to make a statement to camera this morning at 11am.

He has been in office for 72 hours and he has ripped the mini-budget of three weeks ago, to shreds. Nothing in that 'fiscal event' remains.

Income tax will remain at 20% indefinitely.

There will be no cuts to corporation tax.

And even the energy help for rising energy costs will be only for the next 6 months instead of two years as originally promised. Labour always said they would only promise it for six months.

After that Hunt says it will be reviewed and probably targeted on those who need it most. In other words you won't get it for your two empty holiday homes.

Well the markets have stabilised a bit but the black hole of savings required has increased to £72 billion.

So Hunt says that there are still more difficult decisions to come and there will need to be careful savings in public spending.

Wow! This is a U-turn without precedent. This is huge. Even before this announcement three MPs had called publically for her to go, but they are now saying 'what is the point of Liz Truss?' Trussonomics, and all she stood for, has been buried. Everything she stands for has been trashed.

APM Jeremy Hunt is to make a statement to the Commons this afternoon. (Acting Prime Minister!)

****

Headline in *The Times* this morning is "Tories hold secret talks on crowning new leader". OK so not very secret then. Graham Brady of the 1922 committee returns from holiday today, and he will count the letters of no confidence, sigh, and think 'here we go again.' Officially Truss cannot be voted out for another 11 months but Conservatives only recognise rules if they reflect their wishes, so they can be changed as and when.

Names are being bandied about for the next PM such as Rishi Sunak, Penny Mordaunt, Ben Wallace and of course Jeremy Hunt.

But it is a dreadful situation. What about all those who lost mortgages because of that min-budget and what about the rise in interest rates?

My question is how can you cut public spending when so many people are going on strike?

Almost a million NHS workers could go on strike this winter. Christina McAnea, Unison general secretary, said NHS staff were being asked to work double shifts or extra hours at the weekend which left them "exhausted". She accused the government of treating unions as the "enemy within." She said that "They don't want to talk to us—they want to demonise us."

Well I think a lot of talking is going to be required in the very near future as I hear that the BMA junior doctor's committee also intends to ballot for industrial action.

Nick Davies, programme director at the 'Institute for Government,' said "Public services are in a fragile state. These are not isolated problems in specific services but interconnected structural failures. In many cases there are too few staff, with excessive workloads, working on outdated equipment in rundown buildings."

He goes on to say that **"This has been a lost decade for public services, with performance worse now that it was in 2010".**

We are a laughing stock across the world. Jo Biden threw in his pennyweight when he said that "helping the wealthy was a big mistake." He doesn't believe in "trickle down" economics. Global investors see Britain as the new Greece or Italy. We are out of the EU and India freezes a trade deal. Exactly who are our friends?

The Archbishop of Canterbury, Justin Welby, is extremely worried about the future cost of living which he likens to "a monstrous wave coming at us" and can see "no moral case" for budgets that hit the poorest people hardest.

The Conservative Party has few supporters.

****

12.30pm. Breaking News.

Penny Mordaunt will answer the urgent question from Sir Keir Starmer about the economy this afternoon instead of Liz Truss.

Weird. There is no other word.

The Deputy Prime Minister was there sitting beside Mordaunt but not saying a word. The main questions were "Where is the Prime Minister?" to which the reply was "she has been detained on urgent business and I wish I could tell you but I can't." The one we will all remember was when she replied, "No, she is not hiding under her desk". Yes it has come to that.

Penny Mordaunt did look as though she was auditioning for the job of PM but I am not totally sure about her.

Eventually the new (the fourth in four months) Chancellor arrives and so, goodness me, does the Prime Minister. She sits impassively beside the Chancellor and doesn't say a word. She blinks a lot and has a fixed grin and I suppose is there to show that she supports her Chancellor..... as she used to do for her previous Chancellor until she sacked him.

Chris Bryant, Labour, calls for a point of order, saying that as the PM is now present she should speak, but it was overthrown by the Speaker.

So we listen to Jeremy Hunt repeat what he said this morning as he ripped up the mini-budget line by line. A soon as questions began Liz Truss scuttled out.

More difficult decisions to come, he says.

This evening there was a reception at Number 10 when the 'One Nation Tories' met Liz Truss and then, wait a minute, what is this? She gives an interview at about 10pm to Nick Robinson of the BBC. So she is unable to speak to Parliament but can talk to him. And what do we hear? Just more of the same. "**I have made mistakes and I apologise but I now want to stay and deliver.**" Deliver what exactly? More chaos and confusion? And yes she does want to lead the Conservatives into the next election.

So as we go to bed she is still in office but not in power.

****

18TH OCTOBER

I'm not sure how many people realise just how dangerous this government is. Ministers are saying today that Liz Truss cannot afford to make any more mistakes. But the mini-budget of just three weeks ago was not a mistake. It was what she had been saying all through the six weeks of the leadership campaign.

It was her ideology and it was lauded by all of her supporters. No-one in the Cabinet had been consulted but when told about it they all thought it was a good budget. Mr James Heappey, Armed Forces Minister, said ministers viewed the mini-budget as "coherent with a desire to drive growth".

Headlines in *The Daily Mail* said "At last a real Tory budget".

Mark Littlewood, Director General at free market think tank the Institute of Economic Affairs, said: "This isn't a trickle-down budget, it's a boost-up budget. It's refreshing to hear a Chancellor talk passionately about the importance of economic growth and supply-side reforms, rather than rattling off a string of state spending pledges and higher taxes. This is a very encouraging start, but the government must not take its foot off the pedal. If this was the Chancellor's 'mini' budget, I look forward to the 'maxi' budget."

Allister Heath, editor of the finance and business free newspaper City AM said "This was the best Budget I have ever heard a British Chancellor deliver, by a massive margin. The tax cuts were so huge and bold, the language so extraordinary, that at times, listening to Kwasi Kwarteng, I had to pinch myself."

So many Conservatives said this was true conservative thinking.

I repeat: It was NOT a mistake.

****

This was the way of the true Brexiteers and at last they have been rumbled. But we hear that Truss will meet with the ERG today which makes my blood run cold but brings me to another important fact about the present so-called Conservative party.

Who runs the Conservative Party?

This is a really important question and I hear Peter Oborne (author of 'The Assault On Truth') talking today and it is chilling. He tells us to be in no doubt about the fact that this present Conservative government is run and owned by the super-rich. It has been bought whole-sale by a very small group of hedge-fund managers and property developers who are only interested in increasing the money in their own pockets. Instead of giving money directly to the Tories because of disclosure rules, they donate to think tanks and then dictate the policy lines that they want them to follow.

One of the favourite places of Liz Truss is **5 Hertford Street in Mayfair** which is where these people like to hang out. It is a private member's club and has been described as London's most secretive club. It has an annual membership cost of £1,800 and is owned by Robin Birley.

Truss loves going here and it is her sort of place. As Peter Oborne says, her whole career has been one of self-promotion and she lacks all the qualities needed for Prime Minister. "No judgement, no empathy, no understanding, no humility." And, he says, the mind boggles at the damage she and Kwarteng did when she sacked the most experienced chief treasury official Tom Schollar, within days of becoming PM.

We need cool heads at the heart of government and he worries about instability on the continent of Europe and the fact that it is Truss's finger on the nuclear button.

It really makes grim reading.

And Ryanair boss, Michael O'Leary, has just described the economic situation in Britain as a "car crash" caused by the country's vote to leave the European Union in 2016.

"The mini budget was a kind of spectacular failure of the whole concept of Brexit," he said at a news conference in Rome, adding that the first thing Britain needs is what he called a sensible trading agreement with the EU.

Of course it does.

He expects Truss to be out of a job within a week or two.

Well we are hoping it will be by the end of this week.

****

But there is another address we should be concerned about.

This is 55 Tufton Street in London.

I have just seen, on Twitter, a huge ladder being erected outside this address and a large blue plaque being fixed to the wall. It says:

"The UK economy was crashed here. 23rd September 2022 (mini-Budget day)." I had never heard of this place so I look further and am horrified. How do I not know about this?

The plaque has been put up by the group called 'Led by Donkeys'.

55 Tufton Street is the spiritual home (and often the physical base) of a loose coalition of nine think tanks and campaign groups and organisations, many of which are Eurosceptics or climate change deniers. Among them are the 'Global Warming Policy Foundation' and the 'TaxPayers' Alliance,' whose founder Matthew Elliott was a mastermind behind 'Vote Leave'. It has, through soft power and indirect influence, had perhaps more influence on the course of UK politics over the past decade than many departments and most political parties. This is where so much of the money from Tory party donors ends up.

These groups have great influence on the government, and it just so happens that one of their own became Prime Minister just five weeks ago.

The other seven groups are the office of Peter Whittle (former deputy leader of UKIP), 'Civitas,' the 'Adam Smith Institute,' 'Leave Means Leave,' 'Brexit Central,' 'The Centre for Policy Studies' and 'The Institute for Economic Affairs'. (IEA)

Well that's a nice little collection of right-wing Britain bashers if ever I saw one. And of course there is absolutely no information as to who funds them.

Bob Ward, who is the policy director at the London School of Economics Grantham Institute, told *The Independent* that "This zealous ideological clique are trying to imprint their extreme agenda on government policy. It's clear they enjoy preferential access to some parts of government and, considering their small size, they are having a disproportionate impact... [which] is undermining the democratic process".

We really do need to know about them.

Ms Truss has appointed a number of senior advisers recently and apparently they are all connected with these groups in one way or another. They include Matthew Sinclair, Alex Wild, Caroline Elsom, Ruth Porter and Julian Jessop. It is also reported that Liz Truss has spoken at more IEA events than any other politician in the last 12 years, emphasising just how entwined its influence has become within the Tory hierarchy.

And the mini-budget seemed to confirm that Liz Truss is more aligned with the ideas floating around No 55 than any of the previous recent occupants of No 10.

Well she, and they, are all now exposed. 'Extinction Rebellion' protested outside their doors recently and whilst I do not approve of some of their tactics I will watch them carefully before I condemn them in future.

******

There is no governance going on and the following story is the sort of thing that compels me to write my books. This was highlighted on ITV news this lunchtime.

Children are eating rubbers and stealing food from their classmates because they are so hungry in school, teachers have reported. 'More than 80 per cent of primary school teachers polled by the charity 'Chefs in Schools' said children are coming to school hungry because their families cannot afford food. A quarter said children are skipping lunch entirely due to poverty.

"The situation is appalling and getting so much worse," Naomi Duncan, chief executive of the charity said. "Schools are again on the front line, seeing the impact of more families unable to afford nutritious food."

Currently, around 800,000 children living in poverty are not eligible for free school meals.

I write to my MP, Oliver Dowden, about this and I point out to him that he of course gets a subsidised meal at the restaurant in the House of Commons where a typical summer menu consists of spinach soup for 55p and steak and mushroom pie for £2.90.

All primary school children should get a free school meal and all secondary school children on universal credit should also.

But as I say in all my books this government does not care about our children. And I won't get a reply from my MP.

******

19TH OCTOBER

Today, we are all waiting for PMQs with a sort of ghoulish frame of mind. Will Truss be there? Will she take the questions? What on earth can she say?

For, just today................

Inflation has risen to 10.1% the highest for 40 years.

The cap in **social care** has been delayed for a year and maybe indefinitely. "I will fix social care once and for all" said Johnson three years ago.

The triple lock on **pensions** could be scrapped.

No decision yet on whether **benefits** will rise in line with earnings or inflation.

Another **maternity hospital**, East Kent, is under investigation. A report found "dozens" of babies died or were left brain damaged by poor care. "An overriding theme, raised with us time and time again, is the failure of the trust's staff to take notice of women when they raised concerns, when they questioned their care, and when they challenged the decisions that were made about their care," the report said.

How dare they keep on ignoring women when they show concern?

Therese Coffey has been told by an NHS doctor to think very carefully before she gives advice. Dr. Dan Poulter claims Coffey's hostility to what the extreme right call "nanny statism" is stopping her from taking firm action against the "major killers" of tobacco and bad diet.

The controversial **Public Order Bill** has been passed at Westminster by 276 votes to 231. This bill will give police the right to arrest anyone they think looks likely to protest.

Suella Braverman said "I'm afraid it's the Labour Party, it's the Lib Dems, it's the coalition of chaos, it's The Guardian-reading, tofu-eating wokerati – dare I say, the anti-growth coalition – that we have to thank for the disruption we are seeing on our roads today." **The House erupted in gales of laughter.**

Just read that again because it really is bonkers.

The good news is that over **70% of Tory voters want Truss to go**. The bad news is that they want the serial liar, criminal, ignorant, incompetent, lazy, blinkered, blustering and blithering idiot of a former PM by the name of Boris Johnson to return.

Where is Johnson by the way? I know you're asking. Well he is on holiday (again?) in the Caribbean having earned £150,000 for a speech in the US.

Michael Gove (Oh hello Michael. I thought you had been a bit quiet recently) has just said "it is when, not if" Liz Truss goes.

****

So on to PMQs. I am sure that that will go really well.

Well the consensus is that she has bought herself a bit of time. She turned up, she stood up, and she spoke which is all positive. Her Chancellor sat beside her and nodded away. Having told everyone yesterday and this morning that there was no guarantee that the pension triple lock would be implemented, so causing huge worry to millions of elderly people, she said she was "absolutely committed to the triple lock." But then she also said that she was "committed to social care reform" as well which as we have seen in bold print above, is a complete and utter lie. I think Hunt was still nodding.

Her stock answer was "I have been very clear. (Laughter). I am sorry. I have made mistakes (no, this is what you said you would do all along.) I must get on with the job and deliver? (She sounds like Deliveroo).

She kept asking Starmer questions (it is called PMQs which means the PM should be asked questions) and saying he has done nothing. Starmer replies "she keeps asking me questions because we are a government in waiting and they are an opposition in waiting."

She also talks about militant unions and about curbing some workers' rights to strike. She doesn't seem to understand that people are in unions and striking in order to try to get a better future for their families and conditions for their work place. I think this is beyond her.

But she lives to fight another day. **"I am a fighter not a quitter".** Yes, it is always all about her. But I think that was a dangerous remark.

Some are saying that Labour would be wise to wait before striking a fatal blow because of the awful mess they will inherit. But I say actually shall we think of the country for a change? The sooner some grown-up, serious minded, compassionate people get into government the sooner we can get to grips at sorting it all out.

"We are compassionate conservatives they keep saying."

"We will help the most vulnerable".

Someone needs to burst their bubble and the sooner the better.

****

Well that was all this morning. This afternoon there is to be a debate and vote on the fracking bill. The government wants to overturn the ban on fracking and allow it wherever possible. So many people are against this as it goes against the net–zero goal of climate change. So there is a three line whip. If anyone in the Conservative party votes against it they will have the whip removed. William Wragg, a sort of decent Tory, says he has to vote against the bill but if he does so, he will have the whip removed and the letter of no confidence in Liz Truss which he has just delivered to the 1922 committee will be null and void. Then we have Chris Skidmore who says that as the former Energy Minister who signed NetZero into law he cannot personally vote tonight to support fracking. He is prepared to face the consequences of his decision. A Tory with principles.

I would like to know if Boris is back from holiday yet. If not then he should have the whip withdrawn.

****

Then we hear that Liz Truss has pulled out of an event this afternoon at an electronic factory due to pressure of work. Strange because she usually loves getting on her hard hat and posing in front of a camera.

Hang on. 3.25pm and Breaking News.................................

Suella Braverman has resigned. Oh my word what is going on? So this is the reason for the cancelled event.

The story is that she inadvertently broke the ministerial code and Liz Truss is trying to show that she runs a tighter ship than Boris.

She is the shortest serving home secretary since the war.

Grant Shapps is the new one.

Chaos and confusion abounds everywhere you look.

****

But that was all this afternoon. This evening there is complete meltdown.

You really need to sit somewhere quiet with a large gin and tonic, (if you are over 18) and try to follow this.

We had the vote on fracking and it was a complete shambles. It was billed as a confidence vote in the Prime Minister until the very last minute. As they were walking through the lobbies it was suddenly announced that it wasn't. So some MPs were confused and undecided about which lobby to walk through.

But Chris Bryant (Labour) raised a point of order after the result was announced, (a win for the Tories) to say that he had photographic evidence of Ministers pushing and shoving and shouting aggressively and actually manhandling MPs into the government lobby. The Speaker is very concerned and is going to investigate. Jacob Rees- Mogg and Therese Coffey can be seen in the photos and are said to be two of the perpetrators. **Therese Coffey says that she never manhandled anyone, and that is a phrase I never thought I would write.**

We then hear that the Chief whip and her deputy have both resigned.

The story goes that Liz Truss pulled the chief whip's arm and ran round the estate in order to persuade her not to resign and in the resulting chaos she never voted herself.

"I am a fighter not a quitter" we remember her saying yesterday but we did think that she was speaking figuratively.

I hope you are keeping up with all of this. We then see an interview with Tory MP Charles Walker. He is a very dignified and serious man who is resigning his seat at the next election. He is appalled at the spectacle which is unfolding and says he has had enough of "talentless people putting their tick in the right box not because it's in the national interest but because it's in their own personal interest to achieve ministerial position."

Then we hear from the headmaster of Truss's old school in Leeds which she is always so very quick to criticise. She said, only this summer that "pupils at Roundhay School were let down by "low expectations, poor educational standards and a lack of opportunity."

But Alan Taylor, headmaster, says, "May I on behalf of all alumni of Roundhay School apologise for letting the whole of the United

Kingdom down. She should never have been let in nor should she have been let loose on such an unsuspecting world."

Then in a Facebook group for alumni, other former students have hit back in the past few days. They are so angry at the way she has tried to denigrate what was actually a really good school.

****

10pm. Oh no. We hear that the whips haven't resigned after all.

Tune in tomorrow for the next instalment of this unprecedented political storm.

****

THIS IS THE DAY!

20TH OCTOBER

Well we wake up to thunder and lightning this morning as the weather mirrors what is happening in Parliament.

Ken Clarke, former Father of the House until cruelly rejected by Boris Johnson tweets, "**we are even having U-turns on resignations now**".

Another tweet says that she knew it would end in riots and rebellion but thought it would be outside Parliament not inside!

There was a message at 1.33 this morning saying that the fracking vote **was** a vote of confidence after all.

MPs are angry and are giving Truss 12 hours to turn things round. But she has to go. Simon Hoare, a senior Tory, said on the radio this morning that there is a "growing sense of pessimism in all wings of the Tory party". She has no authority and they think the next two days are "crunch time."

And she is planning further confrontation with her MPs as she says "proportionate disciplinary action" will be taken against those who failed to back the government on fracking.

Well that will be interesting because we have the list of those who failed to vote. There was a total of 33 but I will just list the names of those whom I think you will know:

Ben Wallace, John Whittingdale , William Wragg, Alok Sharma, Chris Skidmore, Theresa May, Priti Patel, Boris Johnson, Kwasi Kwarteng, David Davis, and Nadine Dorries.

Liz Truss **was** on that list but has since been deleted as she did in fact vote but in all the kerfuffle it wasn't recorded. I **think** that is the story.

And I also think that this is the day!

And Boris? Where is Boris I ask again? Correct, yes, still on holiday in the Caribbean. In fact would it surprise you to know that he hasn't attended Parliament for one single vote at all since he resigned in July? But still very happy to accept his salary of £84,000. Oh I forgot. He said this was peanuts and not nearly enough to live on. But then he does have a lot of children to support.

His constituents should remove him forthwith.

****

The 1922 committee is expected to meet later today to discuss the leadership crisis. Good luck with that one guys.

11.30 am. We hear that Sir Graham Brady has just walked into Number 10 to meet the Prime Minster. It is being said that it is at her request. We will see.

He is in there for a long time.

1.15pm and the lectern has come out of No 10 and we hear that Liz Truss is to make a statement at 1.30pm. She must be going.

And yes! She's gone!!!!! The shortest serving Prime Minister ever.

Oh my word this is amazing.

She says she cannot deliver the mandate she was elected on and so has spoken to the King and resigned from being party leader. She will remain as a caretaker PM until a successor can be found.

It was fairly short and to the point. No apology nor contrition for making such a mess and tanking the economy.

So what happens next?

Sir Graham Brady has a word and explains the process. MPs have until 2pm on Monday to put their names forward but must have the backing of 100 MPs by then. MPs will vote and hopefully we could have a new PM by Monday evening.

If no-one drops out then there will be an on-line vote from party members with MPs saying who they would prefer. Then the result will be announced by Friday at the latest. That is a week tomorrow.

****

But what else is going on?

The new prime minister will have a lot to address.

I see a tiny paragraph in the paper from the Care Quality Commission which says, "The health and care sectors need to recruit more than 295,000 staff because shortages are paralysing services and putting people's health at risk."

****

Then there is a headline which says that **more than half of maternity units are now judged unsafe.**

****

The Independent Inquiry into Child Sexual Abuse is published at last. You may remember that it cost millions of pounds and Boris Johnson said it was money being "spaffed up the wall" as it was all about the past. To the question has it been worth the eight years and the millions of pounds spent on it the answer is yes **but only if politicians are prepared to turn the recommendations into meaningful legalisation**. The main one is that it should be a legal requirement to report claims of abuse. I cannot believe it has taken eight years and so much money to come up with that. Obviously there were other recommendations but what an indictment on our society. It disgusts me.

****

Then there are people trying to get **child-care** onto the agenda. There is a very long full-page spread by Rosie Kinchen in *The Sunday Times* when she says that "**The country can't grow if we don't fix child care.**"

The number of childcare providers fell by 4,000 in England in the year to 31st March this year. The charity 'Pregnant then Screwed' found that 18% of parents were not able to find child care to meet their needs and 17% had to reduce their hours due to lack of availability. Researchers have found that young children benefit from formal childcare before they start school as it is associated with better cognitive and social development.

****

But what is the government concentrating on now? Trying to find a passable leader, the third in as many months, who can unite their party. None of the above is being discussed or acted upon and meanwhile people are suffering from the rising costs of mortgages, food, heating and fuel for transport, whilst small businesses and hospitality sectors are in a state of collapse.

Be in no doubt, they only care about themselves and how they can stay in power.

****

Bring Back Boris.

Yes there are some people actually saying this. But it would mean him packing his swimming trunks, leaving the beach and returning to the House of Commons. He hasn't been there since July and we know he has no interest in politics at all. As pointed out on Twitter he can make lots of money giving speeches, still be the centre of attention and still be on perpetual holidays. As I quote in *Behind the Headlines* we all know that the only things he is interested in are "being King of the world and shagging."

But I find myself shouting at the television when I hear people saying, "Oh he got all the big calls right. Oh he got us through Covid and he got Brexit done. Oh we all make mistakes."

NO. He caused thousands of avoidable deaths by dithering and delaying over lockdown, he failed to fix social care, he has overseen the collapse of the NHS, he refused to give free school meals to primary school children in England, there has been delay after delay in starting the public inquiry on the pandemic, he refused to give education the funding it needs, he took us out of the largest trade block in the world which is on our doorstep, he appointed a home secretary who viewed all those seeking asylum as criminals, his government passed some of the most draconian laws which curtail workers' rights and the right to protest.

He received a fine from the police for attending an illegal party in the middle of lockdown, he failed to appoint an ethics advisor after he had caused two to resign, he re-wrote the ministerial code in an attempt to water it down and he is under investigation for lying to parliament.

If the standards committee find him guilty he will be suspended as an MP and probably lose his seat. They are sitting in November with the verdict out hopefully in January.

We all know he is guilty so IF he was elected PM there would have to be another election in the New Year.

As David Davis says "GO BACK TO THE BEACH"

I really needed to get that off my chest!

Around a dozen Tory MPs have said that they will refuse to serve under Johnson and will resign the whip or convert to Labour.

William Hague, former leader of the Conservative party has said Johnson's return would send the Conservative party into a 'death spiral'.

Sir Charles Walker, Tory MP said, 'I've had enough of talentless people'.

Sir Roger Gale, Tory MP has said he will resign the whip if Johnson becomes PM.

However some will support him if he stands and we hear that some MPs are being bullied and threatened in order to get them to support him. Goodness does this sound like our Conservative party? Rhetorical question. We have not yet heard about his intentions. He has not formally declared yet.

The entire world is watching us and shaking their collective heads in disbelief.

Peter Oborne writes in the *New York Times* that "The party is so riven by internal feuds, personal hatred and ideological disagreements that it has become ungovernable." He says "This is a perilous time. Britain is facing perhaps its biggest economic, political and even constitutional crisis since World War II".

Italians are furious as the UK is compared with them and being accused of reaching Italian levels of chaos. They say that Westminster is in a league of its own thanks to Brexit.

Moscow says that Britain has "never known such a disgrace as prime minister" after the resignation of Truss.

Germany says "The chaos in Britain has reached perfection". They say that "Brexit has created the problems we always told you it would --- social division, economic turbulence, and permanent political chaos." Or they say to put it another way, "We told you so".

France and Macron says he hopes for a return to stability in the UK.

And so it goes on.

The other contenders for the post of PM are Rishi Sunak, Penny Mordaunt, Suella Braverman and Kemi Baddenoch. Well Braverman, Mordaunt and Baddenoch will be the choices of the ERG.

If the Tories are serious they will choose Sunak. He is probably the best of a dreadful lot.

But whilst we wait there is some good news.

'Privilege Style,' the airline whose plane was ready to fly to Rwanda has confirmed they **WILL NOT** be flying refugees to Rwanda. They've pulled out. They no longer want to be part of that deal. Congratulations to 'Freedom from Torture' the charity who has headed this campaign.

I think that whole venture has cost the tax payer £140 million.

****

It is Saturday 22nd October and we see Johnson arriving at Gatwick airport this morning.

He has not yet officially put his name forward for PM but has had endorsements from Priti Patel, Nadine Dorries and Jacob Rees-Mogg amongst others. Six weeks ago he left office in disgrace as nearly 60 ministers and junior ministers resigned because of his dishonesty.

He has spent all that time away from the UK on holiday, first in Slovenia, then Greece and then the Caribbean and he now thinks he can swan back as a hero to save the Conservative party. Not the country mind you, the party and the careers of Tory MPs.

I am almost out of words. (But not quite!)

****

And just let us have a break in these proceedings to report on a march/rally in Parliament Square today by over 50,000 people calling for us to rejoin the EU. **"We want our star back" is the cry.**

"We know this chaos started with Brexit, it's only going to end when we reverse Brexit and we rejoin the European Union."

The latest polls show that 61% believe it was wrong to leave the EU, and 56% want to rejoin now. The Rejoin movement will only grow from here.

This is reported in some papers but I have not seen it reported on the BBC.

****

Back to the main news. During the day we hear that Rishi Sunak has over 100 supporters and Penny Mordaunt has 23. With Boris Johnson things are more difficult. People are saying he has over 100 supporters but when asked to name them the names are not forthcoming. It is recorded at the moment as actually about 52. Could it be, could it possibly be that they are all lying? Oh of course it is Boris Johnson we are talking about here.

Tweets on Twitter are going ballistic. There is no comprehension whatsoever as to how it is that this corrupt, dishonest, narcissistic shambles of a politician who was hounded out only 6 weeks ago can possibly be allowed back in the country let alone in to politics.

We all feel physically sick.

But late this evening we hear that rumours have it that Johnson is out. That has to be true. Surely we, as a country, haven't sunk so low as to give him any room at all? But then we hear that there is to be a meeting between him and Sunak. Are they trying to broker a deal? It was tabled for 3.30pm then at 5pm and now it seems to be happening at 8pm.

Well tomorrow maybe things will be a little clearer and Johnson will retire humiliated and beaten? Is that too much to hope for?

****

3RD OCTOBER

Actually I don't think it is! As you can imagine, the columnists and journalists of the Sunday papers have been honing their linguistic skills this morning and absolutely lacerating Boris Johnson. This is just a flavour.

Camilla Long: "He has killed his party, killed Conservative politics, killed an entire generation of politicians by screwing the party over so comprehensively it cannot function." And as she goes on to say he took so much time over all of this that no policies could be executed.

Matthew Syed: "Few political parties are bereft of a crazed element" and he cites the Corbynite wing of the Labour party, "but I am not sure any British party has engaged in such a bizarre episode of self-immolation."

Sunday Times editorial: "The normal process of government is grinding to a halt as yet more rounds of ministerial musical chairs delay legislation."

As someone points out on **Twitter** "my son has lived through four chancellors, three home secretaries, two prime ministers and two monarchs. He is four months old."

Andrew Rawnsley: "The toxic twins of Brexit and Borisology turned the Tories into a party prey to delusions." He says that "I am usually averse to using the word insane, but the Conservative party really will be fit only for a straightjacket if it chooses to restore Mr. Johnson to Number 10."

Observer editorial: "Of course the main impact of Brexit has been to make Britain's structural economic problems even worse: to make exports harder, growth worse and economic inequalities sharper."

"This tale of reckless incompetence must end."

"Their political implosion must not be allowed to wreak fresh harm on the rest of the country."

The Mirror: 100,000 readers have signed a petition to say 'enough is enough' and to demand a general election.

The Independent: Relations with Ireland will be "plunged into the freezer" if Boris Johnson returns as prime minister" says Jonathan Powell who was Tony Blair's chief of staff and chief negotiator on Northern Ireland from 1997-2007.

Of course there are pages and pages about the demise of Truss and the state of the Conservative party. Dominic Cummings and others are saying that Johnson supported Truss knowing that she would be rubbish and wouldn't last five minutes, would plunge the country into chaos, and so then he would be asked to return. **Can we believe that?**

Yes unfortunately we can.

Breaking news: 10.30am. Rishi Sunak has officially entered the race to become Prime Minister as his talks with Johnson last night had obviously broken down.

He now has 145 backers, Johnson has 57 and Mordaunt has 24. But listen to this. Suella Braverman has come out in his support. Not going to stand herself as she says "now is not the time for fantasy, I want a leader of our Party and our country to inspire hope for a better future and raise our spirits. And I need a leader who will put our house in order and apply a steady, careful hand on the tiller. That person, for me, is Rishi Sunak." You cannot get more right wing than Braverman. And Kemi Baddenoch is also supporting Sunak. She is another Brexiteer right wing MP who initially thought she might stand.

And the headline in *The Sunday Times* is "Tory Right spurns Johnson as Sunak supports surges."

I think they have looked into the abyss and realised that Sunak is their only hope of survival.

In Sunak's statement he says, "I want to fix our economy, unite our Party and deliver for our country." He goes on to say that, **"there will be integrity, professionalism and accountability at every level of the government I lead** and I will work day in and day out to get the job done."

Well he is their only hope of any sort of comeback from the brink and should have been voted in initially instead of Truss.

2.30pm. There are now less than 24 hours before nominations close. It must be remembered that Johnson has not yet formally decided to run.

But it is about a whole lot more than just getting into office although you would not think that if you listened to what they say.

****

BELOW THE RADAR

We now look at the problems any future PM will have in his or her in-tray. Whoever it turns out to be, he or she are going to have their work cut out as they will inherit one almighty mess.

We all know about the economy but just to bring you up-to-date, the UK's economic outlook has been lowered to "negative" by Moody's, a global integrated risk assessment firm, who says this is due to political instability and high inflation.

But there is so much more.

22ND OCTOBER

Children are always my first concern and there are two stories which are appalling.

Head Teachers have said that nine out of ten schools will have run out of money by the next school year when their reserves will have run out. Paul Whiteman general secretary of the National Association of Head Teachers said that "Schools are cut to the bone. This will mean cutting teaching hours, teaching assistants and teachers." He has just returned from a trip around the country talking to union members and heads and he says the mood has changed "from anger to desperation". "At each of these meeting there was at least one Head in tears."

Jonny Uttley is CEO of the Education Alliance Academy Trust which runs seven schools in Hull and the East Riding of Yorkshire. He has recently met his Head Teachers and said they have to make an impossible choice. **Do they cut vital teaching staff or feed hungry children?**

So if you ever meet someone who says that Boris got all the big calls right just quote this to them.

****

23RD OCTOBER

Then we come on to care homes for children.

An article in *The Observer* today by Tom Wall highlights the news that Ofsted has decided to let staff from private firms inspect and rate children's homes. As Clare Bracey a care charity worker remarks, "Given that 80% of homes are run by the private sector, it feels like marking your own homework." Many of these homes have been previously classed as inadequate and Anne Longfield, former children's commissioner for England says "It is vital that Ofsted inspections are independent and that confidence in their findings is not eroded by using serving managers from big private provider chains as inspectors."

I find this absolutely and astonishingly obvious.

****

So how is the NHS getting on?

Like children, this gets mentioned in all of my books all the time.

Just today there are real concerns, as in education, about any plans to cut the NHS budget, or indeed to raid it, in order rebuild crumbling hospitals. If this were to happen it would plunge the health service into its deepest crisis in decades.

And hospital consultants are balloting for industrial action which is really unheard of.

Also ambulance services have started balloting for strike action.

In fact Prime Minister, whoever you are, there are very many people either on strike or balloting for industrial action or on rolling strikes so what are you going to do for them?

And a very pertinent letter in *The Times* states that the chief problem with the NHS is lack of staff and a very simple and quick solution would be to **provide free child care to doctors, nurses and other medical staff as this one reason why many are unable to work. Child care often exceeds their earnings.** Oh goodness this would be amazing. But it would also, under this government, be a miracle.

****

Then I read about this which I seem to have missed. It is about a drug which is still being given to pregnant women called **Sodium valproate**.

It is a drug to treat epilepsy and bipolar disorder. **However it causes disabilities and deformities in new born babies if taken when pregnant. About six babies a month are being born after exposure to this drug.**

In April this year Jeremy Hunt as chairman of the health committee backed calls for compensation. But campaigners are saying that they have had meetings cancelled and emails and phone messages not responded to due to the inaction at the heart of government because of the ongoing changes of Prime Ministers.

I am appalled to read that there are still none of the legally required warnings on the packets of this drug. NHS data shows that 286 pregnant women were prescribed this drug between April 2018 and March this year exposing a total of 31 unborn babies to its damaging effects. A week ago the pharmacy regulator wrote to 91,000 pharmacists to express their concern and they held its own survey into its usage in June but so far no outcome has been published.

So absolutely no real concern, no sense of urgency, no enforcement of regulations, and not one jot of care for pregnant women and deformed babies. I do not understand how such cruelty is allowed to persist.

A spokesman for the department of health said "Our sympathies remain with all those affected by sodium valproate --patient safety is our top priority and we are committed to improving how the system listens to people." Unless you are a woman of course and particularly if you are of child-bearing years.

****

The cost of living and energy bills.

Well this will go on and on. The number of households today (23rd) who are in arrears with their energy bills have risen to a record high of over 2 million.

****

Musicians are having to cancel concerts and entire tours due to skyrocketing costs. There is a massive labour shortage and the cost of hiring vans and trucks has risen dramatically. The costs of flights and visas are so exorbitant that organisers of smallish venues say that local bookings are now the only viable option

****

A new law. I had a whole chapter on draconian new laws in my book *Behind the Headlines*" but I have only just seen the details of this one which has its second reading in three days' time. It is called the **EU law (revocation and reform) Bill**. It is all about cancelling laws which we were bound to abide by when in the European Union.

Now we are out from under their jurisdiction we are free to go our own way. Are you happy with that? Hmm well let us have a closer look as to what this could mean and then I will ask you that question again.

Toby Helm political editor of *the Observer* gives us a list of some of the laws that are at risk.

1.   Controls that prevent cancer causing materials from being used in cosmetics.
2.   Rules guaranteeing major sporting events such as the Olympics are free to watch on television.
3.   Protection for part-time workers so that they do not get less favourable treatment as full-timers.
4.   Minimum standards that ensure that aircraft are safe to fly. Are you still happy? There's more.
5.   Compensation for travellers in the event of delays and lost luggage.
6.   Minimum requirements for maternity leave.
7.   Protection for staff pensions when companies go bust.
8.   A ban on trafficking of illegal weapons.

This, you will not be surprised to hear, is facing mounting criticism from business groups, environmentalists, legal experts, unions and opposition parties. **I say that numbers 1, 3 and 6 have a direct consequence for women.**

I also say be afraid, be very afraid. But also we need to stop this "ideology driven right-wing experiment by pro-Brexit Tory right-wingers" bill from going through parliament.

****

Then we come to the name **Therese Coffey** once again and we look at the three year stint when she was head of the Department of Work and Pensions. It is important that we detail this story as she is now, for the moment, the Health Secretary and this is about people's health. This information is reported in the '**Disability News Service**.' This is run by John Pring, a disabled journalist who has been reporting on disability issues for nearly 25 years.

When her predecessor Amber Rudd was in charge, literally just four days before she left and Coffey took over, she had secured £106 million for a new DWP Excellence Plan. **One third of that money was allocated to improving safety support for "customers with complex needs and decision making, and learning from its mistakes."**

But an internal DWP document secured under the freedom of information requests shows how **Coffey watered down this plan and how from September 2019 till September 2022 disabled people continued to die as a direct result of her department's failings**.

This makes for very distressing reading. One of the decisions taken under Coffey's leadership was to abandon a pilot scheme called 'SignpostingPlus' which would have tested ways of supporting claimants who were "beginning to struggle to cope before they became harder to help through entrenched disadvantage". When asked about this the DWP said there was no information about it and blamed the pandemic for the decision to abandon it.

Other parts of the plan were for staff to be given extra time to respond to signs of "customer vulnerability" and refer them to specialist support and these conversations would have been measured and acted upon. Again there was "No information held for these two questions on complex needs conversations".

We hear about three people who were seriously ill and who died after their benefits and support allowances had either been stopped or were about to be stopped by Coffey's department. One was a possible suicide. DWP's own figures show that the department started 133 secret internal process reviews into links between its actions and deaths and serious harm caused to benefit claimants between July 2020 and June 2021.

A 'Disabled People Against Cuts' spokesperson praised the original plan which he said would have "saved lives, misery and hardship for millions of disabled people." He added "it's a desperate crying shame that Coffey took a hammer to it. Will these people ever get some humanity and compassion?"

To which of course the answer is no, not under a right-wing Conservative party and not if Therese Coffey is anywhere around.

As John McArdie, who is co-founder of the grassroots group '**Black Triangle**' said "she had caused a catastrophe for sick and disabled people at the DWP and now she has moved to the DHSC, which is going to be equally catastrophic, if not more so."

Well I think we have already seen sufficient evidence of that.

But I just look up the grass roots group called 'Black Triangle' and I am shocked. They have a long and detailed web site and I urge you to look it up. Its basic premise is about the fact that **people like Coffey refer to the disabled as "workshy".** They refer to the "current vicious attack on the fundamental human rights of disabled people by Government using 'Work Capability Assessments' to re-classify sick and disabled individuals as 'fit for work'."

Apparently the Nazis used to put black triangles on disabled people and called them workshy, hence the name of this group. This group was started because a friend of theirs had had his allowance stopped and he subsequently died.

There are no words.

****

So this and more is all in the in-tray. There is a lot to do. There will be more stories and these will run and run but these are the ones I have just unearthed today.

Breaking news: 9pm (still the 23rd October!) Boris Johnson has just issued a statement saying that he will not be putting his name forward for the role of prime minister.

Oh my goodness I just need to pause while I digest that piece of news. We really have to look for the positive wherever we can. But.......here we

go. I have now just read his statement and it is the work of a narcissist.
|It is all about him and how wonderful he would have been as the next
PM. He says he has been "overwhelmed" by the number of people
who want to support him and yes he has definitely got over 100
nominations in order to run.

Then why can we only see about 60 names on his list?

He thinks he is "uniquely placed to avert a general election now". And
"A general election would be a further disastrous distraction".

Unlike the rolling elections for prime minister we are having at the
moment of course.

"I believe I am well placed to deliver a Conservative victory in 2024".
And "There is a very good chance that I would be successful in the
election with Conservative party members—and that I could indeed
be back in Downing Street by Friday."

I really don't think he has read the room. As a friend of mine has just
said "he has an ego the size of Europe".

But then we read this: "Sadly I have come to the conclusion that this
would simply be not the right thing to do. You can't govern effectively
unless you have a united party." He goes on to say that he reached out
to Sunak and Mordaunt but nothing could be agreed between them.

You are too right it couldn't. He basically asked them both to pull out,
give him all their votes and he would give them a place in his cabinet.
They both told him to go away. Or words to that effect.

**Has he seen the numbers? A third of all Tory voters say they will
never vote Conservative again.**

So what now for Johnson? Some are saying he might come back in
the future as he still has a lot to offer. I can only suppose they mean
more incompetence, more recklessness, more selfishness, more

division, more lies and more parties. Ah yes the parties. **The words "All guidance was followed completely" will be coming back to haunt him as the Privileges Committee gets under way and he will be called to testify.** That would not have been a good look for a Prime Minister.

And Liz Truss is having a party at Chequers this evening following the party she gave yesterday for all those who helped her in some rather oblique way. No doubt about it the Conservatives are 'world beating' at giving parties. Usually, it has to be said, at the tax payers' expense.

But my prediction is that Johnson will resign his seat within the next month before he is pushed. He has no interest in politics or in the welfare of his constituents. He only wanted to be prime minister. He just wanted the fun, the attention, the money, the dressing-up box, the photographers and the acclaim. It will be so much more fun to go on to the speech circuit interspersed with holidays and parties. And so much more money. Come on it's a no-brainer. (No comment!)

I really hope that we can genuinely celebrate the back of this destructive politician.

And it is still the 23rd! As they are saying:

"A day is a long time in politics."

****

CORONATION. (NO NOT THAT ONE)

24TH OCTOBER, AM

It is looking as though there will be a 'coronation' this afternoon just after 2pm. Apparently the King is in London this evening! But whilst we hear that his coronation will be in May, this one will very likely be for............

Rishi Sunak.

He has now got the support of over half of all Tory MPs.

Many fervent Johnson supporters have switched to Sunak including Priti Patel and Michael Gove.

Penny Mordaunt is still in the race but has fewer than 30 votes. She says she is "in it to win it" and has actually got more than the 30 or so but just not saying who they are at the moment. Oh where have we heard that one before?

So who is Rishi Sunak? He was Chief Secretary to the Treasury from 24th July 2019 to 13th February 2020 and Chancellor of the Exchequer from 13th February 2020 to 5th July 2022. So basically he is the one who has been in charge of our economy for the last few years. He had to cope with the pandemic and was praised for his furlough scheme and then for his 'eat out to help out' scheme. He is good-looking and we all called him 'Dishi Rishi'. I think he is basically straight-forward and obviously understands economics. I think he is the best chance the Tory party has of limping along to the May elections.

But he needs to be looked at very closely.

He is, as we all know extremely wealthy, and is married to a billionaire. I do not begrudge him his wealth but I think he should spend a month with his family, living in a two bedroom flat on minimum wage, just in order to experience what so many are going through at the moment.

For those of you who have my first book *Beneath the Bluster* just look at page 84. Here I describe my shock and anger when I discover that instead of giving the education tsar, Sir Kevan Collins, the £15 billion over three years he said was needed the Treasury refused and offered only £1.4 billion over three years. This was such an insult to Sir Kevan Collins that he immediately resigned. He had been appointed in order to find out what was needed to improve the education system and they ignored him. Rishi Sunak was, of course, the Chancellor at the time. and I was, and still am, disgusted at this decision.

However there are other things you need to know about him if you are not already aware.

He was heavily criticised for axing a £20-a-week increase to Universal Credit that had helped some of the poorest families through the pandemic. More than 200,000 have been pushed into poverty as a result of the cut, according to the 'Joseph Rowntree Foundation.' He did increase in-work benefits in his Autumn Budget – but not by enough to offset the cut.

He also has strong links to right-wing think tanks such as the 'Centre for Policy Studies', 'Policy Exchange' and the 'IEA'.

He is, or certainly was, **a staunch Brexiteer**.

And in *The Times* this morning we read that he has assured Eurosceptics in private that he will maintain the Northern Ireland protocol bill, stick with the Rwanda policy and introduce new legislation to prevent the ECHR blocking deportations.

We haven't heard any of this as he hasn't given any speech, he hasn't answered any questions or made any reference to what he would do if elected other than to work hard and with integrity.

I am sure we will hear more very shortly but I repeat............we need to keep a close eye on him.

****

12 30pm. Penny Mordaunt is being urged to pull out. Ian Duncan Smith is supporting Sunak. Mordaunt supporters are saying she has 90 followers although we still only know of about 30.

And 2pm we hear that there is only one contender as Penny Mordaunt dropped out at the very last minute. And so.....................

Rishi Sunak is the new leader of the Conservative party.

He will be Prime Minister after the King has asked him to form a government.

So we have our third Prime Minister in two months.

But as you might expect opposition parties said a coronation was "anti-democratic" and demanded a general election, as pressure mounts on the government to give voters a say.

****

25TH OCTOBER

Exactly seven weeks ago Liz Truss went to Balmoral where she met the Queen who asked her to form a government. Conservative members had voted for her over the other candidate who was Rishi Sunak.

Boris Johnson tendered his resignation.

Today, Liz Truss will tender her resignation, and Rishi Sunak goes to Buckingham Palace to meet King Charles who will ask him to form a government.

Just after 12 midday Rishi Sunak gave a speech outside No 10 as Prime Minister. At 42 he is the youngest PM for 200 years and is the first PM of colour being a Hindu of Indian extraction. Yesterday was the beginning of Diwali the festival of light and we are hoping that there will be some lighter and brighter days to come.

Yesterday I did a bit of a hatchet job on Sunak but today I am prepared to cut him a bit of slack. His speech was good and he actually mentioned the NHS, schools, environment and safer streets as a start and said that he will be judged by actions rather than words. He talked about integrity and professionalism which we all took to be a reference to Johnson's time and he said mistakes had been made which was a reference to Truss. I think he is a decent and honest person but we will see.

He is now in the process of choosing his cabinet and this will tell us a lot.

If Therese Coffey is still there by the end of today and if Suella Braverman gets Justice as is rumoured I will be hammering him again.

We think Jeremy Hunt will stay as Chancellor and I will be watching closely about the decision on benefits. Will they be increasing in line with earnings or inflation? That is my other bench-mark.

2pm. We are hearing about resignations now, or are they just going before they are pushed? **Oh Hosanna, Rees-Mogg has resigned as Business Secretary.**

So we spend the afternoon hearing about those who have left the cabinet, as Sunak sacks them in the privacy of his office in the House of Commons, and watching hopeful MPs arriving at Number 10 to hear about which position they are being offered. And my hosannas soon die from my lips. Here we go.

Dominic Raab has got his old job back of Deputy Prime Minister and Justice Secretary. This is bad, very bad and barristers and judges throughout the country will be in despair.. Those of you who have read the chapter on the criminal justice system in my book *Behind the Headlines* will know what a dreadful justice secretary Raab was.

Alok Sharma retains chair of Cop 26 but has to relinquish Business Secretary.

Grant Shapps has been appointed Business Secretary. This makes him the shortest serving Home Secretary ever, being in the post for roughly three and a half working days. The civil servants there had given him a cautious welcome and now do not know who will be thrust upon them next.

Jeremy Hunt stays on as Chancellor. That, I believe to be good.

Simon Hart is the new chief whip as Wendy Morton has gone, following the debacle at the voting on the fracking bill.

James Cleverly stays as Foreign Secretary.

Ben Wallace stays as Defence.

Michael Gove gets his old job back as Levelling-Up Secretary. We are still waiting to see signs of this happening.

Gillian Keegan, a junior minister has been promoted to education. She has been given a 'cautious welcome' from Bridget Phillipson the brilliant shadow education minister. But she is the **fifth education secretary** since July of this year.

Penny Mordaunt retains her post as leader of the House. She was really wanting promotion.

Well reaction to all of this is that Sunak is wanting experience, continuity and stability.

But then we see **Suella Braverman** and **Therese Coffey** walking up to that black door and we freeze in disbelief.

No, no, no, no, no! Braverman is back at the Home Office. She resigned from the Home Office less than a week ago having breached security guidelines and broken the ministerial code. **She had been in the job for about six weeks but in today's climate I can only suppose that, that looks like experience and continuity.** But mark my words people are angry about this appointment. Maybe Sunak thinks he can keep her in check and better to have her there than making trouble on the back-benches. But I don't think he will be happy with her remarks about Indian immigrants over-staying their visas.

We send our condolences to the civil servants at the Home Office.

Then a bit of good news. **Steve Barclay** has got Health and Social Care. That means that Coffey has gone and the NHS will be marginally happier. **BUT where has she gone?**

Oh No! Therese Coffey has got Environment and Rural Affairs. I can hear the howls of despair of farmers across the country from here. She should be no-where near any government ministerial position and how she got elected as an MP is beyond my comprehension.

I just quote a text from a civil servant at DEFRA: **"Haven't we had enough pain? Everyone at work absolutely depressed."** Always remember there are hard-working committed civil servants who have to endure these clowns, Coffey in this, case hour after hour.

And what is this I am hearing? A name I thought had been thoroughly and comprehensibly abandoned for ever due to incompetence, ignorance, and stupidity.

Gavin Williamson has been given Minister without Portfolio. Sacked three times, twice by Theresa May as Chief Whip and Defence Secretary and once by Johnson when Education Secretary, he had been shuffled up to the Lords never, we thought, to be heard of again.

What on earth is Sunak trying to do?

When I watched him making his speech outside Number 10 this lunchtime and listened to his words of "**integrity, accountability, professionalism and compassion**" I was really encouraged and I actually thought for one brief minute that maybe this book would be a slimmer volume than I had originally thought. I imagined how proud his parents must be and how meteoric his rise to the top had been, having only entered politics five years ago. He was able to speak in sensible sentences and appeared smart and intelligent and genuine. This might seem a low bar but is something we are not used to.

But even as I thought all of this I couldn't help thinking, somewhere at the back of my mind, "I am really sorry Mr. Sunak but I don't think you are going to be in this job for very long".

That was before I knew about all of these cabinet appointments.

Keir Starmer, meanwhile, is preparing for government, talking to business leaders, having 'master-classes' for all and receiving large donations, as Labour gains trust from the City. Labour are now viewed as having 'economic credibility' and there are more and more articles about their front bench in the media.

We now wait to see what happens in PMQs tomorrow.

****

26TH OCTOBER

Surprise, surprise, it is all about Suella Braverman and how is it possible for her to be re-appointed to the Home Office after having to resign just a few days ago for compromising security and breaching the ministerial code?

Sunak was welcomed by everyone before they all piled in with their questions. The answer to the one about Braverman was: she made a mistake, said she was sorry, stood down, and has now moved on. Is Sunak trying to please the ERG, is he sure that the Rwanda plan will not happen anyway so it doesn't matter, or has he made his first really enormous mistake by re-appointing her so soon after he spoke about integrity?

We also heard him say that he would stick to the manifesto commitment to ban fracking. But we also heard him say something to the effect that there would be a strong NHS, good schools, investment in infrastructure etc. etc. to which I want to shout **"Then why after 13 years of Tory government is everything such a mess?"**

Keir was in fine form and very relaxed and at one point accused him of being beaten to the post just six weeks ago, and then, of course, his predecessor was beaten by someone who had the shelf life of a lettuce.

And when Sunak accused him of being soft on crime he replied that he had been a prosecuting council for many years and indeed he was head of the CPS so that is really not a good line to take.

Straight after PMQs there was an urgent question called for by Labour to the Home Secretary about her appointment. The Home Secretary scuttled out of the Chamber leaving another cabinet minister to answer the questions on her behalf. She is a lawyer for goodness sake and yet is unable to defend herself.

When asked, the cabinet minister did say that the PM will be appointing an ethics advisor. But I do remember him saying it would be the first thing he did. The opposition parties have asked for an inquiry to be held into the security breach that triggered the sacking of Braverman and then her re-appointment but I am pretty sure that I heard the cabinet minister say that that would not be happening.

All over Twitter there are messages saying that they were prepared to give Sunak the benefit of the doubt after the speech yesterday but have since changed their minds because of Braverman. Did he promise her a top job if she moved away from Boris to him? Very probably.

It's not looking good.

****

But we must get the better news when we can. The fiscal statement that was due to be out on the 31st will now be presented as a full autumn budget on the 17th November. It will have the OBR forecast. Although this is a delay it would appear to be necessary in order to consult all departments in a thorough manner.

And Mr. Sunak has already spoken to the Welsh and Scottish First Ministers. That is good because Liz Truss did not speak to either of them at all during her six weeks in the job.

And just an interesting nugget of information which you might not be aware of. I certainly wasn't. It's about the **lecterns** which we have been seeing a lot of recently outside Number 10. Did you know that every prime minister has his or her own lectern especially made? In my ignorance I thought they wheeled out the same one every time. But no they are all different. They take three or four weeks to be made and cost between **£2,000 and £4,000 of tax payers' money.** Poor Rishi Sunak had to use an old one because there wasn't time to make him a new one. I remember Liz Truss's lectern. It was all swirly whirly. I don't think that will be used again. But I think if prime ministers keep changing at such a fast rate they will have to keep using the same one. To be honest I've never heard of anything so ridiculous.

****

WORDS, WORDS, WORDS

28TH OCTOBER

Well that was just the first 24 hours. It does not appear to be getting any better. There is a lot of talk and most of it is cause for concern. **The triple lock guarantee on pensions** is continuously mentioned in order, I think, to get us used to the idea that this manifesto promise will be broken. What really concerns me is that the think tank, 'Policy Exchange,' says in a paper published today reconsidering of pension and benefits spending is "essential to ensure that frontline services are not asked to make disproportionate savings." They say that the government should scrap the triple lock. You will remember that 'Policy The triple lock guarantee on pensions Exchange' has its home at 55 Tufton Street.

The PM insists that his government will protect the most vulnerable and he also says we must judge him by his action as "actions speak louder than words."

Oh don't worry Mr. Sunak we will.

****

We also hear today that the PM is not going to **Cop 27 in Egypt** next month. There is a lot of anger at this decision. Apparently he has too many domestic problems to sort out. And apparently Liz Truss told the King not to go. So our new Secretary of State for the Environment, Therese Coffey, does the rounds on the media this morning. As we all know her answer to most questions is "I am not aware" and there we go she says she is not aware that Liz Truss told the King that he must not go. Well **we** all knew. Don't worry, she said, **she** will be going.

She was also 'not aware' that Biden and Macron are going. Well it was all over the news this morning. And she asks us not to worry.

Many people are concerned that climate change is not being given enough attention. On BBC Question Time last night Julia Hartley-Brewer who is a TV talk host, **dismissed climate change as being "mere weather".** The guests were debating a report by the UN Environment Programme that said the world, and especially richer carbon polluting nations, remains "far behind" and is not doing nearly enough to reach any of the global goals limiting future warming.

She called the report "a load of nonsense". David Lammy (Labour MP) who was also on the programme, put his head in his hands in despair.

Then I see a Twitter from former neuro-surgeon Henry Marsh. He wrote the book 'Do No Harm' and is a colleague of a surgeon who once operated on me so I notice him whenever he is vocal. He has just been out to Ukraine with Dr Rachel Clarke to give medical support there and he has also recently been diagnosed with cancer.

He says "**Have you noticed the weather? It's warm enough to be summer. I find this more frightening than the economic mess the country is in, more frightening than my cancer."**

****

The **Suella Braverman** story runs on. It is beginning to look as though rather than immediately resigning she was shown the evidence of her 'mistake' and **then** resigned.

Senior civil servant, Simon Case is reported to be 'livid' over her re-instatement.

Some are saying she'll be gone by Christmas.

We then hear of some dreadful conditions in which asylum seekers are being held at Manston airport in Kent. Because she had blocked the transfer of thousands of refugees from this processing centre during her first six-week spell as Home Secretary it had become seriously overcrowded. There are reports of outbreaks of scabies and diphtheria. She is also being accused of breaking the law as the refugees are being held for up to 32 days and it is only designed to accommodate people for up to 24 hours during security and medical checks. At one point this month more than 3,000 people were being held there which is three times its original capacity.

During his three and a half working day tenure at the Home Office Grant Shapps found more places for the refugees to move to very quickly.

Sunak is now liaising with Macron in order to try to find solutions to the small boat crossings. Of course we all know what the solutions are and have been saying so for years as my letter published in *The Times* in March clearly explains.

18/04/22

Sir, As Priti Patel is devoid of any humane ideas for asylum seekers I offer her this. There needs to be an assessment centre in Calais and then those who qualify for refuge in the UK can come across the Channel safely on the ferries. This idea was first suggested in 2015 by the United Nations when Peter Sutherland their special representative on migration said, "You could set up an immediate system for assessing how many of these people are refugees. You could do it in a very short time and you could do it as a joint responsibility." Or is any co-operation with the French impossible since Brexit? And to talk about the inhumanity of a scheme which will forcibly deport vulnerable and traumatised people to a country to which they do not want to go is not talking politics, it is talking morality.

Suella Braverman, Liz Truss and Priti Patel all refused any meaningful discussion with France so nothing was achieved. Let's see what Sunak can manage. But be in no doubt, Suella Braverman is a disgrace to British politics.

****

So back to the **economic mess** we are all in and which is going to take so much of the PM's time that he is unable to attend Cop 27.

The Director General of the British Chambers of Commerce, Shevaun Haviland says that he believes the time is right for a renegotiation of the EU-UK Trade and Cooperation Agreement signed in December 2020, as the UK economy and businesses would benefit from a deeper trading agreement with the EU. He is also concerned with the tensions surrounding the Northern Ireland Protocol. This problem goes on and on and the deadline by which power sharing should have been restored at Stormont passed last night without a solution so there are now no longer ministers in office in the Northern Ireland Executive. It is now up to senior civil servants. There will now be an election but so far no date has been set.

This ridiculous situation too, could be solved at a stroke, if we rejoined the single market and customs union.

****

29TH OCTOBER

There is a protest rally in London today by the charity 'Pregnant then Screwed' against the **rising cost of child care**. This is a recurring theme in all of my books and continues to be ignored and side-lined by all those in government.

Some facts:

* The UK has one of the most expensive child care systems in the world behind Switzerland and Slovakia.

- The average cost of a fulltime nursery place for a child under three is about £14,000 a year. (National Childbirth Trust).
- In the UK there is no free childcare help until a child reaches the age of three.
- Many mothers are forced out of work because it is not economically viable to keep their job.
- Whilst on maternity leave women typically receive no pension contributions from their employer.

So Mr. Sunak what are you going to do? Holly Mead in *The Times* today says that "childcare is rigged against women," and "the childcare system needs ripping up entirely and restarting from scratch."

There are still a million miles to go before women are treated as equal citizens in our society. Listening to us would be a start.

****

And again in every book I write I have to mention **children's care homes.** I am indebted to Martin Barrow who is writing about these nearly every day on Twitter.

This is just one.

Overly Hall Ltd

This is a privately run home for 22 children with severe learning disabilities, sensory impairment, autism spectrum disorder and/or challenging behaviour. They can stay till they are 18 to complete their education.

It is on the same site as a special school and a separate residential home for young adults. It has just had an Ofsted inspection on its social care provision. It was classed as inadequate in all areas.

The report concludes "There are serious and widespread failures that mean children are not protected or their welfare is not promoted or safeguarded and the care and experiences of children are poor and they are not making progress."

"We will take a compassionate approach to government" says Sunak.

Councillor Ian Forster of South Tyneside council said: "Rishi Sunak is a man with a proven track record of financial competence and compassion."

I say, good. There is a lot which needs compassion and financial competence at the moment and you, Mr. Sunak, are going to have your work cut out.

****

30TH OCTOBER

This is really concerning.

We hear that Liz Truss had her phone hacked whilst she was Foreign Secretary. This breach was only discovered during the summer while she was running for the Tory leadership. Boris Johnson and the cabinet secretary Simon Case, however declared a news black-out and so it was never reported. **Apparently spies suspected of working for Putin gained access to sensitive information including listening to discussions about the Ukraine war**. Also, conversations between Truss and Kwarteng criticising Johnson, were hacked into.

Opposition parties are insisting that there should be an urgent investigation in order to uncover exactly what went on.

This is the woman who went on to become Prime Minister.

****

Our Children

I cannot begin to tell you how angry this makes me feel. There is still anger over the fact that during the pandemic pubs were opened before schools. Funding for the school holiday food voucher schemes in England now has to come out of councils' household support fund which was introduced last October by the government. Local councils are saying that they are using too much of this money on this scheme and they are having to axe the food vouchers scheme because there is not enough money left. The government is saying it is up to individual authorities as to what they do. So no accountability there then.

Local authorities including Reading, York, Birmingham, Leeds, Stoke-on-Trent, and Wakefield have dropped the voucher scheme. So parents face a post code lottery as others have managed to keep them going.

At the end of half-term children will be returning to school tomorrow hungry.

Then we see an article which is very excited because it reports that the first launch of a rocket strapped to a jumbo jet will take off from Cornwall in a few weeks' time. It is intended to be the first of many launches from centres around the UK.

How wonderful is that? **We can jet off into space but we cannot feed our children.**

****

Then there is an article about the lack of interest in education by all political parties in *The Sunday Times* by James Kirkup director general of the Social Market Foundation. He reports that research by the Nuffield Foundation shows that spending per pupil will be 3% lower by 2024-2025 than in 2010. And these figures were drawn up before we see the budget on the 17th November.

We already know that health spending is roughly double the spending on education but what is so alarming to me is the fact that a recent poll discovered that just 8% of the public considered education to be a high priority. That's the lowest since 1984.

He says that "unless the country and its leaders start to notice and act, prosperity and fairness will elude us. And young people who feel that the country doesn't treat them as important will be – sadly – correct."

****

But we already know that. 15 years ago the government set a target to end inappropriate admissions of children to adult psychiatric wards. However last year there were 249 admissions of children to adult wards which is up 30% from the year before. 'YoungMinds', a mental health charity for young people, said the figures showed that the burden on the system was "unsustainable" and that improvements were needed "not only to inpatient care but also to community services that help prevent young people becoming so ill that they need to be hospitalised."

We can never accuse the Conservative Party of acting hastily when children are involved.

****

We have to talk about Brexit yet again. And we will go on talking about Brexit until some government or other sees sense. The government in its wisdom has decided to stop accepting the European Union's CE mark and instead has created a new Conformity Assessed (UKCA) mark to show that a product is safe. When this system is in place manufacturers will have to pass one set of tests for the EU and another for the UK. This will increase the red tape enormously. But at the moment this can't happen because the UK has no facilities to test some building products such as glue, sealants and glass, or some medical supplies. The 'Construction Leadership Council', representing the building industry has warned the Business Secretary Grant Shapps and the Housing Secretary Michael Gove that plans for new homes, hospitals and schools were being affected. Innovators and entrepreneurs are saying that because of the excessive red tape they are leaving the UK and doing business overseas.

But even more worrying are the delays to medical supplies. The Medicines and Healthcare products 'Regulatory Agency' said it was recommending a delay to this change until 2024 for medical products. All manufacturers want ministers to phase in these changes and three-quarters of them want the CE mark to be continued to be recognised.

To me it sounds completely crazy and I think that is because it absolutely is. As William Keegan puts it so clearly "Brexit is madness. We need to re-enter the single market and customs union".

And he also goes on to say "The Labour party should stop shilly-shallying over the issue. Or is Labour scared that if the government did have a change of heart, the beneficial impact on the economy would improve the Conservatives' electoral chances?"

Well the chances of that happening mate are zero. And my thoughts about the Labour position is that they think if they start talking about Brexit it will muddy the waters. However I do think that they need to step up and stand up for what they truly believe.

But at the moment it is all words, words, words when what we need is some action from someone. Anyone?

****

TWO WEEKS ON

MONDAY 31ST OCTOBER

So one week into his premiership how is Sunak doing?

Well the editorial in *The Times* this morning thinks he is doing OK and that all the little spats over this, that and the other are insignificant so long as the economy is stabilised.

So let us look at this, that and the other and decide for ourselves.

Asylum: We return to the situation at the Manston airport centre. Yesterday some fireballs were thrown at a Border Force jetty in Dover where refugees were being picked up in the Channel. So 700 refugees were moved to Manston where, as we know, conditions are already appalling. The immigration minister Robert Jenrick and Sir Roger Gale Conservative MP for North Thanet rushed down there last night to assess the situation.

Mr Jenrick said he had been left "speechless" by the safety problems at the overcrowded site and Sir Roger Gale said that Manston was "working as it was intended" five weeks ago but was "now broken and it's got to be mended fast". In fact he actually thought that it is almost as though it has been allowed to deteriorate in this fashion "deliberately."

Apparently morale at the Home Office is at rock bottom. Insiders are saying that a lot of Home Office staff are looking for new jobs and some have already left rather than work for Braverman. The entire department is shambolic.

****

Cop 27

Pressure is growing for Mr. Sunak to attend and it is being reported that he could make his first U-turn and make an appearance.

****

Women

Maria Caulfield MP has been made Minister for women. Let us be clear about her and what she stands for.

She supported cutting the abortion time limit and voted against buffer zones outside clinics and was previously an officer of the all-party parliamentary "pro-life" group and voted against legalising abortion in Northern Ireland.

As you can imagine this appointment has provoked an enormous backlash and has prompted criticism from charities and women's rights groups everywhere.

The British Pregnancy Advisory Service, a charity that advocates for access to abortion, said: "Caulfield's views are out of step with members of the public and her own parliamentary party. Recent amendments to establish buffer zones around clinics and secure at-home early abortion care have passed despite the opposition of MPs including Maria Caulfield."

The shadow secretary for women and equalities, Anneliese Dodds, said it was "deeply troubling that Rishi Sunak has appointed a minister for women who supports limiting women's rights to abortion. The government must be clear that a woman's right to a safe and legal abortion is not under threat," she said.

And let us hear what the government spokesman has to say in reply: "The minister for women has a strong track record of delivering for women in her previous ministerial roles. We will continue to pursue a compassionate approach to equality, ensuring that everyone is able to live their lives free from discrimination."

Well good because we have noted what you say and will be holding you all to account.

****

And then the issue of maternity rights raises its ugly head again. Mel Stride MP, who was appointed Work and Pensions Secretary last week, has called for a slashing of maternity rights to "provide a massive shot in the arm for British Business." He says "They are too onerous."

Jonathan Ashworth shadow Work and Pensions Secretary said last night that this remark showed why "working people simply can't trust the Tories."

****

This is why the Retained EU Law Bill could be so detrimental to the health of us all. With EU laws we would not have sewage in our seas and rivers, we would not be concerned about the safety of food imports, and working hours and paid holidays would be protected. Every one of us and every business would be affected.

And I am just hearing that "Rishi Sunak is considering deprioritising Jacob Rees Mogg's controversial bill to switch off 2,400 retained EU laws covering everything from holiday pay rights to environmental protections and aircraft safety."

Well that is very good news Mr. Sunak and I will always report good news when I find it. We applaud the fact that Jacob Rees-Mogg is now on the backbenches and his Brexit finding-opportunities have gone with him. But he really should not have been allowed to bring this dangerous bill forward in the first place.

****

Meanwhile the economy continues to be in a mess. There is a furious article by Kevin Maher in *Times 2* today where he says that he is now paying £1600 a month for his mortgage instead of £500. And in another article I read that one third of all public sector workers are ready to resign from their jobs. The TUC says that "the government has only itself to blame." They say that "it has chosen to hold down public servants' pay while giving bankers unlimited bonuses."

"Enough is enough. It's time to give our key workers in the public sector the decent pay rise they are owed."

****

The hospitality sector is highlighted in the travel section of *The Times*.

It makes grim reading. Hotels, pubs and restaurants are facing their biggest crisis in living memory with one in ten at risk of closure this winter. This is largely due to the rising energy and service costs but also to the shortage of labour and Brexit.

According to the latest 'Hospitality Market Monitor' 2,230 premises closed down between June and September this year which is about 24 a day.

David Weston of the Bed and Breakfast Association said that for some guest houses this winter could be "the final straw."

****

Then I see the following, reported by *The Express* political editor David Maddox. It really makes depressing reading.

He writes that "Rishi Sunak is facing a major crisis with "deeply unhappy" Conservative Party MPs already preparing letters of no confidence in the Prime Minister, led by a furious backlash over his massive Cabinet reshuffle."

They don't like the fact that some ardent Brexiteers have been left out of the cabinet. You see it really is the ERG party.

Can you believe this? "An exasperated MP said: "Don't rule out another leadership vote next year."

I almost feel sorry for Rishi Sunak as he inherits an unsustainable government. But my real sympathies are with this country and the dreadful time that so many people are having to go through because no one in government seems to care. Everything now depends on what the autumn budget will say on the 17th of November.

****

Suella Braverman is to make a statement to the House this afternoon. Yes it is still only the morning! I take a much needed break for lunch!

****

Well Suella Braverman gave her statement to the Commons at 5.15pm. I found it absolutely shocking and so did very many others. The reply from the Opposition was given by Yvette Cooper. This was followed by questions.

Braverman acknowledged that the whole asylum system was broken which after 12 years of Conservative rule is a damning admission.

She has also been accused of using inflammatory language as she described the small boat crossings as "an invasion on our southern coast." An invasion Ms. Braverman, just to be clear, is what is happening in Ukraine by Russia. These asylum seekers are traumatised people who need help and care and kindness, similar to that which was given to your parents when they migrated to the UK in the 1960s from Kenya and Mauritius.

Many of these people would love to be allowed to work and to contribute to our economy as your parents did so successfully, one as a nurse and the other who worked for a housing association. There are so many job vacancies all over the UK and there are over a quarter of a million long-term empty residential properties in the UK at the moment.

There is no thought or competence or will to sort this problem out.

And I have just seen a graph showing how the number of boats crossing the channel has risen from about 299 a year in 2018 to the 28,500 so far this year. This is nearly 100 times higher than 2018.

So why is this? I hear you ask. Well, let us think back to what it was that happened round about 2018/2019.

Could it, I wonder, could it have anything to do with Brexit?

Surely not, because Brexit was all about taking back control and in particular control of our borders.

However it is important to remember that when the UK was part of the EU, there was something called the Dublin Regulation. This meant that the UK could ask other EU countries to take back people they could prove had passed through safe European countries before reaching the UK.

The UK could make "take charge" requests and officials were often able to prove that asylum seekers had passed through other countries thanks to the Eurodac fingerprint database.

But since Brexit the UK no longer has access to that database, so it is harder to prove definitively which other European countries small boat arrivals to the UK have previously passed through.

For some reason the UK has not so far struck any bilateral agreements with other EU countries to enable it to replicate the Dublin arrangement. Instead, officials have labelled many claims where they suspect people have passed through other European countries before reaching the UK as "inadmissible".

So leaving the EU has had the complete opposite outcome from what we were told would happen. The number of small boat crossings continue to rise. No surprise there then.

And a letter in *The Times* this morning states that the lack of part-time judges has meant that there is a huge back-log of hearings in the First-tier tribunal of the Immigration and Asylum Chamber. This results in considerable delay in the courts deciding whether a person has the right to stay in the country.

This is all due to lack of funds of course.

No money anywhere you might think?

Well I am seeing reports that the Manston processing centre is run by a company called 'Mitie Care and Custody'. Their directors are registered at The Shard. This company has two Tory peers on its board and was apparently given loads of illegal contracts during the pandemic. They seem to have plenty of money as they made a profit of £6 million in tax payers' money this year.

All I will say is that none of that money seems to be being used to make conditions at Manston habitable.

There is so much incompetence and corruption that Suella Braverman is on a hiding to nothing. She ended her appearance by saying that there are some who would like to get rid of her. (Well yes that is correct.)

But then she said "Let them try."

All I say is that the last person to say in parliament "I'm a fighter not a quitter" quit the very next day.

I don't think Rishi Sunak can win on this one. If he sacks her, one wing of the Tory party will go mad, but if he keeps her the other wing of the party will go mad.

****

2ND NOVEMBER

The beginning of week two Just one day:-

Rishi Sunak decides that he **will** attend Cop 27 after all. One week in and his first U-turn.

****

Decision on Cumbrian coal mine is delayed for the third time. Apparently the decision will now be made "on or before 8th December 2022"

****

There is an enormous sewage slick off the north coast of Cornwall at St Agnes Bay.

****

A large proportion of Britain's international development budget is being spent at home on housing refugees, mainly from Ukraine, according to the Centre for Global Development. Of the remaining £7bn, which is administered by the UK directly, more than half will be spent domestically in 2022, including about £3bn on housing refugees, according to CGD's analysis.

****

Richard Walker, managing director of Iceland, who is also standing to be a Conservative MP, said he would like to see free school meals extended as a "critical priority". He says that, "Rishi Sunak should extend free school meals to all families on universal credit ".

****

Police chiefs are failing to stop sexual predators and other criminals from joining the force despite repeated warnings, the official watchdog has found.

****

Mat Hancock, Conservative MP and former Health Secretary, is to take part in the television programme "I'm a celebrity ---get me out of here" so has had the whip removed.

****

An article by Alice Thomson in *The Times* today discusses our new environmental minister mentioned at the beginning of this chapter. She says she needs an ABCD to save rural Britain. This stands for "Agriculture, biodiversity, climate change and drains" she suggests.

But no, all we get is Alcohol, Balderdash, Cigars, and a double D for Dither and Delay. (Yes, she smokes cigars).

****

220 child refugees have gone missing from hotels after being processed at the 'inhumane' refugee centre at Manston.

****

BP have made profits of £7 billion and has said it will pay £2.2 billion in taxes for its UK North Sea businesses this year, as well as £695

100

million to the energy profits levy, which was imposed in May.

****

The British government has reportedly "war gamed" emergency plans to deal with week-long electricity blackouts amid concerns over the security of power supply this winter due to Russia's war in Ukraine.

****

Suella Braverman is pushing ahead with controversial plans which risk forcing vulnerable child refugees to undergo x-rays to prove they are not lying about their age.

****

A group of asylum seekers were taken from the Manston centre to London and forced off the coach at Victoria station. Whilst some managed to contact friends or family, a group of 11 were left stranded with inappropriate clothing, no food, no money, no help and no idea where they were. They were from Afghanistan, Syria and Iraq and it was only thanks to a volunteer from the charity 'Under One Sky' who was there helping the homeless that they were given help.

****

A young girl threw a letter over the boundary fence at Manston pleading for help. A judicial review is being launched against the Home Office over the conditions at Manston.

****

So, just a typical day in the life of a country led by the British Conservative Party.

****

3RD NOVEMBER

The Economy.

The Bank of England increases interest rates today to 3% which is the biggest increase since 1989. The UK could be facing the longest period of recession since records began if their predictions are correct. This, they say, is to try to control inflation which is now at 11%. They say that if they don't do this now it will only all get worse.

The Governor of the Bank of England said that the UK was just hours from potential total financial meltdown in the wake of Liz Truss's disastrous mini-budget. He said the Bank was forced to step in "quickly" and "decisively" to mitigate a "very real threat to financial stability" after markets were spooked by the calamitous £45 billion tax giveaway. He also suggested the chaos that followed the mini-budget was a "particular UK issue", rather than the result of global shocks.

He argued that the former business secretary Jacob Rees-Mogg was "wrong" to blame the turmoil in the markets partly on the Bank's failure to raise interest rates.

"Certainly, global markets have had shocks this year, we've had common shocks, Ukraine would be an example, but this was a particular UK issue," he said.

John Curtice, a professor of politics at Strathclyde University tells *The Guardian,* **"No government in power during a financial crisis has survived an election."**

He is viewed as the UK's foremost polling expert and he goes on to say that, "They have lost ground because public opinion feels it can no longer trust [the Conservatives] to lead the country."

****

The Environment.

We are all clinging on to the fact that the PM has said he would not let the scrapping of all EU laws go ahead. But there are so many concerns in this particular area. James Bevan who is the head of the Environment Agency has signalled he wants to change a key regulation on water quality which repeatedly exposes how English rivers are being choked in a cocktail of sewage and agricultural pollution. This regulation provides a tough testing regime and requires that at least 75% of all English rivers be in good health. However, would you believe, at the moment not one single river passes this test.

But I'm afraid we do have to mention Therese Coffey who is in the news once again today as environment minister, as the headlines say that there has been **a sewage spill every 2 minutes in England and Wales since 2016.** This is an unbelievable statistic and Feargal Sharkey, a former singer and now campaigner said, "The utterly chaotic, collapsing government we have surrounding us continues damaging the environment."

It is obvious to all that these regulations are absolutely vital and I really do not understand the thinking behind this announcement.

If only we had stayed in the European Union we would have had to abide by their strict environmental rules and our seas and rivers would be clear and sparkling.

****

Then Grant Shapps (the new Business Secretary) is saying that he really doesn't want to blast more tunnels through the Pennines and so the HS3 Northern Power House railway between Manchester and Leeds will be scrapped. As a letter from the Mayors of North of Tyne, West Yorkshire, and Greater Manchester says in *The Times* today "For years, prime ministers and transport secretaries have promised to construct Northern Power House Rail and for years these promises have been watered down, or broken, on a loop."

Indeed, and I was writing about all of this on November 16th 2021 in *Behind the Headlines*.

****

And that is not all. Do you remember the Cumbrian coal mine? Still no decision on whether to allow it to go ahead or not. With Cop 27 about to start a decision has been postponed for the third time.

****

3RD NOVEMBER

Well Suella Braverman has actually visited Dover and Manston at last. Her team arrived at Dover in four cars and she then took a Chinook helicopter to travel the 30 miles to Manston near Reigate.

A helicopter engineer has said that the Chinook would cost £3,500 an hour to run, 2,640 lbs of fuel an hour, involve 2 military pilots, 2 crewman, air traffic control, groundsmen, pre-flight checks, take off, land and further checks so the whole process would be at least £10k.

So concerns for the environment or the economy are obviously not troubling our Home Secretary.

****

But it is this which concentrates my mind at the moment.

A letter signed by scores of doctors, nurses and health experts have called for a major expansion of free school meals to combat the growing risk of malnutrition, obesity and other health conditions affecting children in low-income families hit by the cost of living crisis.

Martin Godfrey, a GP in south London, said he increasingly saw malnourished children. "We are seeing thin, pale children who lack the energy of a normal child. There isn't much clinically we can do to help other than signpost parents to people and places that can. We all need to do more right now. Extending access to free school meals would make a huge difference." **Jonathan Tomlinson, a GP in Hoxton, east London, said inadequate nutrition was manifesting as fatigue, recurrent infection and behavioural problems in youngsters. "One thing I do notice is that most children seem to have iron, folate and vitamin D deficiency and when I ask them, they don't eat anything green."**

The letter urges ministers to extend free school meals to an extra 800,000 children on universal credit whose families are in poverty and unable to meet the cost of an adequate lunch but under current criteria are deemed not vulnerable enough to qualify for free meal provision.

Some schools have described pupil hunger as the biggest single challenge they face this winter, with some having dipped into emergency cash reserves to feed pupils ineligible for free school meals. Teachers have told of desperate children stealing food from fellow students, eating rubbers, and even "pretending to eat out of an empty lunchbox".

I have written about this before but am indebted to Patrick Butler and Rowena Mason of *The Guardian* for highlighting this issue once again. Nevertheless I do not see it mentioned in other media outlets which I find appalling. We also hear that British five-year-olds are up to 7cm shorter than children of the same age in Europe. Some experts are suggesting nutrition- and especially a lack of quality food - could be stunting the growth of children in the UK.

There is so much talk about education reform and I get so cross that I write **two** letters to *The Times* about different aspects of children's hunger.

I am often asked what it was that made me start writing about this government. It is a sense of burning anger.

****

There really does seem to be a paralysis in the government at the moment. This is partly because everyone is waiting for the budget on the 17th November but it is also due to the long summer recess which was dominated by the leadership election campaign and of course the six weeks of chaos under Liz Truss. It is being likened to a "zombie" government.

And the high turnover of ministers under three different prime ministers has just added to the chaos. Some are saying that this is having real world effects, with some jobs being done by four different MPs in the space of months.

When Truss entered No10 one of the first things she did was to slash the number of policy aids working in the building. Civil servants working in the policy unit were also shipped out of No 10 into the Cabinet office.

Well Sunak is trying to reverse this but it all takes time and at the moment Downing Street is very short-staffed.

The 2019 manifesto is no longer being implemented and so many Tory promises are in doubt.

****

Sorry Prime Minister what was that you said? You will build a government of "integrity, professionalism and accountability."

So Prime Minister, why have you not yet appointed an ethics adviser?

I give them till 17th November but then I think that is when the fireworks will really go off.

Nurses are going on strike before Christmas. If the debate is between the nurses and the Tory politicians then the nurses will win. I need to add here that no A & E staff will strike and no one with life threatening conditions will be denied treatment.

As Andrew Rawnsley writes in *the Observer* today, "Some may have thought things couldn't get worse, but Rishi Sunak and his Chancellor will soon rid them of that illusion". He goes on to say that, **"We are the only G7 country to be poorer today than we were pre-pandemic."**

****

Brexit.

And this is one of our main problems of course.

Professor John Curtice, president of the British Polling Council, said "Probably Brexit is now less popular than it has been at any point since June 2016."

According to a new poll, only 43% of the British population consider that the UK's departure from the European Union was a good decision, while 57% believe it was a mistake.

A recent survey by the British Chambers of Commerce found that half of small businesses are finding it harder to export to the EU.

Post-Brexit supply chain problems worsen in UK.

Tighter immigration rules since Brexit have compounded the labour shortage in the UK.

Amsterdam has overtaken London as the largest financial trading centre in Europe. The Tories, in power since 2010, still remain 30 points behind Labour in the latest polls.

The boss at the port of Dover says delays due to Brexit will continue for the foreseeable future.

An old clip of Boris Johnson (from before his time as prime minister) has resurfaced on social media. Dated June 21, 2016 – two days before the general public hit the ballot boxes for the EU referendum – Johnson spoke to LBC and promised he would apologise if the country went into recession after Brexit. Ha, we will await that one in vain.

Research from *The Financial Times* has found that the UK officially has the worst healthcare in Europe.

****

4TH NOVEMBER

And then at the end of an Editorial in *The Guardian* today we read this:

"Mr Sunak is trapped. He cannot give an honest appraisal of the nation's economic predicament, since doing so would mean abandoning vacuous rhetoric around Brexit "opportunities", recognising instead that Britain's severance from EU markets is a wound that needs healing. "The upshot is that leaving the EU has caused long-term scarring to the country's productive capacity and competitiveness. Asinine ministerial denial of that reality is a further deterrent to investment. Economic decline stokes political volatility, which makes recovery harder. That vicious cycle will be broken when Britain has a prime minister who is willing to deal in facts about Brexit and set pernicious fictions aside. Rishi Sunak, it seems, is not that man."

The difference today is that at last Brexit is a topic of conversation. I think we are on the road back to sanity and the re-joining of the single market and customs union. It will be a long and twisting road all right but maybe this is the beginning of the beginning.

****

This evening King Charles is holding a reception at Buckingham Palace for 200 people connected with environmental issues. Business leaders, NGOs, experts and decision-makers, will all meet up to mark the end of the United Kingdom's presidency of COP 26 and look ahead to the COP 27 summit in Sharm el-Sheikh.

The King really wants to go to COP 27 but I think the government want his first official visit to be to the USA or somewhere. So this reception is a brilliant idea.

****

6TH NOVEMBER

There is an article in *the Observer* today by Will Hutton on a subject that I have written about so many times. He begins his article with the following sentence, **"Judge the vitality and health of a society by the way it treats its young."**

A report from the Institute for Fiscal Studies released two days ago states that the single most influential determinant of an individual's life chances is their experience when young. It is about their birth weight, what they eat, the strength of family ties and parenting and their access to excellent early years' education.

I have flagged this up so often and so have all those involved with education and the early years such as the Princess of Wales.

So just two points of interest here. It is being forecast that it will take a year longer than the original goal of 2024 to get education spending in real terms back to the 2010 levels.

The incomes of Britain's top 10% are five times higher than the bottom 10% whilst in the rest of Europe the average ratio is three times. Will Hutton points out that, **"There is no route to improving the condition of the 4 million disadvantaged kids without improving the incomes of their parents."**

Then there are the teachers. At the moment the main concern of teachers is about making sure the children are getting the proper nutrition. He asks, "How, as a society, have we allowed this to happen?"

I would like you to answer this one.

****

Asylum seekers and the Home office.

As Suella Braverman so rightly says the immigration system is broken. The backlog of unprocessed applications has risen alarmingly since 2012. In 2010 there were nearly 6,000 cases awaiting an initial decision and by the second quarter of this year there were 100,000. This is not because of an increase in those seeking asylum. In fact there has been a drop in numbers. In 2002 there were more than 100,000 people claiming asylum whereas there were almost half, just more than 50,000, last year according to Oxford University's Migrations Observatory. No, the backlog is because the number of officials working on these applications has fallen enormously since 2016. In 2014 almost 80% of applications were dealt with in six months. Today it is less than 10% and in some years it has only been 4%.

I think there are at least three things that should be done.

*There need to be safe legal routes with visa centres in France.

*There needs to be an enormous recruitment drive for more officials to process applications, and

*asylum seekers need to be allowed to work when they are here.

David Neal, Chief Inspector of Borders and Immigration has written a critique for *the Times* in which he says decision making must be speeded up and the teams need to be carefully recruited, nurtured and re-trained. He has found low morale, a high employee attrition rate, unstable management and no service standard in which to base performance.

Basically it looks as though the whole department needs a rapid overhaul.

There are plenty of job vacancies. In the present situation refugees are sitting in centres or other accommodation doing absolutely nothing for days on end. 18 and 19 months in some cases. Again it is interesting to note that individuals arriving from Ukraine are able to live and work in the UK for up to three years and access healthcare, benefits, employment support, education and other support.

A sealed border is not a possibility so we need more realism, less vitriolic speech and more humanity.

****

Then there is a report concerning **Therese Coffey** and her new department of Environment and Rural affairs. The deadline for producing new nature and polluting targets was yesterday and was not adhered to. This however was not the first time that deadlines had been missed. The Office for Environmental Protection was created to replace the enforcement role of the European Court of Justice on Environmental Law. Oh so we are back to Brexit again. The chairman, Dame Glenys Stacey, said "We remain concerned that there is a pattern of missing legislative deadlines."

She said that formal enforcement action against the government would be kept under "active review". **Failing to produce the targets by the end of the year could trigger action. The National Trust, Friends of the Earth and Woodland Trust have all complained.**

Two weeks? Not a brilliant start I would say.

****

UP TO THE JOB PRIME MINISTER?

8TH NOVEMBER

Things are not looking good. Suella Braverman failed to turn up to answer an urgent question put to her by Labour about over-crowding at Manston. I think this is contempt of Parliament. Then we hear further complaints about Gavin Williamson and his bullying. He (allegedly) told a civil servant to "Jump out of the window" and "slit your throat."

It has also just been revealed that during her failed bid to become Tory leader, Suella Braverman received funding which was linked to the climate-change denying think tank based at 55 Tufton Street. Well we know all about them and this is not a good look at any time but definitely not during Cop 27. This group goes by the name 'The Global Warming Policy Foundation' and is being investigated by the 'Good Law Project.'

"So these people are filling the news at the moment.

Oh wait a minute, what is this we are hearing on the eve of the next PMQs? **Sir Gavin Williamson has resigned.** Well we think he should be put into the Guinness Book of Records as he has been sacked (or resigned if you prefer) three times under three different Prime Ministers.

There are calls for him to be stripped of his knighthood of course.

And it is a gift for Starmer.

****

9TH NOVEMBER

PMQs

He roasted Sunak but the really interesting thing here was that after a question from Starmer, when Sunak should jump up with an answer, there was silence. The cameras focused on him and there he was, still sitting down reading his notes with his head buried in his large file. Someone behind poked him in the back and the front bench all turned towards him. "Ooops, I think I am still the PM" he must have hurriedly thought as he jumped up and murmured something about "integrity, professionalism and accountability."

But we saw Dominic Raab, who was sitting beside him, mouth the word "wanker" at Sir Keir.

It really is utterly pathetic and, pleasant enough as Sunak most probably is, he is just not up to the job. And the language of some of his ministers is utterly disgraceful

****

10TH NOVEMBER

Public Finances and the Economy. And then I read a really frightening article in *The Guardian* by Aditya Chakrabortty.

She says that all the Conservatives are the same at the moment and their ideology is universal across the party. They all basically protect the interests of the wealthy, the company bosses and all those at the very top of the food chain.

I think we all knew that but she puts it very eloquently when she says, "Picture brutal metal studs embedded in the sole of a shiny black Oxford brogue: that is the form of government we face now."

She talks about the forthcoming budget and the kind of austerity we should expect. This, she says, is when the public services will bear the brunt of the cuts.

She goes on to say that, "It will be not the second but the third wave of austerity since 2010 (many forget the cuts made by Sunak at No 11 as the pandemic eased).

Each has been about disciplining poor people and protecting the rich, and each has come with a fresh wave of authoritarianism. Just look at what they introduced this year in the Police, Crime, Sentencing and Courts Act, banning protests and locking up those who take part in them for a year."

And right on cue we read about the journalist **Charlotte Lynch.** She was standing on a bridge in Hertfordshire over the M25, where there was a protest by the 'Just stop Oil' group who were holding up the traffic. Police approached her and she showed them her press card. But they searched her, took her phone, hand- cuffed her, put her in to the back of a police van in a sort of cage and took her to Stevenage police station. There she was searched again and put into cell where she stayed for five hours. There was one flat bed and a metal toilet. She was never questioned. She was terrified, and listening to her on LBC you could hear the trauma in her voice. Some other reporters were also arrested and the Crime Commissioner of Hertfordshire Police will be investigating.

If this doesn't scare you to bits then nothing will.

As *The Guardian* article says, "A clampdown on public finances, a crackdown on public disorder: the two went together in the 80s, in the 2010s – and they are what lie ahead now."

****

16TH NOVEMBER

Inflation has reached 11.1% the highest since 1981.

William Keegan in *the Observer* says he does not know how further austerity policies are going to encourage the business investment we need. As for public sector capital spending, the former Treasury permanent secretary Lord Macpherson said, during the 1976 IMF crises this did "fall off a cliff and has never truly recovered."

But there are reports of more cuts to public investment coming in the autumn statement and he ends his article with the following sentence:

"Whom the gods would destroy, they first make mad."

****

The Grenfell report

On the night of the fire on 14 June 2017, 72 people died in the greatest loss of life following a residential fire since the Second World War.

An inquiry into the Grenfell fire was launched in August 2017. All the permitted evidence has now been marshalled. The final report will be published, possibly in 2023. But inquiries such as this one always take an inordinately long time to be completed and criminal charges can only be considered after the full report is published.

The residents knew that the building was unsafe and expressed their concerns to the Tory council often.

All companies involved and accused have denied any wrongdoing but Stephanie Barwise KC named a "rogues gallery" including 'Arconic,' the US-owned firm that made the highly combustible cladding panels, the architect 'Studio E', fire engineer 'Exova' and Kensington council staff and contractors.

Adrian Williamson KC named some more of the companies who were culpable which were: 'Celotex', which made most of the combustible insulation, and 'Kingspan', another manufacturer, charged with testing and certifying the building products.

Imran Khan KC accused them all of "a callous indifference to anything – morality, honesty, life safety – that was not related to the bottom line of the business." Words such as "fraudulent", "grossly negligent" and "reckless" were used by these lawyers who also said there had been "a merry-go-round of buck passing" between companies, public authorities and professionals.

In the final statement by Richard Millett KC, counsel to the inquiry he declared that: **"Each and every one of the deaths that occurred in Grenfell Tower... was avoidable.**

You might remember that our then Prime Minister, Theresa May didn't even bother to meet the traumatised residents and refused to speak to them after the fire. She carried out a private visit to the scene and spoke with emergency service crews and blocked media access. The decision was taken due to "security reasons", it was claimed, but local residents were furious that she did not stop to listen to their concerns. Compassionate Conservatism.

The Queen on the other hand met firefighters and police officers who had worked around the clock and she and Prince William spent 45 minutes greeting people before leaving. The Duchess of Cornwall also sent her "thoughts and prayers" to the victims of the Grenfell Tower tragedy.

The costs of the inquiry are over £150m and rising.

****

The NHS

And the other most important self-afflicted headache for the government is the crisis in the NHS.

Nurses in nearly all Trusts in England have voted to strike. Emergency and life- saving care will not be affected but the backlog for elective surgery will be even higher than it is now and cancer referral and chemotherapy treatment and scans etc. will be delayed.

They are asking for an increase of 15% in pay and the government are saying sorry not possible. The pay review body advised 4% and the Health Secretary Steve Barclay is very sorry and he feels their pain but that is it. They were given a rise last year and they need to make do with that.

But do not fear, Oliver is here. He is all over the media and he says, "We have well-oiled contingencies in place for the strikes". What? Where? How?

Where will all these spare strike-breaking nurses come from exactly? This is Oliver Dowden my MP. I might have mentioned him before.

This will be the first strike in the history of the RCN.

Oh I just hear that the Health Secretary is meeting some nurses to discuss it all. Good heavens that **is** a good idea. Who would have thought? How much do we pay our politicians? £84,144. My goodness do we think they are worth it? Are we getting good value for our money? I leave that with you.

****

Then we mustn't forget the social care problem.

You will remember the flagship policy of Boris Johnson was to put a cap of £86,000 on the amount that people would have to pay for their social care as well as increasing national insurance to help fund the social care plan. Well this latter idea was ditched by Liz Truss and we are hearing that the cap could be delayed until 2025 or maybe even indefinitely.

Are you beginning to get the picture that there is absolutely no sustainable governing going on, that all manifesto pledges are being broken, that this government hasn't got a clue and that they really do not care?

****

And whilst we are talking about the NHS here are some figures you might be interested in.

In a transparency drive ordered by the Health Secretary (yes you did read that word 'transparency' correctly), it has been discovered that NHS England has 30 managers on six figure salaries. This includes Amanda Pritchard, the chief executive who earns **£260,000 a year**. There are 109 employees who earn at least **£150,000** a year including many working on IT, and Sir Chris Whitty, chief medical officer, earns **£210,000** a year. Sir Chris Wormald, permanent secretary at the department of health earns **£175,000** a year. Nice work if you can get it.

The current starting salary for a Band 5 nurse in the UK is £24,907.

And between 2010 and 2021 a nurses pay decreased by 7.4% in real terms.

****

Then there is more on our maternity services. As I have previously reported, although ministers keep saying they are perfectly safe, many hospitals, as you know, have had dreadful records of safety.

But there is a study, by an international team of researchers including academics from the University of Oxford, who examined data on millions of live births across Denmark, Finland, France, Italy, the Netherlands, Norway, Slovakia and the UK. **They found that mothers in the UK are three times more likely to die around the time of pregnancy compared with those in Norway.** They found that

Slovakia had the highest maternal death rate among the countries studied and the UK was the second highest. In a linked editorial, Prof Andrew Shennan of King's College London warned that **variations in maternal mortality "remain one of the starkest health injustices in the world".**

****

Then there is still no movement on the scandal that is social care. You can get more money shifting boxes around in a supermarket than for shifting elderly poorly people around.

At the moment there are 13,000 people well enough to leave hospital but cannot because of the lack of care in the community. They are actually being harmed by being kept in hospital as their muscles are weakening and their mental health is suffering.

So this is how we look after sick people today. Be in no doubt, this government wants to destroy the NHS and privatise it. I never used to believe this but I'm afraid it is becoming obvious even to me.

So the NHS crisis is all over the news and will be for the foreseeable future.

****

Levelling up going well?

Not if you are a cyclist it isn't. Our roads have deteriorated dreadfully over the past five years or so. A mass freedom of information request to all local authorities responsible for repairing roads in England and Wales showed that local authorities in England and Wales have paid out more than £32m in compensation over the past half a decade due to pothole-related injuries.

At least 425 cyclists have been killed or seriously injured due to poor or defective road surfaces since 2016.

So a lot more levelling of roads is required but not much chance of that happening at the moment. As someone sad "We don't drive on the left anymore. We drive on what is left of the road."

****

But how is the more important levelling- up going which always meant, or so we were led to believe, the boosting of the north to level it with the more prosperous south?

We will focus on the town of Barnsley which is a deprived northern town and which was promised £3.6 billion and which has not yet seen one penny of it. A third of Barnsley's children live in poverty and this money was going to be used to help increase their life chances. And if we had stayed in the EU South Yorkshire would have received £900 million.

The really interesting thing though is that this former mining town was not even placed in the top tier of towns needing help, whilst Richmond, a relatively prosperous town in Yorkshire, secured highest priority status.

Oh wait a minute. Richmond is the constituency of our former Chancellor, now Prime Minister, Rishi Sunak.

****

As I have previously said Brexit is at last being talked about and not before time.

Lord Wolfson chief executive of Next, and prominent Brexiteer has said that there needs to be a relaxing of rules on immigration. Pardon? Yes, restricting the supply of migrant workers threatened a "fortress Britain" he said, and it would hamper economic growth. Oh my goodness did you not foresee this at the time of Brexit? The lack of brain power is hugely worrying.

Many employers are struggling to fill vacancies and the result, according to the 'Commission on the Future of Employment Support' is that the country is failing.

Yes I think we can all agree on that. In 2023 the UK will be the only big economy in which employment is lower than before the pandemic because so many people left the labour market.

****

Then, hold your breath, we hear this. George Eustace, the Environment Secretary in the Johnson era, is now a back bencher and has the luxury of actually speaking the truth. Now that's a novelty.

He talks about the trade deal that Liz Truss, the then Foreign Secretary did with Australia.

"The first step" he says "is to recognise that **the Australia trade deal is not actually a very good deal for the UK,"** adding that **"the truth of the matter is that the UK gave away far too much for far too little in return".**

Well yes that is exactly what everyone concerned with this deal thought at the time particularly British beef farmers. We will now have to eat cheaper cuts of meat at more expensive prices.

The agreements with Australia and New Zealand are the only new trade deals signed since Britain left the European Union and Eustace says that we need to learn from our mistakes to make sure it doesn't happen again.

The trouble is, Mr. Eustace, your government never, ever admits to making any mistakes so it will never learn and it is continuing to make mistake after mistake after mistake, everywhere you turn.

****

And here it is from the horse's mouth. Well one of them anyway. Michael Saunders former member of the bank of England's monetary policy committee says that "The UK economy as a whole has been permanently damaged by Brexit." And, "if we hadn't had Brexit we possibly would not be talking about an austerity budget this week."

****

And Paris has overtaken London as Europe's biggest stock market, new analysis has revealed because Brexit has reduced the country's potential output and resulted in reduced investment into UK businesses. Indeed we are all aware of that.

****

18TH NOVEMBER

The on-line safety bill has been delayed yet again. It was due to return to the Commons next week, but has been withdrawn from the parliamentary schedule because of the chaos surrounding the resignation of Liz Truss as prime minister. It had previously been planned for late summer, but was then delayed to the autumn as a result of the chaos surrounding the resignation of Boris Johnson as prime minister. This bill is being designed to protect children from viewing harmful images such as children suffering sexual abuse and rape and practising self- harm. With no known date for when the bill will return to the Commons, internet safety groups warned that any further delay would continue to place children at risk.

Labour's Lucy Powell, the shadow secretary of state for digital, culture, media and sport condemned the delay. "It is disgraceful that one of the first acts of Rishi Sunak's government is to, yet again, pull the online safety bill."

Of course you get the blinkered, cruel, and intellectually challenged MPs worrying about free speech. But it is important to see what those who actually care about our children say.

Barnardo's Chief Executive Lynn Perry MBE said: "Every day the Bill is delayed is another day that children are exposed to extreme pornography, which harms their mental health and their understanding of healthy relationships. The Government has said this legislation is a priority and we would urge Ministers to act swiftly to protect children. The bill would require pornography websites to introduce age verification, which will help prevent millions of young children from stumbling across harmful videos online. These vital changes must come back to Parliament urgently. **Children cannot afford to wait any longer."**

****

A two year old little boy has died of a respiratory and cardiac arrest caused by having to live in rented accommodation which was uninhabitable due to excessive mould.

His name was Awaab Ishak and his parents had repeatedly raised the issue with Rochdale Boroughwide Housing but no action was ever taken.

"We shouted out as loudly as we could, but despite making all of those efforts, every night we would be coming back to the same problem."

RBH chief executive Gareth Swarbrick said they would learn hard lessons from this but he won't resign.

But I have questions of my own. How is it that no one at the RBC took any notice and no-one in the health services took any notice? How is it that on the 13th January 2016 the Conservatives voted **against** a Labour amendment to the current Housing and Planning Bill to ensure houses were kept to a decent standard, by 312 votes to 219, a majority of 93? Could it be that at least 71 of the Tory MPs who voted against an amendment to force landlords to make sure their properties are "fit for human habitation" are private landlords themselves? **And, Mr. Swarbrick, do you really think you deserve to keep your salary of £170,000?**

****

Ha! We have just heard that he has been fired.

****

I have no words for those who seek to harm our children and this government, as I keep on saying and will continue to keep on saying, have no regard for our children whatsoever.

****

More Strikes

Civil servants are threatening months of disruption as they have voted to strike. 100,000 of them including staff in the courts, the Border Force, Passport Office, DVLA and job centres have said they will set dates very soon unless they are offered more money by the end of November. It includes staff in the Cabinet Office and Mark Serwotka, general secretary of the union, warned of a 'prolonged industrial action reaching into every corner of public life.'

The Fire Brigades Union and its members have rejected their bosses' pay offer of an insulting 5% – less than half the rate of inflation – inching the union further towards strike action. It comes as the UK is facing a winter of industrial action across many major sectors – and the Fire Brigade could be next to join.

****

So just to be absolutely crystal clear about the calibre of this government we have:

Gavin Williamson who has just resigned over allegations of bullying.

Suella Braverman being investigated over sending confidential documents on personal emails, possibly lying on her CV and possibly breaking the law with over-crowding at Manston to which I would add being in contempt of parliament for failing to turn up for an urgent question. Oh and she has just found £63 million in her back pocket to sign a deal with France for more patrols on the beaches in order to try to stop the small boat crossings. Well even **she** is saying that it won't actually sort out the problem. No, Ms. Braverman we know.

Dominic Raab who is also accused of bullying. In fact top civil servants were told they did not have to work directly for him when he was reappointed as their boss last month as Whitehall bosses feared some were still traumatised from his first year-long stint in charge of the department which ended in September. And we see him mouthing "wanker" at the Leader of the Opposition in the House of Commons. (He says he said "weaker" as he is being called to account about it but I saw it and I recognise wanker when I see it.)

Steve Barclay our Health Minister who says that doctors and nurses need to work harder and for longer, especially at weekends. The nurses' demand for more money was "neither reasonable nor affordable". That has gone down well.

Oliver Dowden who never answers my emails but says once again on TV that they have well-oiled contingency plans for the nurses if they strike but no, he won't tell us what they are.

Matt Hancock our previous failed health secretary who is in Australia earning £400,000 from a TV show whilst still drawing his MP's salary. Oh wait a minute. He has just returned to the UK and his constituents have just told him to go. So he will not be standing at the next election.

Then we have yet another Tory MP **Julian Knight** being investigated after a complaint against him and he has just had the whip removed

And there is Rishi Sunak himself. Nesrine Malik *The Guardian* columnist has said it has taken only three weeks to expose Sunak as "yet another underqualified and over-promoted prime minister. **There is now no doubt that he does not have the mandate, the appetite or the nerve to deliver what was expected of him.**"

Well, that is a very succinct and pertinent summing up of our new Prime Minister and I think I was right when I said that I was not sure about him and that I would watch and wait. And no Mr. Sunak, I don't think you are up to the job.

****

THE AUTUMN STATEMENT

17TH NOVEMBER 2022

Jeremy Hunt, Chancellor, announces that the UK faces a two year recession.

As forecast, taxes are going up and public spending cuts are introduced. There is some more money for the NHS and for schools but many changes will not occur for another two years. In other words just before the next general election. Aha! I have news for them. My prediction is that there will be a general election in October 2023. I cannot see how this corrupt and useless government can continue.

Inflation is now at 11.1% Even the Treasury's own analysis shows half of British households will be worse off next year – with taxes hiked to the highest levels since the end of the Second World War, the country in the grip of recession and inflation remaining high. So after a winter like that people will be in despair. I just don't think it will be sustainable.

The OBR says living standards will fall by 7% in total over the two years to April 2024, wiping out the previous eight years of increases, and households are really going to notice how bad things have got. But I think they will notice long before then.

In fact they are noticing now.

The extended freezing of tax allowances and the spending cuts in non-protected Whitehall departments are bad news and of course there is nothing said about free school meals.

Again in this statement, he pledged to double annual energy efficiency investment with new funding of £6bn.

Wonderful you might think. But this doubling does not happen until 2025, when the energy bills crisis may be over and the climate crisis will be even worse. It is ridiculous and deceitful.

Hunt is the fourth chancellor since the beginning of 2022 and the chaos in the Tory party has meant unnecessary delays in making people's homes warmer and cheaper to heat. The trouble goes back almost a decade in fact, when David Cameron's ditching of "green crap" saw insulation rates fall by 95%; a decision that has cost bill payers billions. On the supply of low-carbon energy, Hunt backed expensive nuclear power as well as offshore wind, but said nothing on the fastest and by far the cheapest sources: onshore wind and solar. They have no idea and are completely out of tune with ordinary voters who of course have far more common sense than any government minister.

But as I have said nearly all the austerity cuts are to take place much later and after the next election. As one minister put it: "This was the day we lost the election." Actually mate I have news for you. You lost the next election months ago.

As Tom Peck of *The Independent* says "It is not a government, it is a rolling experiential performance art piece, of which the latest character to take centre stage is Jeremy Hunt."

"Boris Johnson, Liz Truss, Kwasi Kwarteng, Suella Braverman, Rishi Sunak, Dominic Cummings, Gavin Williamson, the absurd list rolls on and on, and endlessly on – to the point where its idiocy has become tedious".

Indeed it does. He forgot to mention Dominic Raab, George Eustace, James Cleverly, Therese Coffey, Grant Shapps, Michelle Donelan, Mel Stride, Gillian Keegan, Michael Gove and Nadhim Zahawi.

I leave you to add your favourite incompetent idiots to this list.

The shadow chancellor, Rachel Reeves, said when replying to the statement in the House: "What people will be asking themselves at the next general election is this: 'Am I and my family better off with the Tories?' And the answer is no."

And an article about **Sir Keir Starmer** in *The Times* makes very interesting reading. He is quoted as saying "The transition from law to politics is a very odd one, because you're used to a courtroom with evidence, with rules, with rationality, with a decision. And suddenly you go into politics where none of that really counts for very much. The number of people who do fantastic speeches describing the same problem without actually fixing it, drives me mad. That's where my passion is --- let's identify what the problem is, let's be really accurate about what needs to change, then just let's get on and do it, rather than talking about it."

This is music to my ears. And to many other ears I would imagine. The fact that the cap on social care has just been delayed for another two years in the autumn statement is a scandal. The Dilnot report recommending a cap on social care spending was published in 2011 hoping for it to be implemented by 2014. It will now not be discussed again until 2024 unless there is a Labour government before then. There are so many heart-breaking stories of people having to pay sums like £2,000 a week in order to get the care they need.

Also music to my ears is when he says that **there should be more arts and creativity in schools.** "If you are playing in an orchestra you've got to work as a team. These are the subtle skills that children need to go into modern day work." To which I would add singing in a choir. He does think the education curriculum needs to change and reform.

Be in no doubt, the Labour party is ready for government. And be in no doubt, the Conservative party is a spent force.

****

THE LAST 10 DAYS OF NOVEMBER

20TH ---- 30TH

Women

So we return to the general attitude to women and girls in this country.

For some insane reason Eton College invited Nigel Farage to give a talk at the school and they also invited some girls from a nearby state school.

Apparently the girls were subjected to a barrage of misogynistic language, racial slurs and jeering.

The school has apologised and "sanctioned" a number of pupils. This is the school that spawned Boris Johnson and it creates an atmosphere of self-entitlement and arrogance amongst all its male pupils.

And just to be clear about the sort of school it is, they had also cheered Farage's "worst comments on migrants and Covid".

For this type of 'education' the parents pay £46,296 a year.

There is a growing consensus which says that all privately paid education (public schools) should be abolished and all children should attend state schools. Well this won't happen but Labour will attempt to force a binding vote on ending private schools' tax breaks and use the £1.7bn a year raised from this to drive new teacher recruitment.

****

The Independent Office for Police Conduct published its investigation last week into a specific case and they found that **West Midlands police** "materially contributed" to the murders of a young woman and her mother, through their repeated failures to address the threat that a former partner posed to their lives.

They state that this was not an isolated incident.

There is a police culture of misogyny and some police treat violence against women as a joking matter rather than a serious crime. A woman is killed by a man every three days in the UK and many of these deaths are preventable. But not with the present culture of misogyny in the UK police force. The new Commissioner of the Metropolitan Police, Sir Mark Rowley, has said he will reform the Met and will be ruthless in removing those who are corrupting the integrity of the Metropolitan police. Meanwhile the West Midlands Police issued an apology to the families of the murdered women.

****

Midwives are marching again and it is not surprising because,............ has this government improved maternity services since their campaign a year ago? Well what do you think? I think you could write this book as well as I can actually, because you must be getting the message by now. As midwives are saying. **"Not much has changed — actually, things are worse! Maternity services across the UK are in a state of emergency and women and birthing people are in catastrophic danger."** And the group 'Mothers and Babies: Reducing Risk through Audits and Confidential Enquiries' — this month revealed maternal death rates are rising in the UK and there are increases in the suicide rate of new and expectant mothers. Very few of them had a mental health diagnosis but significant numbers had a history of trauma.

So I think it is obvious that this government hasn't done a thing and doesn't intend to do a thing and doesn't care about doing a single thing to help expectant mothers and their babies.

So midwives are talking about strikes, although the Royal College of Midwives executive director, Dr Suzanne Tyler insisted that any strikes would not put women or babies at risk and safe services will be maintained. But, she warned: "Our members are sending a very clear message to the Governments in England and Wales and one that must not be ignored any longer."

****

Farming

Eggs are in short supply, say the supermarkets, because there is an outbreak of avian flu. Apparently we consume 37 million British eggs every day and we are capable of producing 42 million. So this is looking serious. And indeed it is. But when we delve further we realise that the main cause of the shortage is actually because farmers no longer have enough money to pay for their chicken feed, the energy bills for heating their sheds, or for higher wages for staff and so they have not restocked their hens. As Jennifer Turnball, a fifth-generation farmer says, "Production costs have soared and supermarkets haven't covered it so farmers have decided it is not worth it."

I think it is important that we know the real facts behind the headlines.

****

20TH NOVEMBER

So Cop 27 at Sharm el-Sheikh comes to an end, and although there were a few positives there was plenty of disappointment as well.

There was agreement to set up a "loss and damage" fund which is meant to help vulnerable countries cope with climate disasters, and it was agreed that the world needs to cut greenhouse gas emissions by half by 2030. **It was reaffirmed that the goal of keeping global warming to 1.5 degrees Celsius above pre-industrial levels should be kept.**

So some progress but not enough.

So good that Sunak decided to go in the end and whilst there he would have met one of his predecessors which was Boris Johnson. Not sure why he went except, wait a minute, isn't Sharm el-Sheikh a lovely holiday venue? We know how much Boris likes his holidays.

****

Politics, Brexit and the Economy

Brexit is really the absolute crux of the problems this country is facing but to get our politicians to understand this is impossible.

Just read what people are saying right now.

Will Hutton in the *Observer* writes that, "Babble about exploiting Brexit opportunities is just babble: trade is shrinking and with it private investment. There is no plan, no vision, no institutional architecture that might offer better, and none anticipated."

He says that "Britain needs a serious national conversation for which the precondition is truth telling."

But we know that this is impossible with this Conservative government.

Will Hutton says, "Eight weeks ago a Tory chancellor promised the biggest tax cuts for 40 years; now, facing reality, there is a proper reversal on the same scale. Even Ruritania," he says, "could not do worse."

Their editorial says that "real wages will not return to the levels at which they were before the 2008 crisis until 2027." They go on to say that, "it is dishonest to pretend that Britain's grim growth outlook is purely a product of global shocks. Other countries have proved more resilient, even as Britain's economy is showing its fragility. The reason for that is 12 years of Conservative economic policy and political instability; what the Institute for Fiscal Studies has described as a series of 'economic own goals'."

They say that the Brexit offered to the country was based on "a series of lies."

The NHS will continue to be under-funded and under-staffed, education catch-up for disadvantaged children will not be adequately funded and these children will feel the consequences for the rest of their lives.

"Britain is getting poorer and it is the Conservative party not Vladimir Putin that is largely to blame."

The 'Organisation for Economic Co-operation and Development' says that the UK is facing the worst downturn of major economies next year and is set for a recession which most of the rest of the world will avoid.

And a man on BBC's' Question Time' spoke passionately about his import/export business which he says is a massive struggle now of bureaucracy, red tape, massive expense and loads of paper work. Before Brexit, he said it, was easy. None of this was there and everything went through so smoothly. **"I don't want to trade with Australia or New Zealand" he said. "I want to trade with the markets on our doorstep just 20 miles across the channel."**

That explains it in a nutshell.

And every time someone said we need to re-join the single market and the customs union the entire audience burst into spontaneous and rapturous applause.

****

24TH NOVEMBER

So what does Rishi Sunak say at the CBI? This is their Annual Dinner where more than 600 senior business leaders will be wanting to hear words of wisdom about the economy.

Well he has rejected any move to rebuild damaged trade with the EU that would undermine the UK's freedoms, insisting that Brexit is "delivering" for the country. He also said: "Let me be unequivocal about this. Under my leadership, the UK will not pursue any relationship with Europe that relies on alignment with EU laws."

He also rejected the CBI's call for fixed-term visas to allow businesses to bring in more overseas workers to plug labour shortages – insisting his priority is to curb illegal, cross-Channel migration.

In fact this was his number one mission at the moment as he kept saying in answer to questions. "The number one priority right now, when it comes to migration, is to tackle illegal migration" and he kept saying he wanted to stop the small boat crossings.

There had been talk about copying the Swiss style relationship with the EU, but no, that was certainly not open for discussion.

However, the government is under pressure to explain how it will mitigate the forecast 4 per cent hit to GDP, with a 15 per cent loss of trade, from Boris Johnson's hard Brexit deal.

Matthew Syed sums it up at the end of his article in *The Sunday Times* when he says that we seem to have had the worst of all possible worlds with the Tories. "We have had low quality politicians deriding expertise and thereby taking the nation from crisis to contradictory crisis. That is why we have endured the gravest mismanagement since the overreach of the post war consensus in the 1970s, perhaps since the Second World War. **And here's the thing we should never forget: a critical mass of Tory MPs cheered it all.**"

I have never read so much damaging criticism across the political divide about a UK government before. This is very frightening and people are saying that there is worse to come.

****

25TH NOVEMBER

We have just heard that nurses have voted for strike action on the 15th and 20th of December. So many questions were being asked of the Chief Nursing Officer on the radio this morning as to how patients will suffer and how will they alleviate disruption but the question that was never asked and which was the most pertinent of all was, 'What is the government doing about it?' This is the first strike in their history and the government is not even talking to them. All they say is, well we are abiding by the pay review body.

BUT THAT IS NOT ENOUGH. THAT IS NOT WORKING.

There are so many strike actions with the railways, train drivers, the Royal Mail, all teachers in Scotland, all University lecturers, and many more to come. GPs want to shorten their hours from 8.30 am to 6pm to 9am to 5pm.and the editorial in *The Times* today makes my blood boil as they tell the government to remain firm and brook no compromise with "a new generation of union militants." Well that will help won't it?

****

Rishi Sunak is looking weaker and weaker. He is facing his first Tory Commons rebellion since entering 10 Downing Street. After 47 Tory MPs threatened to back an amendment on planning reform which would oppose compulsory housebuilding targets, the government has pulled the vote until further notice. There is such a lot of criticism about this. Successive governments' failure to build enough homes is legion and I was campaigning about this years ago. But to quote an editorial in *The Times,* "House building is as close to a textbook case of market and political failure as any student of economics or public administration could wish for.

"We are not building and never have built enough homes and as long as that remains the case legally binding targets, however unpalatable, are the bare minimum a responsible government can do."

So why exactly do some MPs object to this bill and these targets? Because it would mean more homes being built in their leafy southern constituencies, their constituents wouldn't like it and they might get voted out at the next election.

Do they not know? Do they not hear? Do they not listen? There is a by-election coming up in Chester on the 1st December due to the resignation of the present incumbent Labour MP Chris Matheson, after allegations of sexual misconduct. Well my forecasts are not always very accurate but I would think that the Tory candidate would lose his deposit. We will see and I will take note.

(No lost deposit but a drop from 20,000 to 6,000)

****

And there is another rebellion brewing for Mr Sunak about onshore wind farms. He is opposed to more building onshore for the same reason; he thinks local communities do not want their beautiful views spoilt by large turbines. At present there is a ban on building wind farms onshore would you believe and he is trying to work out just how big the rebellion would be if he did lift it. But they are already rebelling about the ban so it looks to me as though there is a rebellion whatever he does or doesn't do.

Well I've got an idea. Why doesn't he go into a quiet room, think carefully about what would be best for the country, and then go out, stand up straight and tell the country and the Commons his firm decision. I thought that was what being a leader was all about.

****

All MPs wanting to stand for the next election have until 5th December to declare their intent. Well eleven Tory MPs have announced their intent to stand down so far. Some of them have served for many years but some are surprisingly young which is causing some worry.

Dehenna Davison has only been an MP since 2019 and was considered to be a rising star, William Wragg is 41 and a sort of decent Tory as he has been very critical of Johnson and Truss. Chloe Smith was 27 when she was elected in 2009 and became the youngest MP and Douglas Ross, leader of the Scottish Conservatives since 2019, is also going. And I have just heard that Sajid Javid is standing down.

I wonder why they don't want to stay.

And it is becoming more and more obvious that MPs such as Boris Johnson and Jacob Rees-Mogg will lose their seats.

Oh what a night that will be.

(40 now declared they will stand down. June 2023)

****

So what other stories are circling around?

Well here is one which I nearly wrote about in my last book so it has been around for a while. Certainly last April her residence in Belgravia was involved in an early morning raid and police and the CPS are looking at a lot of electronic material to see whether they can bring a case of fraud and bribery to court. The reason I didn't include it was because I wasn't absolutely sure that it could be verified. But oh my word it is all over the place at the moment so here it is.

It concerns a Tory peer called Michelle Mone.

During the pandemic the government had what was called a VIP plan for the quick purchase of PPE and I have written about this before. It was extremely controversial, (that is polite speak for 'probably unethical') because many ministers were lobbied by friends with companies making PPE so giving them an unfair advantage. Certainly, when taken to court by the Good Law Project, a judge ruled it was unlawful to give two companies preferential treatment as part of this VIP lane.

One company placed on this fast track lane was one called Medpro and they were recommended by Michelle Mone and they received £203million worth of contracts. Now according to documents seen by *The Guardian*, tens of millions of pounds of the manufacturer's profits were crammed into an offshore trust that Mone and her adult children benefited from.

It gets worse.

£122 million was for gowns from China which proved to be sub-standard so were never used. She is already under investigation by the House of Lords Commissioners for Standards for allegedly not disclosing an interest in and lobbying for PPE Medpro. Labour are using a vote in parliament to force the publication of all secret texts and emails relating to this matter.

She refutes all allegations so we will see. For the moment she retains the Tory whip.

I have just heard that MPs have voted in favour of releasing all records relating to this PPE firm linked to Michelle Mone. That is brilliant. Believe me the tide is beginning to turn.

Aha I have just heard that the whip has been withdrawn and she seems to have disappeared from the face of the earth. Her house (mansion) is up for sale and Honduras has been mentioned. An awful lot of people are saying that she really should be in prison.

****

Two senior MPs are under investigation for rape.

This seems to be an ever increasing problem with MPs just now. And the Conservative party is facing calls to suspend an MP who is being investigated over allegations of rape and sexual assault. It is understood that none of the alleged victims have made a formal complaint, but some Conservative MPs have reported the accusations to the police and the Party.

At least six Conservative MPs have had the whip withdrawn or quit politics in the past 18 months over allegations of misconduct. One backbencher is currently under orders to stay away from parliament after having been arrested on suspicion of serious sexual offences also including rape.

Chris Bryant, the Labour chair of the standards committee, said: "I don't think it should be political parties investigating this type of complaint. It should be done confidentially, to a shared set of criteria, and the parties need to sit down and agree them."

Mike Clancy, the general secretary of 'Prospect', raised the issue of whether an MP facing allegations of sexual offences should be allowed to continue in their job in parliament while an investigation is ongoing.

"The report that another MP has been accused of sexual offences raises important questions as to who knew what, when, and what have they done about it," he said. "This MP remains free to visit the House of Commons and interact with staff despite these very serious allegations. This highlights yet again that there is no fit-for-purpose process in place to deal with this type of case and make parliament a safe place to work."

He added: "The Commons commission is finally looking into excluding MPs from parliament when they are under investigation for this kind of thing. That inquiry needs to be expedited."

I presume he means completed as quickly as possible. Unfortunately as we keep seeing that is not how this government works. But I find it incredible that they are allowed to carry on working whilst being investigated for such a serious crime. I don't think this would happen in any other profession. Surely they should be reported to the police.

****

Then I am really sorry but we have to mention Suella Braverman again. A refugee has recently died of diphtheria in the Manston detention centre. And we hear that the Home secretary has moved dozens of refugees with suspected diphtheria to hotels all around the UK. What is worse she did not consult with the local authorities before-hand. Jim McManus, president of the Association of Directors of Public Health, said it had "put asylum seekers and potentially hotel workers at avoidable and preventable risk". Claiming an offer to help the government deal with the outbreak was "rebuffed", Mr McManus said **the lack of "information, coordination and engagement from the Home Office has made the situation far worse than it could have been".**

****

It doesn't stop there.

The Home Office is routinely changing the birth dates of refugee children so as to classify them as adults.

The Refugee Council said interviews with 16 children released from Manston revealed that even in the cases of some boys who had identity documents stating they were children, **the Home Office changed their dates of birth to make them over 18.** Renae Mann, executive director of services at the Refugee Council, said: "This is a misuse of power by the government. These children are very vulnerable and have been through so much already."

If you can read this and not be appalled and frightened by it then I am not expressing things as clearly as I think I am. **This must be illegal. And to me this borders on Nazism.**

****

And the government continues with ridiculous plans to try to bring the immigration numbers down. International students may be barred from Britain unless they win a place at a top university.

Downing Street indicated that plans to bring overall numbers down could include putting up barriers for international students' loved ones and family members. **But university bodies have said that any plans to curb record immigration by launching a crackdown on foreign students would be "an act of economic self-harm".**

Well that would not be the first time. As we all know this is what this government does best.

Which right on cue brings us back to **Brexit**. The first major free trade agreement signed by Britain after Brexit has been branded a failure after new figures showed exports had fallen since it came into force. **Liz Truss signed a "historic" deal with Japan as trade secretary in October 2020, describing it as a "landmark moment for Britain".** It was claimed it would boost trade by billions of pounds and help the UK recover from the pandemic. So what happened? Figures collated by the Department for International Trade show exports to Japan fell from £12.3bn to £11.9bn in the year to June 2022.

The new figures follow evidence that Britain's economy is set to struggle compared to its international counterparts. According to the 'Organisation for Economic Co-operation and Development', **apart from Russia, we will be the weakest performer of the world's big economies next year.**

****

The Arts.

We not only have a corrupt and incompetent government, but those of you who have read my books will already know that we also have a philistine government.

In order to 'level up' and cut costs, Nadine Dorries, the so-called Culture Secretary, together with the government, have chosen to destroy the arts and in particular the opera. The steps she has taken this month indicate and confirm that she has absolutely no idea

how the arts work and that this government has no idea how to level up anything.

In Newbury, Berkshire, the **Watermill Theatre** is in "deep shock" after they discovered that there was to be a **100% cut to its Arts Council England funding.** They do an enormous amount of work with the local community and they say that, **"It threatens the work on stage and our hugely popular community engagement programme, which works with more than 20,000 people a year including refugees, young people with autism, adults with additional needs and our inclusive youth theatre."** Is the Arts Council aware of any of this or do they simply not care? It must be one or the other. The theatre company is currently playing to hundreds of school children throughout the UK including Darlington, Blackpool, Glasgow and Cardiff.

As they say "There is a dearth of mid-scale touring work – it's where the real issue is. Surely this is what levelling up has to be about?" Indeed, but the phrase "levelling up" is completely meaningless as we have seen over and over again. It is quite obvious that the Arts Council hasn't got a clue about the way in which the theatre works with other organisations.

We see the same problem with the **Welsh National Opera**. The opera company is based in Cardiff and also receives funding from the Arts Council of Wales and also works **and tours widely in England visiting Plymouth, Bristol, Southampton, Oxford, Milton Keynes, Birmingham and Liverpool. Its annual ACE allowance has fallen by a third, to £4m.**

"We were steeling ourselves for a cut, but not for one at this level," says general director Aidan Lang. "We don't know how the gap is going to be filled." He goes on to say, "We are struggling to understand what the opera policy is at ACE with both ourselves and **Glyndebourne Touring Opera** being so heavily cut."

Because yes, as he says, there is Glyndebourne's Autumn Touring Company which travels to **Milton Keynes, Canterbury, Norwich** and **Liverpool** and which **has lost 50% of its funding**. It is worth remembering that their summer season receives no public funding. And the company's activities extend far beyond just staging opera. **There are family concerts, visits to care homes and schools in Wales and England, a long-standing dementia choir and a long-Covid project, plus work with refugee centres in Cardiff and in Birmingham.**

"We were well on our way to migrating our Birmingham hub to the Black Country," he adds, "creating a localised presence that enables us to deliver engagement projects and become involved with local practitioners, really embedding the company in the community."

The Black Country was identified by ACE as an "underserved priority place" – somewhere with less cultural provision, and yet Lang is no longer able to say if the company will be able to tour there, and "if we're not going to take opera to the West Midlands, there's little point having a hub there without the singers and chorus and technicians to support the work".

Then there is the **English National Opera at the Coliseum**. The Arts Council has suggested that it moves to Manchester. This is absolutely crass, deluded and actually totally impossible. It is complete fantasy.

The ENO is the premier gateway opera house. It is the only company that always performs in English, fifty per cent of its audience are opera first timers, one in seven are under the age of 35, eleven per cent are ethnically diverse (more than any other United Kingdom opera house), and tickets are totally free to under 21s – and start at £10 for everybody else. It is the model of accessible art but does the Arts Council understand any of this? Obviously not.

The announcement was made with virtually no consultation or notice. Again that is so obvious. It would appear that a rigid dogma to redistribute funding away from the capital at any cost, coupled with a fundamental misconception of opera as a high, esoteric and inaccessible art form has led to ENO being a regrettable but, ultimately, expendable victim of levelling up. But you can't shift the hundreds of employees with their expertise away from the capital like that and has Manchester even been consulted? No of course not. And what about Opera North?

No consultation with anyone involved and just continuing ignorance, incompetence and wilful destruction from a government composed of philistines.

****

DECEMBER

Well that was November so now let us see how December is going. Well it is going very well so far as my book is concerned but not, I'm afraid, for the country.

The most frightening story I think I have ever read is one about the lack of preparedness for another pandemic. Not just the lack of planning but the fact that according to Dame Kate Bingham she thinks this is "deliberate." You will remember, I am sure, that her task force was central to procuring a range of vaccines so that we could begin vaccination before the rest of the world.

But we have now been overtaken by the rest of Europe and, she says, "Our approach seems to have been to go backwards rather than to continue the momentum." Apparently ministers have ignored all her recommendations about working with industry and experts and have handed control of key policies to civil servants. The vaccines policy is now run by a civil servant with a background in defence and no health expertise at all. As she comments, **"I'm beginning to think this is actually deliberate government policy just not to invest and not to support the sector."**

She goes on to say that, "Our vaccines currently are not good enough. We need to improve the quality of the vaccines' durability, the ability to stop transmission, the way in which we give vaccines, lots of things that need to be improved."

There needs to be a senior figure to bring together research and manufacturing and she cannot understand why this has not happened.

Well I think we all know why this has not happened. It is because we have the most negligent and incompetent government in our history.

****

Some interesting headlines:

"Northern rail delays hit trains en-route to meeting about northern rail delays."

I thought you would like that one.

The rail chaos in the north is worse than it has ever been and business groups say this near-constant disruption is costing the northern economy more than four hundred million pounds a year.

Here is another one:

"Fire chief will sack racists and sexist workers."

I honestly cannot think what to say about that one.

****

And then we hear the name Suella Braverman again and again. First of all the former head of UK counter-terror policing has called Suella Braverman's language on migrants "inexplicable" and compared it to Enoch Powel's "rivers of blood" speech. Yes, indeed her language is provocative and an incitement to violence.

But we also hear from the 'Public Administration and Constitutional Affairs Committee' which has said that reappointing Braverman 'sets a "dangerous precedent" for how breaches of the code are dealt with.

Its chair, Tory MP William Wragg, said: "It is incumbent on the Government to ensure a robust and effective system for upholding standards in public life is put in place, with proper sanctions for those who break the rules."

He also says that "The Prime Minister is rightly the ultimate arbiter of the rules in our system. We urge him to show leadership and give legal status to all the ethics watchdogs."

But we know that he has no leadership qualities and apparently no-one wants to be the new ethics adviser. Well, are we surprised?

Labour leader Keir Starmer has demanded the Home Secretary's sacking, accusing Sunak of brokering a "grubby deal trading security for support" in the Tory leadership contest, which he won after receiving Braverman's backing.

But the Prime Minister has insisted Braverman has "learned from her mistake" and that he does not regret the appointment.

Hmmm. He might come to regret that remark however as there are signs that some back benchers are not too happy about her appointment.

It really isn't looking too good for this Prime Minister at the moment.

****

They really should all be put in prison but we can't even do that because the country has apparently run out of prison cells. The government has made an emergency request for the use of 400 police cells for the first time in 14 years. And guess what............they are putting all the blame onto the barrister's strike. Of course always, always, blame others for your incompetence. Anyone who has read the chapter on the criminal justice system in my book *Behind the Headlines* will know the truth.

Only 3,100 additional prison places have been created as part of the government's promise to build an extra 20,000 new cells by the mid- 2020s.

The Prison Governor's Association said using police cells would reduce the number of officers available to carry out frontline duties. **He said that "a police custody suite should never be considered an alternative to prison."**

****

The chief economist of the Bank of England has sounded the alarm over the UK's shrinking labour market and he says that Brexit is the cause of Britain's weak economy.

I say, tell us something we don't already know.

And the London School of Economics says that leaving the EU has added £200 to food bills.

And people will go on talking about the disastrous effect of Brexit until someone has the gumption to take us back into the single market and the customs union.

The Office for National Statistics have published revised figures for the three months to September showing economic activity contracting by 0.3 per cent, compared with a previous estimate of 0.2 per cent.

The slowdown also extended to the first half of 2022 with previous growth estimates revised down in the new numbers.

This performance puts the UK well behind its neighbours. Bank of England governor Andrew Bailey last month contrasted the UK's performance with that of the eurozone area, whose economy is now 2.1 per cent bigger than in 2019, and the US economy which is now 4.2 per cent.

****

2ND DECEMBER

The world of education continues to be in a mess under this government which always upsets me. Figures published yesterday by the Department of Education says that the number of trainee teachers has plummeted to "catastrophic" levels. Only 17% of the targeted number of trainee physics teachers were recruited in this academic year. The number recruited from all subjects and stages of school was 71% of the target down from 97% last year. Geoff Barton of the Association of School and College Leaders said "The government has consistently missed its own targets for recruitment over the last decade but this is a new low."

Dr. Mary Bousted, of the National Education Union blamed the government for an "abject failure."

****

My attention is drawn to a letter in *The Times* from the advocacy director of 'Liberty'. **He talks about Dominic Raab's new bill of rights.** This is something we are all worried about and, as he says, the bill is such a "complete mess" (the government's words) that it will weaken everyone's rights. This includes victims of violence against women and girls and disabled people. It is not being updated, it is a complete overhaul which will actually make things worse for everyone.

Well that seems to follow this government's manifesto, not yet printed but yes can be summed up in a few words: we will do our best to make everyone's lives a great deal worse than they already are. In fact we will be world beating at that.

And believe me, they already are.

****

So that is December. Oh goodness what am I saying?

It is only December 2nd!

Today we have the result of the Chester by-election. Well the Conservative candidate didn't lose their deposit, just their credibility. Over 6,000 people voted for them which must mean that there are over 6,000 people in Chester who have not read my books. Outrageous.

Labour increased their majority by 10,974 majority, and a 61% vote share. It was the worst defeat in Chester for the Conservative party since 1832 and was Labour's best ever result in the seat.

Even Conservatives are now saying that Sunak is just a manager not a leader. Actually it would be good if he could even actually manage something.

****

Well this is a new styled advent calendar. **Every day from now until Christmas, has been marked by the number of strikes taking place.** Some days have three different strikes a few just have one and on three days there are four different strikes.

The strikes are by: rail workers, Eurostar guards, buses, education, NHS, driving examiners, postal workers, cash delivery, road maintenance and breweries. Those are the ones whose dates we know. But there are others lurking and it certainly looks as though it is going to be a **'winter of discontent.'**

Not a good look and not a lot of negotiation going on.

****

And then we hear of a new report about 'illegal' asylum seekers by the right-leaning Centre for Policy Studies that says "**if necessary Britain should change human rights laws and withdraw from the European Convention on Human Rights in order to tackle Channel crossings**

by small boats." Basically it says we should lock up all asylum seekers and throw away the key. Maybe not in so many words but that is what they mean.

Suella Braverman has pledged to do "whatever it takes" to end the small boat crossings. Everyone who enters the UK illegally will be detained indefinitely and banned from ever settling here. As the government says there are no legal routes so that means everyone.

There is no such thing as an 'illegal asylum seeker'

How many times do we have to say this?

****

Then I can hardly believe what I am reading. Except unfortunately I can. This is another story about the dis-functioning and incompetent Home Office that is just outrageous.

Only four Afghan refugees have been brought to safety in the UK on the government's flagship resettlement scheme since the fall of Kabul, Home Office figures show. Announced last August, the Afghan citizens' resettlement scheme aimed to resettle 5,000 Afghans in the first year, and up to 20,000 over five years.

But while 6,314 refugees who are already in the UK have been granted indefinite leave to remain, only 4 people who fled Afghanistan after the Taliban takeover have been resettled.

Charities have condemned ministers for "abandoning the Afghan people" and effectively closing any safe routes to the UK for those at risk abroad. As we know...........no safe and legal routes.

The Home Office said the situation is "complex and presents us with significant challenges".

Oh for goodness sake. Just admit that none of you are up to the job and call a general election.

****

Levelling Up secretary Michael Gove has sent a letter to Tory MPs confirming that the government will water down housebuilding targets.

Mr Gove told the MPs the Levelling Up bill would be amended to abolish mandatory housebuilding targets. He recognised that "there is no truly objective way of calculating how many new homes are needed in an area" but that the "plan making process for housing has to start with a number".

However campaigners fear that housing secretary Michael Gove's decision to scrap mandatory targets for local councils in rural and suburban areas puts at risk the government's promise to build 300,000 new homes a year.

Mr Gove's climb-down comes after behind-the-scenes talks with leaders of more than 100 Tory MPs threatening to vote against his flagship Levelling Up and Regeneration Bill. Mr Gove's Labour counterpart Lisa Nandy has said that the climb-down was "unconscionable in the middle of a housing crisis".

Sunak is performing so many U-turns he is going round in ever-decreasing circles.

****

5TH DECEMBER

And Rishi Sunak is facing further criticism this morning from the head of Britain's biggest business organisation, **the Confederation of British Industry.** Tony Danker, the director-general of the group, has warned that the government is "going backwards" on the green growth agenda. An agenda, which he argues, provides the best opportunity to lift the country out of recession over the coming years.

He has said that businesses were "confused and disappointed" over the failure of Mr Sunak's government to foster green growth measures such as lifting the ban on onshore wind farms in England and making the City of London a global centre for sustainable finance.

Yes, well, we have missed the boat on that one.

****

And we now hear that the government has decided that the proposed new coal mine in Cumbria is to go ahead. I first wrote about this in January 2021 when Robert Jenrick initially approved this mine. Then on March 12th he decided to put it on hold.

Michael Gove has just now approved it saying that it was "the right thing to do" it will create loads of jobs apparently and he insisted he was satisfied that it would be "net zero -compliant".

Well the government has been accused of "environmental vandalism" as you would expect, and experts question the signals the move sends.

Opponents warn it will create more greenhouse gas emissions and say is hypocritical in the wake of UK efforts on the international stage to show climate leadership and urge the world to give up on coal.

Former government chief scientist, and chair of the independent 'Climate Crisis Advisory Group' Sir David King, labelled the decision as an "incomprehensible act of self-harm." Yet another one.

This is the government of self- harm for the UK.

Apparently the coal in Cumbria has a lot of sulphur content which will mean that most of it will be exported so won't even by used in the UK.

Professor Stuart Haszeldine, from the School of GeoSciences at University Edinburgh, said: "Opening a coal mine in Cumbria is investing in 1850s technology, and does not look forward to the 2030s low carbon local energy future. Most, and maybe all, of this coking coal will be exported outside of Europe to escape environmental constraints on its use. England will become a global dirty fuel supplier."

Shadow communities secretary Lisa Nandy said that the people of Cumbria deserved well-paid jobs but the Government had recently rejected a plan to bring new nuclear to Cumbria, creating 10,000 jobs.

****

8TH DECEMBER

And then in the House of Commons today the Speaker suspends parliament when Michael Gove stands up to explain this decision.

The government failed to provide Mr Gove's full statement to Labour's shadow ministers and opposition MPs at least 45 minutes before the debate which is the standard practice.

The Speaker was really angry and said: "That is not according to the ministerial code – we don't work like that. I am going to suspend the House ... This is not the way we do good government."

Surely the gross incompetence of this government is becoming more and more obvious to everyone, even those who do not normally engage with the news.

****

And the very next day we hear that, due to the chaos in government, the Schools Bill has been dropped. Gillian Keegan, the Education Secretary, told MPs on the education select committee that the Bill would not progress to a third reading. Her reason was that parliamentary time had been taken up by measures to provide economic stability. **So this is the third U-turn in a week.**

This Bill was drawn up by Boris Johnson's government to "raise standards across the country". Remember him? He who kept saying "let me get on with the job." He achieved nothing. This legislation, for schools in England, was originally intended to cover issues including school funding, the regulation of academies, tackling truancy, and banning unsuitable teachers.

Children, as I always say, are at the bottom of the barrel with a Conservative government.

****

10TH DECEMBER

Rishi Sunak has just avoided being the shortest Prime Minister on record as he passes the 44 days of Liz Truss.

So how is it going Rishi? Well we do hear that some of your back benchers, particularly those who voted for Truss, are not too happy and are searching around for an alternative PM.

****

Ministers are set to scrap a scheme that was set up by Sunak when chancellor and which has cost the taxpayer £2.37million. This was an apprenticeship training scheme for work placements for people aged between16 to 24 year olds. There had been concerns about the scheme as it did not offer people any payment for going on placements and so it was not taken up in sufficient numbers.

****

Then it's back to Suella Braverman. One of her advisers has decided to quit as she says she is "on a completely different planet" from the

Home Secretary. Well for goodness sake aren't we all?

And then we hear that 14,000 staff from the Home Office and Border Force have written a letter to the Home Secretary to say that last month's high profile deal with France which cost the tax payer £63 million would fail and should "no longer be pursued."

They say what we have been saying for ages, which is that the only solution to the small boats crisis is to create a safe passage visa that allows refugees a secure route to the UK. They go on to add that the whole approach and attitude of the Home office with policies such as the hostile environment is making their jobs "deeply unpalatable in a variety of ways." It was compounding a sense of misery amongst the staff. They have also concluded that any plans for Rwanda deportations plus other policies for cracking down on these crossing would not survive a legal challenge. High court judges are shortly to give their verdict on this scheme.

A different planet? Suella Braverman is off the radar.

****

11TH DECEMBER

Doctors and health officials are saying that the NHS could collapse this winter. Pat Cullen, general secretary of the RCN, said she was prepared to press "pause" on the nurses' industrial action if the health secretary, Steve Barclay, agreed to meet and negotiate and discuss pay.

She says that five times her offer to negotiate has been turned down. A deal agreed in Scotland has averted a strike there and a similar deal in England and Wales could do the same here.

Well that has put the government in the firing line. Something needs to happen and to happen fast.

****

No money? Don't you believe it.

In *The Sunday Times* today there is article by Gabriel Pogrund and Jack Clover about the contracts given to companies for PPE at the beginning of the pandemic. I have written about this before but this article names the different companies and explains exactly how much money was paid to each of them and how much money was wasted because the equipment was faulty and not fit for purpose. They highlight the British firms which got the biggest deals.

They got these details from the 'Good Law Project', 'Spotlight on Corruption', and from the government's insights service 'Tussell'. Figures for unused PPE are from the Department of Health and Social Care estimates on the number of units marked "do not supply" as of June 2021.

Here is the major part of their list.

FULL SUPPORT HEALTHCARE LTD: PPE contracts £2 billion.
Government estimates of **unused PPE, £84.7 million.**

UNISERVE LTD: PPE contracts £877 million.
Government estimates of **unused PPE, £179 million.**

UNISPACE GLOBAL LTD: PPE contracts £684 million.
Government estimates of **unused PPE, £3.67 million.**

GUARDIAN SURGICAL/ROCIALLE HEALTHCARE LTD: PPE contracts £445 million.
Government estimates of **unused PPE, £63.8 million.**

PESTFIX LTD: PPE contracts £349 million
Government estimates of **unused PPE, £84.4 million.**

P14MEDICAL LTD: PPE contracts £276 million.
Government estimates of **unused PPE, £184 million.**

AYANDA CAPITAL LTD: PPE contracts £253 million.
Government estimates of **unused PPE, £138 million.**

PURPLE SURGICAL UK LTD: PPE contracts £238 million
Government estimates of **unused PPE £35.8 million.**

MEDLINE INDUSTRIES LTD: PPE contracts £228 million
Government estimates of **unused PPE, £11.691**

PENINE HELTHCRE LTD: PPE contracts £228 million
Government estimates of **unused PPE, £3.7 million**

PPE MEDPRO LTD: PPE contracts £203 million.
Government estimates of **unused PPE, £125 million. This is the one that Michelle Mone is connected with.**

RAMFOAM LTD: PPE contracts £149 million
Government estimates of **unused PPE, £108 million.**

INIVOS LTD: PPE contracts £127 million
Government estimates of **unused PPE, £124 million.**

Where exactly did all this money come from? And what a colossal waste.

****

12TH DECEMBER

And today we hear of more tax payers' money being spent by this profligate government. The Department of Health and Social Care who do not have enough money to pay the nurses, are about to spend thousands of pounds of our money to block the release of a document which sets out what lessons have been learnt from the pandemic. It has been blocking a *Times* request for this report since August 2021.

Previous transparency releases show that these cases can cost as much as £130,000 in legal fees each time.

The official Covid-19 inquiry is starting in 2023 and the number of deaths in the UK where coronavirus is on the death certificate, currently stands at 21,000.

****

Steve Barclay has turned down the request from Pat Cullen to meet the nurses and negotiate about pay.

I get so angry that I write to my MP.

Dear Oliver, I understand you are chairing a couple of Cobra meetings this week and encouraging unions to get round the table to negotiate and to think about the disruption they are causing to working people.

I really think you need to understand that all the people on strike actually ARE the working people. And they HAVE offered to get round the table to talk. It is the government who refuse to discuss anything in a sensible way. Pay review bodies are just advisory and anyway this last one for the nurses was drawn up months ago and is well out of date. I am really surprised that these meetings are only happening now. This crisis has been in the making for months if not years.

No money? You have shed loads of money when you want it. Billions of pounds wasted in a failed track and trace system, billions of money wasted on unusable PPE, millions of pounds spent on agency staff for the NHS because you don't train up enough doctors and nurses and just today we hear of thousands of pounds of tax-payers money about to be spent on blocking a report setting out what lessons the government has learnt from its pandemic failures.

I don't expect a reply to this email because why would you reply to this one when you haven't bothered to reply to many others? I am waiting especially, for a reply to my emails about free school meals. I would still like to know why you think it is OK for you all to have subsidised meals and a bar in the Commons when so many children are going hungry.

But you do not reply because you have no answer.

Well I really needed to get that out of my system.

****

And Libby Purves writes in *The Times* that the decision to haul in the army to help out in the strikes is not necessarily a sensible one. She quotes former head of the army, Lord Dannatt, who said that in a natural disaster "everybody understands why the military needs to be helping the blue-light services," but he asks how reasonable it is for them to paper over the cracks "in the context of industrial disputes that many people think government could resolve but for political purposes choose not to."

****

So just in case you think we are not quite completely down the rabbit hole you need to read this. All schools classed as outstanding have been exempt for inspection for more than a decade. So Ofsted have been returning to the inspection of these schools which is reasonable enough. But Ofsted have said that the goal posts have changed and they want fewer schools to be classed as outstanding and so are forming judgments accordingly. However it has acknowledged that its gradings could be misconstrued. **Its national director of education admitted recently that for a school to be downgraded from outstanding to good "doesn't mean that the school has declined in recent years; in fact, the opposite can be the case."**

No I don't have a clue either.

****

THE DAYS BEFORE CHRISTMAS

Four refugees drowned in the freezing sub temperatures of the Channel in the middle of the night, including one child, when their small boat capsized.

This, of course sets the PM and the Home Secretary into spasms of nastiness.

Sunak outlined a five-point plan in the Commons including law changes to criminalise and then remove tens of thousands of people who claim asylum after travelling to the UK by small boats, and a deal with Albania to aid removals back there and also to re-install the Rwanda plan. He will then revive data-sharing powers which will stop migrants who have arrived in the UK by irregular means from obtaining bank accounts.

Well the High Court is about to pronounce the Rwanda plan as illegal and an inquiry by a government watchdog in 2017 found that one in 10 people were refused a bank account because of a failed immigration check.

Colin Yeo, the immigration specialist barrister and author, said the development was a "massive" potential problem for those caught up in the Home Office's faltering systems.

"There are huge problems with Home Office data," he said. "Banks have to shut your account if a check against that data flags you.

"There's basically no remedy. That's it, game over, you can't eat, travel or pay your rent."

Keir Starmer said Sunak was indulging in more "unworkable gimmicks" as promised by other Tory prime ministers."

And charities said that the majority of those who arrive by small boats qualify as legitimate refugees fleeing wars and famine.

Tim Naor Hilton, chief executive of charity 'Refugee Action,' criticised the government for failing to commit to creating safe routes for people seeking refuge.

"Most of these changes are cruel, ineffective and unlawful and will do nothing to fix the real problems," he said.

The asylum backlog has ballooned, with 143,377 people awaiting an initial decision on their application and unable to work.

I get so angry that I write yet another letter, this time to *The Times*.

Sir, This government could stop the dangerous small boat crossings tomorrow if they really wished to do so. All they need is an assessment centre in France (already agreed by the French) and then those whose applications are successful could come over on safe and legal routes by ferry or train.

This idea was first suggested in 2015 by the United Nations when Peter Sutherland, their special representative on migration said, "You could set up an immediate system for assessing how many of these people are refugees. You could do it in a very short time and you could do it as a joint responsibility."

This is a political choice and many more people are going to lose their lives if the government does not act in a responsible, sensible and compassionate manner. At the moment there are no safe and legal routes as this government has scrapped them all. New draconian laws and tough meaningless words display weakness and a sense of panic.

Well it wasn't published but a similar letter was and it was from the Executive Director, of the International Rescue Committee UK so I guess she took precedence.

Sunak claimed that triple the number of asylum applications will be processed to clear asylum claims, with a doubling in the number of caseworkers.

"We expect to abolish the backlog of initial asylum decisions by the end of next year," he said.

Oh my goodness, he does set himself up to fail.

****

Boris Johnson has brought in a legal team to help him in his defence in the investigation by the Privileges Committee about him lying to Parliament. He is charging their fees to us the tax payers. This comes to £222,000.

It might interest you to know that last month he earned £750,000 from global speaking engagements, according to the latest parliamentary register of interests. He declared total earnings of £754,652 from three events in November, which were said to have involved 25 hours and 45 minutes work.

It works out at more than £30,000 per hour. This is, of course, on top of his MPs salary of £84,144 and a severance pay for having been prime minister. Are you happy with that?

****

17TH DECEMBER

So just let us look at some headlines from the papers today:

'Sunak needs to get a grip'

'Our nurses are leaving in droves for retail jobs'

'Sunak says no to pay talks'

'Laws stopping walkouts too difficult to bring in'

'We have failed to control borders admits Braverman'

'Raab's office crippled by complaints'

Truss denies claims of drugs at Chevening'

'By-election loss is bad sign for Tories'

'Cost of Strep A drugs increases tenfold amid supply chain row'

'MPs should not be using overseas trips for sex tourism and heavy drinking'

Yes well I think we would all agree on that last one. And these are all from just one newspaper *The Times*.

Here are a few others:

The Independent

'Ministers rip up protections for torture victims and asylum seekers in detention centres'

'Sunak's £150 billion stealth tax raid will cost families £5,000 each'

The Mirror

'Rishi Sunak blasted on shipyard visit for betraying UK workers by using Spanish firm'

The Guardian

'Ex-Foreign Office Advisor says aid cuts are 'dreadful moral choice'

The Express

'Election ID laws to come into play despite just two voter fraud convictions in five years.'

The Telegraph

'NHS hires 'lived experience' tsars on up to £115,000 a year'

'Government scraps its target to improve overall water quality'

'Ambulance strikes pose 'big risk to public' says Oliver Dowden'

This is just one day.

****

19TH DECEMBER

I get so annoyed at the news, as it is all the same subjects and it is just relentless and heart-breaking. So I write this verse instead!

'Twas the week before Christmas and the news has not changed.
It's the same as before but just re-arranged.
Doctors and nurses are burnt out and tired
More agency staff are now being hired.

Rail workers are striking and bus drivers too
Causing chaos, confusion for me and for you.
So many people are going on strike
Britain is broken, there's nothing to like.

Money is short and our budgets are tight
Children are starving, there's no end in sight.
It is snowy and icy and windy and cold
And some people's houses are riddled with mould.

Those MPs who govern are callous and tough
They refuse to negotiate. Well we've had enough.
Those seeking asylum will soon be deported
They'll then wash their hands and say "well that's sorted,

We've got back control of our borders at last."
Their cruel decisions just leave me aghast.
As we start to celebrate the birth of a child
Born in a manger and yes, meek and mild,

A man for all people, for you and for me
We remember Him too, as a young refugee.
We ask those who govern to remember Him too
To govern with kindness and just think things through.

Please sit round a table and listen and hear
What people are saying, so loud and so clear.
They are broken, exhausted and just want to be able
To look after their families, put food on the table.

As I write this book I am filled with despair.
It's all so depressing as I try to share
The sadness and grief, the hunger and pain
Over and over, again and again.

It was published in *The Canary* news web-site.

****

I cannot believe this but the High Court has ruled that the Rwanda
plan is legal. Well there are going to be appeals and further court
judicial reviews so nothing will happen for a long time. But Suella

Braverman is jumping up and down for joy.

But actually not for long. The High Court also found her to have acted unlawfully in failing to give asylum seekers an increase of a 10 per cent cost of living boost.

In a damning high court ruling seen by *The Telegraph*, Mr Justice Fordham said the Home Secretary had acted unlawfully by failing to increase the subsistence allowance from £40.85p a week to £45 a week after inflation spiralled from three per cent to more than 10 per cent.

The judge took the unusual step of issuing a "mandatory order" forcing the Home Secretary to implement an immediate increase in the rate of asylum support to £45, which will affect at least 85,000 asylum seekers at a cost to the taxpayer of £18 million a year.

****

So we have nurses, ambulance workers and paramedics on strike. The government refuses to get round a table to discuss any compromise on a pay deal.

But there are some heartfelt and heart-breaking words from 'the secret consultant' who writes in *The Guardian*.

"We are told that the NHS is at breaking point and has been for years, underfunded and poorly planned by successive Conservative governments," he says.

"But this is different. What is breaking now is not the system, but its people, and in a rapid, tangible way.

"I regularly see colleagues in tears. Every few weeks I hear of someone else I know who is leaving, retiring early, going part-time, moving to a less stressful area.

"All the time I hear how things have changed, that the pressure is too much now, that we wouldn't recommend our children to do the jobs we do.

"The pandemic has accelerated this and we need compassion more than ever. While I regularly see this from our patients and the public, it is notably absent from our leaders."

That a medical consultant is writing in this way is a disgrace and the government should be ashamed. But no. They just tell them to work harder and to be more efficient.

****

Meanwhile traces of cocaine use have been found at Chevening House after some of Liz Truss's parties when she was Foreign Secretary. No wonder she didn't know where the Black Sea was.

Also it looks as though Dominic Raab has now got eight allegations of bullying against him. Doesn't surprise me in the least. His office is scrambling to fill yet another vacancy, as formal complaints against his conduct continue to grow. An internal civil service job advert seen by *The Independent* shows the deputy prime minister's office is looking for another senior mandarin on as much as £76,000 to start in the New Year. It comes after the civil service last week separately advertised for as many as 10 new private secretaries to work in his office.

****

So it looks encouraging that, at last, Rishi Sunak has appointed a new ethics adviser after a six-month vacancy. He is Sir Laurie Magnus CBE and it might be of interest to note that he is an old Etonian, "quango king", a City grandee, a hereditary peer, an investment banker and a Conservative Party donor. Jobs for the boys? However Sunak has been condemned for clinging onto the personal power to veto any investigation into ministers as he ignores calls from the Committee on Standards in Public Life and others to give his top adviser the power to start their own investigation without his permission.

Labour accused Mr Sunak of having chosen to "preserve the rotten ethics regime" that led to the resignations of both Lord Geidt and his predecessor Sir Alex Allan.

Why, oh why would we expect anything different?

****

22ND DECEMBER

Global Britain?

At some point, and essentially very soon, we need to realise that having left the huge trading bloc on our doorstep, we have become inconsequential in the eyes of the world. We are a small island floating around in the North Sea, completely out of our depth, with no successful trade or business and no political integrity or vision.

As Simon Nixon writes in *The Times* today that when "global Britain" first emerged as a political slogan it was clear that it was going to be a delusion. "The risk was," he says, "always that Britain outside the EU would find itself increasingly isolated outside three competing trading blocks, the US, EU and China."

This is proving to be the case. We have no deals with the US or the EU, China is not looking good and the deal with India is nowhere to be seen.

"What Britain needs" he says "is a serious debate about how to respond to the shifting global trading landscape."

Well that is not going to happen under this government.

Simon Nixon concludes his article by writing, "It goes without saying that such a debate must start with accepting the world as it is, and not as some might wish it to be."

****

24TH DECEMBER

Matthew Parris today disagrees with his colleague Daniel Finkelstein who in his column a few days ago advocated a good dose of optimism. Yes I know. None of us thought that that was what the country needed just now.

As Mr. Parris so rightly says, what we need is a good dose of realism. But he says we are all hypocrites because we would not vote for politicians who are honest and tells it as it is. "We force them to lie and then complain they're liars" he says. But we do sense that things are difficult. Polls suggest that "inflation menaces us, government and indebtedness is mounting, strikes punch our economy in the stomach, the NHS is failing, our trade deficit is rising, productivity remains stubbornly low and Brexit isn't working. We know too that we're already poorer than we were a few years ago."

Oh my word. How many times do we need to hear that before something is done? How many times?

I leave you with that unanswerable question as I break off for Christmas.

****

2023
A NEW YEAR. WHERE'S RISHI?

3RD JANUARY

Where indeed? This is the question on everyone's lips. Most people are back to work today but of course MPs don't return to parliament until the 9th. That press room which cost the tax payer £2.6 million has not been seen since the days of Liz Truss.

So what's happening?

Well the crisis in the NHS is unprecedented. Ambulances have just been told to discharge patients in hospitals after a 45 minute wait whatever the circumstances and nurses have been told to discharge patients into the community without giving them a discharge plan. And there are between 300 and 500 avoidable deaths every week because of delays in emergency care. The latest data from NHS England shows that there were more than 3,700 patients a day in hospital with the flu last week – up from 520 a day the month before, and just 34 a day this time last year. A growing number of NHS trusts are declaring critical incidents.

More and more rail strikes are paralysing the country and the government still refuses to talk to the unions. There is talk of all unions working together in order to co-ordinate all strikes in order to cause maximum disruption.

Oh wait a minute Sunak is saying something. Well he is actually making a speech. Could be his New Year Resolution: talk to the public.

It is the 4th January.

He says that he will make it compulsory for all students to learn maths until they are 18.

What? Is that it? Why? How? For what purpose exactly? And how does that help the old lady of 90 who is dying on a hospital floor?

He then continues with 5 pledges.

1. The government will halve inflation
2. It will grow the economy
3. It will reduce the national debt
4. NHS waiting lists will fall and people will get the care they need more quickly.
5. They will introduce more laws to stop the illegal boat crossings. He will stop the boats.

He said that "these priorities are your priorities and we will either achieve them or we won't." Yes he really said that.

And the speech was given, not in the new press room (£2.6 million) but in the Business Park in East London. Why was that do you think?

Well I am grateful to Tom Peck of *The Independent* who explains that it was only when the Tories heard that Starmer was going to deliver a speech there that Sunak hurried forward with his speech in the exact same location but a day earlier. How pathetic.

****

So we then hear from Starmer.

He actually embraces the Brexit slogan of "take back control". He wants to transfer powers from Westminster to local communities. He pledged to devolve new powers over employment support, transport, energy, housing, culture and childcare. Hmmm. Some words there that rarely pass the Conservative lips.

He also said he was "under no illusions about the scale of the challenges we face."

But Tom Peck again says something very interesting. He says he saw something very unusual during Starmer's speech.

"Something strange was happening. Unprecedented even, certainly in recent times. Had anyone else noticed it? Had they realised? That here, on this very day, at this precise moment, it really did appear like a **leading, mainstream, frontline British politician was actually giving a good speech."**

Well yes we are not used to that.

****

4TH JANUARY

Today, after his first speech to the nation and just one week into the New Year, Rishi Sunak has decided to 'take action'. Not before time you might think.

'Action' to him means inviting everyone he can think of to an all-day conference at Downing Street.

Representatives from the public and private sectors will be attending, alongside chief executives and clinical leaders of NHS organisations, local areas and councils from across the country, plus medical and social care experts.

Amanda Pritchard, chief executive of NHS England, and Sir Chris Whitty, chief medical officer for England, are also taking part in the meeting.

****

Then, on Monday the 9th, health unions have been invited to meet Health Secretary Steve Barclay to discuss pay for 2023-24 from April - but union leaders say the government must act on the current pay dispute for 2022-23 and the talks will not stop the planned strikes for January.

Speaking to the BBC's 'Today' programme this morning, Royal College of Nursing General Secretary Pat Cullen said the pay increase nurses would receive in 2022-23 was "fundamental" to the ongoing dispute.

Asked about earlier comments in which she appeared to suggest the union would consider lowering its pay increase demand from 19%, and about reports it would be prepared to accept 10%, she called on Mr Sunak to meet her "halfway".

"I have put out an olive branch to get us to the table," she said. "The ball is now firmly in the prime minister's court. He needs to come to the negotiation table with me and he needs to put money on that table, and it needs to be about the current year."

****

9TH JANUARY

Marine Disaster

There is news of further incompetence, neglect and ignorance by this government leading to disastrous consequences. An article by Jenni Russell in *The Times* today makes alarming reading.

Sixteen months ago there was a massive disaster concerning marine life in the North Sea off Teesside. Along 30 miles of coast, from Hartlepool to Whitby, the beaches were piled with hundreds of thousands of dead and dying crabs and lobsters, some still twitching in agony. Nothing like this had ever been experienced before. Within weeks it was evident that one of Britain's most important fishing areas had been devastated and might never recover.

No-one could work out why this had happened and so people waited for a report from Defra. Well six months later (never in a hurry) Defra reported that there was absolutely no problem and these deaths had just been caused by large algae blooms. As the blooms sank the crabs, lobsters etc. had died from toxic algae or lack of oxygen. They chose to ignore the fact that the dead crabs had extremely high levels of a toxic chemical called **pyridine** and this chemical had been produced in large quantities in factories along the Tees until recently. It is thought that the dredging in this area was releasing this chemical.

The fishermen were distraught at this and they commissioned university scientists and marine biologists, toxicologists and oceanographers to carry out their own research.

Defra's case was blown apart. The scientists' evidence was terrifying. Even a tiny amount of pyridine can kill crabs within six hours and yes of course this came from the factories. The ignorance of Defra was extraordinary. Pyridine isn't routinely tested for in the UK as it isn't officially a "chemical of concern." The other proposed Freeports are also in danger as they all have lethal chemicals and our current safeguards are completely inadequate. These ports are Southampton, Liverpool, Felixstowe and Harwich, the Humber, Plymouth and the Thames.

Now can you remember who the Minister for the Environment is? Close your eyes, lean back and (clue) maybe have a cup of coffee.

Yes it is of course that beacon of hope, efficiency and dynamism, Therese Coffey. (I jest) The Environment Select Committee held a day's hearing about it and then wrote to Therese Coffey calling for urgent action. Coffey agreed to their demands and said that an expert panel would be set up under scientific advisers.

So what happened next? Well as you can guess pretty well nothing. Jenni Russell says, "The panel is a mystery. Defra refused to tell me who was on it, its remit, who it was hearing from, or when it would report." She goes on to say that "**The short-term goals of politicians are driving careless poisoning of the only sea we have. It is torment.**"

Dredging needs to be done with far more care and caution as the environment committee asked for. It will not cost a lot but once the chemical enters the food chain this can never be reversed.

Even with this government I find it hard to believe they can be so cavalier with our safety.

****

Except actually sadly I can. There was a meeting this morning between union bosses and government ministers. This was an hour long meeting in order, I presumed, for them to negotiate about pay in order to prevent any more strikes going ahead. Well surprise, surprise, they broke down without any agreement and the strikes will go ahead as planned.

Onay Kasab, Unite's national leader said "the government only wanted to talk about productivity". Well I really do not know how NHS staff and ambulance staff can be more productive. What exactly do they mean? There was no detailed discussion about pay and he said "It's an insult".

Mr. Kasab, this whole government is an insult. They are an insult to our intelligence, to our work, to our children, to our well-being, to our trust, to everything we do.

More and more strikes are now planned and teachers and junior doctors are balloting this week.

****

Then I read a disturbing article in *The Guardian* by Nesrine Malik. She writes about the state of our public services, especially the NHS and rail services, and says that we now, officially, have a two tier system.

By failing to provide functioning public services, through either privatisation, underfunding or lack of negotiation with striking workers, the government is effectively withholding your rights for which you have already paid through taxes and national insurance. And yes if you are able to afford to use private facilities you will, but you are still giving money to the government. This, she says, is their end game when "the state stops performing its primary function which is to provide basic human rights to health, shelter, energy, water and transport." She goes on to say that it is not poverty that has caused everything to buckle. "We are here thanks to conscious political choices disguised as a fact of nature."

Absolutely. This government could have sat down with the unions and negotiated their pay and conditions months ago. Or they could have looked at the graphs from the 'Kings Fund' and the ' Nuffield Trust' to discover how spending on the NHS rose till 2010 and then steadily declined since then to the present day. Everyone who pays for private facilities rather than relying on the state is playing into their hands.

Oh wait a minute what are we seeing here? Mr Sunak has a photoshoot of him boarding a private jet. Where is he going that requires such extravagance and carbon footprints? Err, Leeds. To visit a hospital. I think he could have worked on the train actually. And this is our money that he is spending quite happily.

****

So he doesn't use the trains and he doesn't use the health service.

He refused to answer the question put to him in the Laura Kuennssberg programme on the BBC three days ago as to whether he is registered with a private GP saying that it would not be appropriate to discuss his family health arrangements in public. He has repeatedly refused to answer this question saying it is "not really relevant" and it is a personal choice.

However, Pippa Crerar of *The Guardian* writes that he **is**, apparently, registered with a private GP practice which guarantees that all patients with urgent concerns about their health will be seen "on the day".

At a price.

She writes that the west London clinic used by the prime minister "charges £250 for a half-hour consultation and, unlike most NHS GPs across the country, offers appointments in the evenings and at weekends, as well as consultations by email or phone that cost up to £150."

Home visits will cost you about £400 and prescriptions £80.

But what is this? Just three days later at PMQs he decided that it **is** OK to discuss his family health arrangements **because he has suddenly discovered that he is registered with an NHS GP after all.**

I do hope you are keeping up with all of this.

But let's hear about something the Tory party does really well. Backbenchers are already saying that there is a possibility of an election this year and Rishi is not the person to lead them there. Plots afoot. The crazy chaos continues.

****

11TH JANUARY

But before we leave the fascinating subject of our present prime minister we hear that he is to speak to the nation on television sometime today. What again?

This is the speech he **will** make:

Good evening everyone. Believe me I do know how tough everything is for you all at the moment. But we **will** get through these difficult times which have been caused by the unprecedented situations of the pandemic and the war in Ukraine. The new laws we are putting through parliament today will ensure that no-one will suffer unduly from strike action by our key public services. This is a common sense approach and I know you will all agree. I love this country and your priorities are my priorities and I will work night and day for the good of everyone.

This is the speech he **should** make:

Hello everyone. I really do need to apologise for the mess we are in and I am going to see the King to ask him to dissolve parliament in order to call a general election. It has got to the state where you cannot tell the difference between strike days and ordinary working days as the chaos, caused entirely by us, is ongoing. It is too difficult for me to sort out so I am going to leave it to someone else, other than the Tories, to clear it all up. Once more please accept my apologies, especially those of you who have lost loved ones, who in normal circumstances would never have died.

This is the speech he will **never** make:

Brexit is the entire cause of broken Britain. We must re-join the single market and the customs union without delay.

I will let you know how accurate I have been when we hear the actual speech!

****

It was not a speech to the nation at all, it was **a Conservative party political broadcast and lasted about three minutes**. It was on the television channels at different times so you probably missed it. The production was poor and the content abysmal. He was wooden and robotic and a lot of the time not even looking at the right camera so that when he was saying "you want this" he was staring off into the middle distance somewhere. As for the content it was shallow, vacuous and dishonest. Always the answer is "we will bring in new laws" never "we will try to sort out the problems". So there will be laws to provide a guarantee minimum safety level during strikes, to criminalise and stop all migrant boat crossings in the channel, and he will sort out the economy and the NHS waiting lists.

He doesn't appear to realise that ambulance strikes and nurses and doctors strikes are **because** they are unable to provide minimum safety levels. He also doesn't seem to be aware of the fact that there is no such thing as an illegal asylum seeker.

He had started by saying "I was brought in to fix these problems". Yes mate you were not elected by the general public and you seem to have forgotten that the Conservatives have been in power for 13 years and that you were Chancellor for a couple of them.

The lack of intelligence is frightening.

****

THINK TANKS

I am sure that some think tanks do what it says on the tin but these two are very worrying and I think it is important that we know all about them.

REFORM UK

We hear of a new political party calling themselves Reform UK. Except that it isn't a new party of course. It is the old Brexit, Ukip party being organised by the ERG and 55 Tufton Street. Be afraid. Be very afraid.

Richard Tice is the leader of this party and he has vowed to "smash and destroy" the Conservative party at the next election. He has said that he is on a mission to ensure the Conservatives never have a majority government again. He is a right wing politician and before joining the Brexit party he was a long-term donor and member of the Conservative party. He was the first to use the phrase, "no deal is better than a bad deal" in relation to Brexit in July 2016.

He is connected to certain people at 55 Tufton Street which, in case you had forgotten is the head-quarters of right-wing, far-right and lunatic-fringe climate-change-deniers.

However times are changing and with a resurgence of remainers their influence is declining. But it is important to know that 'Leave means Leave' has found a home at 55 Tufton St. This group was co-founded by Richard Tice, an active member of the Leave EU hierarchy, and 'Leave means Leave' has now welcomed Nigel Farage who's using it as a platform for his 'return to frontline politics'. **Farage and Tice, a frightening couple.**

But there is one other person you should be aware of.

This is Matthew Elliott who is also to be found at 55 Tufton Street. Let's find out a bit more about him. Matthew Elliott became the chief executive of 'Vote Leave', the official organisation advocating for a 'leave' vote in the 2016 referendum. He was described as "...one of the most successful political campaigners in Westminster today." In 2018, *The Guardian* described him as a central figure in "a network of opaquely funded organisations", mostly based at 55 Tufton Street, that "centre around... the 'TaxPayers' Alliance' – a pressure group that he founded – and 'Brexit Central', an anti-EU website of which [he was then] editor-in-chief.

He also played a significant role in the ill-fated **'Conservative Friends of Russia'**, an organisation whose Tory MP membership later resembled rats deserting a sinking ship when the group's motives were brought into question following the discovery that their head contact at the Russian Embassy, Sergey Nalobin, was a spy who was later expelled from Britain.

Well yes better to disassociate yourselves from someone like that I would think. But he is now closely connected with Farage and Tice and they are all tucked up together at Tufton Street.

So when you hear the name **Reform UK or Richard Tice** and you think well actually that all sounds interesting and maybe you decide to give them your vote, just be very sure that you have researched into exactly what it is that they stand for.

****

INSTITUTE OF ECONOMIC AFFAIRS

This is another right wing think tank that we all need to be aware of with its rather grand and serious sounding title. This one is not actually based at Tufton Street but is based in Westminster and so is very close to the centre of power.

These think tanks are all very mysterious and secretive but they rumble away below the radar and they have more influence on governments than is healthy in a so-called democratic society. So we need to know who they are and what they stand for.

The IEA was founded in 1955 by an Old Etonian (!) called Antony Fisher. **They promote a neoliberal worldview and are climate-change deniers and advocates of total privatisation of the NHS**. The IEA has received more than £70,000 from the tobacco industry (although it does not reveal its funders), and IEA officers have been recorded offering "cash for access" *(Wikipedia)*

And they have connections with national media outlets including our friends the BBC. This means that those who oppose their views very rarely get represented or heard. It really is a case of biased reporting.

We need to look at **Kate Andrews**. She has become a regular interviewee and participant in various news-based outlets, especially the **BBC**. She is now an expert economics editor for ***The Spectator***, but before that, she worked with The **Institute of Economic Affairs in London** for almost four years. She appears regularly on Channel 4, Channel 5, ITV, Sky News and BBC 'Question Time'.

The following is just one example of sloppy reporting from the BBC.

On *Newsnight* some years ago she called in to push for the abolition of the NHS. "It's time to overhaul the NHS and replace it with a system fit for 2018," she said. But the BBC failed to inform viewers that she was a member of the hard right IEA and has a vested interest in privatising the health service. Worse, this isn't even the first time the BBC has done this.

Not only do their views include rejection of the NHS as a publicly funded and provided service, but they oppose any "sugar tax" and any attempt to combat the obesity epidemic by curbing the "freedoms of the giant food monopolies." The government has literally just said that it is postponing any decision on a sugar tax for the time being and Jamie Oliver has gone ballistic. And now, after following the trail for this book, I have found out why.

Many of you will be shocked to find that EU bureaucrats will be replaced by American executives in the tobacco industry, the (cane) sugar industry, the agrochemical industry, animal husbandry and of course the fossil fuel industry via policies that, just as with the Brexit referendum, were discussed in secret outside parliament and cabinet.

Control was certainly taken back, all the way back to the neocon paymasters who've funded the greatest scam in British political history and they're nowhere near finished yet.

And I have not finished yet either.

A BMJ (British Medical Journal) investigation includes infographic charts and diagrams which plot the IEA's financial links to 32 Tory MPs, and argues that the person most closely and publicly associated ideologically with the IEA is one-time Tory leadership candidate.............. drum roll............. **Dominic Raab.**

The BMA study also states that although he "does not have direct links with the IEA", health secretary (and another failed Tory leadership candidate) **Matt Hancock** has in recent years received funding [totalling £32,000] from Neil Record, who became chair of the IEA in 2015.Well does any of this surprise you? It certainly explains a lot.

****

AND SO IT GOES ON

It is so dispiriting to see each day that the stories I have been writing about for the last three years are still being highlighted in the news. Nothing is being solved or corrected or improved, there is no working plan or policy announcement, no ideas, no vision, no clear thinking and seemingly no concern. I keep saying that if they do not own the problem or acknowledge that there is a problem then how can they solve it?

And just when you thought it was safe and a practically **Boris** free zone we hear more about Johnson and those parties. Well we have further information about the party held at No 10 Downing Street the night before the funeral of the Duke of Edinburgh. Apparently Johnson boasted that this was **"the most unsocially distanced party in the UK right now."** Whistleblowers have told an ITV podcast about everything that really went on and most appalling of all that the police only investigated half of all the parties. We always had suspicions that the investigation was not particularly thorough and here is confirmation.

No 10 staff were also alleged to have destroyed evidence of illicit gatherings and had shredded a lot of material.

We also hear that some of Johnson's aides were believed to have had sex at this party which puts lack of social distancing at a completely new level.

And Andrew Bridgen, Conservative MP for North West Leicestershire, has been suspended from the Conservative party for suggesting in a tweet that the MRNA vaccine rollout was as bad as the Holocaust.

So just a brief look at three politicians at this moment in time. One is the PM, one was the PM and would like to be PM again, and the other just an ordinary MP.

But there is always more.

****

We hear that **Boris Johnson** is thought to have secured **an £800,000 line of credit from a millionaire distant relative while he was at No 10**. Well apparently there is nothing illegal about this except (and there is always an 'except' with Boris it would seem), that this millionaire was being suggested for a top role as chief executive of the British Council, a non-departmental public body. Well he didn't get it but Boris has been urged to come clean about his financial affairs and end his Conservative leadership ambitions. He has been condemned for the lack of transparency around the "alleged murky financial arrangements", and people are calling on No 10 to come clean about who exactly Johnson had received money and other benefits from when he was PM.

Yes well that will be the day. At the moment he is busy trying to employ a top lawyer to defend him in the forthcoming Privileges Inquiry. Hopefully he can find one who he has not offended in the past by referring to "lefty lawyers".

It has also emerged that Mr Johnson put a dinner costing more than £4,000 on a government credit card while with staff in New York for a UN General Assembly meeting in September 2021.

The bill for £4,445.07 for the meal at Smith & Wollensky's enjoyed by Mr Johnson and his entourage emerged in a question posed by Labour. "While families are sick with worry struggling to make ends meet, this waste of public money is obscene," said deputy Labour leader Angela Rayner.

Well I think we all know about Johnson and money. He loves it. Especially other people's.

****

And it has been brought to our attention by Matt Chorley of *The Times* that **Andrew Bridgen** should actually have had the whip suspended months ago. **Far from ensuring "integrity, professionalism and accountability at every level" eyes were rolled but no action was taken over various sackable offences.** A High Court judge found that he had lied under oath whilst in court, he has been accused of bullying and he has made many baseless claims about vaccine safety. He claimed that Covid was both harmless and a "manufactured bioweapon" kept secret by spooks. On and on went the lies and no-one did a thing to stop him until his remarks about the holocaust. As Matt Chorley says "Will this do? No. No, it won't."

****

And Rishi Sunak? How is he getting on?

Well, this week he could find himself suffering defeat from two controversial bills going through parliament.

First we have the **Online Safety Bill** which has had delay after delay because of chaos in the top echelons of the Conservative government. The Prime Minister is facing a major backbench rebellion as Tory MPs push for social media bosses to be made criminally liable if they do not block minors from seeing damaging content online. In other words they could face custodial sentences. This bill had been watered down, in essence, as they thought, to appease their back benches but as Lucy Powell, shadow culture secretary said, 'the Sunak government was "incredibly weak", adding: "I think many on their own side feel they're ungovernable, to some degree. On this, there's weakness and real out-of-touchness."

Then there is the **Retained EU Law** (Revocation and Reform) Bill

Ministers are braced for more Conservative backbenchers to join a Brexit rebellion to force the Government to give MPs, rather than just ministers, a say on eradicating the EU laws which are in this bill

Paul Seddon BBC politics reporter says that "official estimates indicate that removing or replacing EU-era laws by the December deadline will require the government to pass around 1,000 new pieces of legislation." Labour wants to push the deadline back to 2026.

Mr Seddon goes on to say that "green groups in particular have warned about the difficulty of reviewing the large number of EU-era environmental laws, covering huge issues such as water quality, air pollution standards and protections for wildlife, to detailed laws on mollusc farming, border checks on imported salamanders, and rules for importing hay."

Craig Bennett of the Wildlife Trusts said "the government was planning to get rid of regulations - such as those concerning pollution on beaches, energy efficiency and chemicals in the home - without a plan of how to replace them."

"Even a five-year-old could understand you should keep what you've got until you work out what to replace it with," he told the *BBC's Today* programme. Absolutely. The young children I know have far more common sense than anyone in this present Conservative cabinet.

He accused the government of introducing a "bulldozer law" ideologically driven by supporters of Brexit. That word again.

It is all looking very dangerous for Sunak.

****

17TH JANUARY

Well we have the first U-turn of the week. Not wanting to be defeated by the **Online Safety Bill,** Sunak has agreed to the amendment which will mean that if social media bosses refuse to take down abusive and damaging material for children they will go to prison for two years.

****

The largest teaching union has voted to strike in February and March.

****

And Parliament is voting to make it compulsory for all strikes to provide minimum safety standards and for those who defy this and strike when not supposed to, to be criminalised and given the sack. What they don't seem to realise is that, especially with the NHS, it is **because** they are unable to provide minimum standards of safety that they **are** on strike. We can't get an ambulance **now** so how are you going to be able to provide them during a strike? And if you **can** provide them during a strike why are you not providing them **now**? Or is this just too difficult for them to understand?

We have my MP, Oliver Dowden, boasting on *Twitter* saying that "Tonight we're voting to restore the balance between the right to strike and the public's right to know that critical services are protected." I think that answers my question.

He then goes on to say "It brings us in line with other European countries."

That is untrue. Other countries do not have the ability to sack workers. And how interesting to see you all taking note of what happens in other European countries.

I thought the whole point of Brexit was so that we could do our own thing.

****

The government announces today also a last minute amendment to the Public Order Bill as it passes through the Lords. It will change the definition of "serious disruption" and give the police the power to shut down protests when they **suspect** disruption could take place.

I don't think they will be happy until we are all in prison. Ooops, there are no prison places, they're full.

****

So how is levelling up going? This was one of the great slogans of the Tory party and Boris Johnson and indeed I have written about it at length. Well we hear that the phrase has now been scrapped. Tory MPs have been told not to use that phrase anymore because no-one knows what it means.

It really does beggar belief. With all the ongoing problems this country is facing and they are talking about a slogan.

This was a great flagship for Boris and he even set up a 'Levelling Up' department and unveiled 12 'Levelling Up' missions.

But they have now been told to talk about 'stepping up', 'gauging up', or 'enhancing communities' instead. Also to say 'difficult decisions' rather than 'tough decisions'.

You really could not make it up.

Labour's Lisa Nandy, the shadow Levelling Up secretary, said that 'screwing up' would be a 'more accurate' alternative phrase for Tory MPs to use. Well yes I think we could all agree with that.

****

But the very next day we hear about the levelling up fund distribution and Michael Gove is wheeled out on the morning media channels as the **Levelling-Up Secretary**. I don't think he got the memo.

But people are not happy. They are saying that more money has been given to the south and south east and London than the more deserving areas in the north. Oh surely not. No, no, Sunak is insisting that despite the south receiving more cash overall than the north-east, Yorkshire or the Midlands, the northwest was getting twice as much per capita. I am really finding it quite difficult to follow this line of thinking.

The Tories are finding the same. Andy Street, Conservative mayor of the West Midlands is very angry at the whole decision process of allocating funds. He said that allowing Whitehall to allocate £2billion to more than 100 projects around the country was "flawed". "I cannot understand why the levelling-up funding money was not devolved for local decision makers to decide on what's best for their area" he said. It is a ridiculous "begging bowl" approach pitting local councils against each other. And privately some Tory MPs are angry too as one has said that "I've got shops without roofs and streets of boarded up houses and some people are getting cash for adventure golf." And I notice that Morecombe Bay in the north-west is getting £50 million for an Eden project in the bay.

I also see that Mr. Sunak's constituency, leafy, affluent Richmond in Yorkshire, has been awarded £19 million.

In fact research by *The Guardian* found **that the money allocated so far would disproportionately benefit people in Conservative seats**. Oh surely not.

A *Guardian* analysis found that "Conservative marginal seats, those with majorities of fewer than 8,000 votes, have received 1.5 times the amount of funding per person than all other constituencies under the £4bn budget – £76 a head compared with £53 a head.

Constituencies that won under the Conservative landslide in 2019 – many of which will be vulnerable at the next general election – have been awarded almost twice as much per person as other seats." Some red wall

MPs in the Don valley, Dudley North, Keighley and Ilkley, Gedling, Wolverhampton North-East, and also Bracknell in Berkshire are all asking how they can get access to cash the next time round as all these areas are suffering enormously and their bids were all turned down. People in Blyth, 10 miles north of Newcastle, have given up on politicians of all colours as they watch their town disintegrate. Some, who voted Tory for the first time at the last election, believing their promises of 'levelling-up', say they will never vote Tory again.

What on earth is going on?

****

Well what is going on is that our prime minister has been handed a fixed penalty fine by Lancashire police for travelling in the back of a car without wearing a seat belt. It was, I'm afraid, an open and shut case as he was recording a piece to camera and it was shown all over social media. He also publicly acknowledged his "slight error of judgement" so here we have it. A prime minister who has had two fixed penalty notices, one as Chancellor and one as PM.

"Integrity, professionalism, and accountability," were his first words to all of us on the steps of No 10.

****

20TH JANUARY

The mystery of the crab deaths.

Well the report about the marine extinction has just been released and the panel admitted they could not find one single clear cause for the incident. They concluded that a new virus, bacterium or amoeba could be to blame. Apparently they did not have the time to conduct a new analysis so conducted a "desk-based study" exploring all avenues of concern over the use of chemicals.

Well fishermen are furious. So also are politicians and other researchers.

Alex Cunningham, Labour MP for Stockton North, has accused the government of hiding behind the algae bloom theory.

Stan Renne, a fisherman based in Hartlepool, was very scornful. "They've just come up with another theory, they're kicking the can down the road until the Freeport dredge is finished." he said.

And **Dr Gary Caldwell of Newcastle University** said there was no direct evidence for the panel to suggest that the deaths were caused by an unknown pathogen.

The report has been criticized for a lack of transparency and thoroughness and for being in too much of a hurry to come to a conclusion. People want to see their reports.

****

23RD JANUARY

So we start another week and move towards the end of the first month of the New Year. I wish I could say that all is going well but the opposite is true. **Nadhim Zahawi** and his tax problems are all over the media and apparently the investigation into his financial affairs all started when he was Chancellor. Civil servants had, it seems, alerted Johnson to an HMRC "flag" over Zahawi before his appointment as Chancellor by Johnson, but it had been ignored.

But we are hearing about something else now. This concerns the loans for the Greensill scandal which I have written about in previous books. According to an article in *The Times* today Zahawi wrongly claimed that he had not exchanged messages on a WhatsApp group with David Cameron, who was prime minister at the time. Except that now it seems that he did! Apparently Cameron asked him to give him details of Richard Sharp who was a Tory donor and former banker at Goldman Sachs and who had been advising Rishi Sunak when he was Chancellor. His messages had been deleted but following an investigation they have been found and after further questioning Zahawi has admitted that he had sent messages to Cameron. And he had no idea as to how they had been deleted. Oh dear, memory playing up again Mr. Zahawi?

****

Wait a minute what was that name again? Richard Sharp? Well his name has cropped up today in a completely separate issue. Connected to Boris Johnson. Yes that always spells out bad news.

As we know Boris is always short of money and so he is always looking for it behind the sofa, or in other people's pockets. Well, well Richard Sharp apparently contacted a long lost relative of Johnson's in Canada and arranged an £800,000 loan guarantee for him in order to be able to fund his lifestyle.

After Mr Sharp reportedly agreed to help, he is said to have met with Cabinet Secretary and head of the civil service, Simon Case at Downing Street at the beginning of December 2020.

Before the loan was finalised, the PM allegedly invited Mr Sharp and Mr Blyth for a private dinner at Chequers. And then goodness gracious me what happened next? **Mr Sharp was recommended, by Johnson, for the role of BBC chairman,** for which he was successful, and he began the role in February 2021.

Well Sunak has asked his new ethics adviser to look into Mr. Zahawi and has asked William Shawcross to speak to Mr. Sharp. Who is **William Shawcross** exactly?

Well he is, the Commissioner for Public Appointments, and he said he would review the competition which led to Sharp's appointment while Johnson was prime minister.

But we need to note that he has previously attacked the Labour Party and expressed open support for the Tories. In an article for the *National Review*, he wrote: "Only a vote for the Conservatives offers any hope of drawing back from the abyss." And hang on a minute what is this? **His daughter, Eleanor, just happens to be Sunak's deputy chief of staff and head of No. 10's policy unit.** It all seems very cosy to me.

****

Then we must also remember **Dominic Raab** who is being investigated for two complaints about bullying. Wait a minute. It is being reported that there are a total of 24 complaints against him for rudeness and bullying from civil servants now.

Mr. Raab, who is justice secretary and Deputy Prime Minister, continues to deny any allegations of bullying whatsoever.

****

5.18 pm: Remember this? Alex Bourne, a publican and former neighbour of the then Health Secretary **Matt Hancock**, had always denied allegations that he had won £30 million of work producing Covid test vials when he offered his services during the pandemic. He had apparently WhatsApped Hancock and in spite of having no previous experience or any medical training he was given the contract. Well The 'Good Law Project' has just announced that the DHSC has been instructed to hand over copies of all WhatsApp messages between the two of them. The information Commissioner's office ruled that the DHSC breached FOI guidelines and have given the department 35 days to respond or risk being in 'contempt of court'.

****

Well, I hope you are keeping up with all of this. This government is dangerously incompetent as the next disturbing issues show very clearly.

BROKEN BRITAIN

But this is what we have come to expect of this government. Incompetence, negligence and destruction everywhere you look.

But if you think all that is bad then this is 100 times worse.

The Probation System

We need to go back in time here to an article written for *The Guardian* on **30th June 2019** by Jamie Doward. And, I am very sorry, but we have to mention one of the names that is always associated with chaos and disaster in the Conservative government and which I know you were hoping never to hear again.

In **2015** the government decided in their wisdom to privatise some of the probation service and it just so happened that the justice secretary who proposed and implemented this crazy decision was none other than .... **Chris Grayling.** I know you remember that name.

As Mr. Doward says "it was an 'unmitigated disaster' that left the public at greater risk from ex-offenders released from jail"

Even then, in 2019, bigger caseloads and unrealistic targets set by Grayling have meant that the probation service were unable to keep to the same standards as before. More than a third – 36% – of those interviewed as part of research by Professor Gill Kirton, of Queen Mary University of London, and Dr Cécile Guillaume, of Roehampton University admitted that "they regularly cut corners and compromise professional standards to meet targets."

In a typical comment, one probation officer told researchers: "I truly believe that offenders will receive a poorer service and staff will struggle to provide the high level of service they have always given. Consequently, the public will be at risk."

Another said: "I do not consider that we are in a position to protect the public, but we will be the scapegoats when tragedies happen."

And we now hear of two dreadful tragedies that are a direct result of this decision. Offenders have been let out on parole deemed medium risk to the public when their threat level was far higher. One man was allowed to go home to his pregnant partner and not only was she killed by him but so also were her young son, her daughter and her daughter's friend who was there for a sleep-over.

Then a young, beautiful aspiring lawyer was assaulted and murdered on her way home in London by an offender who had been released just nine days earlier.

The Probation service is broken and not fit for purpose. Many experienced officers are leaving so that it is now 1,800 officers short, and inexperienced officers are being left without proper supervision to make judgements which are literally of life and death significance. **As the editorial in *The Times* today says**, "**for too long the service has been under-resourced and under-funded and undervalued.**"

Now where have we heard that before?

The young lawyer's aunt was on *BBC's Woman's Hour* yesterday and she accused ministers and the Probation service of having "blood on their hands."

The family are still waiting for an apology from the Justice Secretary.

****

25TH JANUARY

The PM says today in an answer to a question from Sir Keir Starmer that women and girls are safe on our streets because they are working on it all. Starmer had spoken to the aunt this morning. I suggest that Sunak does the same.

****

Women.

So whilst we are talking about the treatment of women by this government we hear that the government has rejected calls for a large scale pilot of menopause leave, in a move described as a "missed opportunity" by a Commons committee. Ministers have also resisted a recommendation from the Commons Women and Equalities Committee to make menopause a "protected characteristic" under the Equalities Act. This was first put forward last July and people are concerned that it has taken so long to be finalised. But this is of course a disappointing result. It is rather strange too, that the government also think that it could inadvertently create new forms of discrimination, for example, discrimination risks towards men suffering from long-term medical conditions.

I've heard it all now.

There are actually disability allowances for men and women with long term problems but only women suffer from the perimenopause/menopause symptoms for goodness sake. According to research by Bupa around one million women in the UK have actually been forced to leave their jobs last year due to perimenopause/menopause symptoms. If it were possible for them to be granted leave whilst experiencing these problems many jobs could be saved. But no. We have to think about men. I honestly do not understand.

****

Rape crisis centres are now being forced to close their doors because lack of funding means they can no longer meet the demand. Waiting lists are closed as the cash runs out.

****

Where is all our money going I would like to know? We are the fifth richest country in the world but our public services and living standards are amongst the worst.

****

Then of course after women come our children and the neglect and cruelty of them is what makes me persevere with this book. If ever anyone says to you that this government wasn't really that bad just refer them to these next two stories.

****

Children.

Unaccompanied young child refugees are going missing and the Home Office does not have the faintest idea as to where they are. A Home Office whistleblower who works for Mitie the Home Office contractor has said that an estimated 10% of children were going missing each week after seeing children from a Home-Office-run hotel in Hythe, Kent being effectively trafficked. The targeting of helpless children by criminal gangs has reportedly become a frequent occurrence. This is also happening outside a hotel in Brighton.

And it has emerged that the Home Office was warned repeatedly by police that the vulnerable occupants of the hotel – asylum-seeking children who had recently arrived in the UK without parents or carers – would be targeted by criminal networks.

****

Then there is this. I have written previously at length about what I call **Children's We Don't Care Homes** and here are some more appalling reports. The Hesley Group of residential homes and special schools are based in Doncaster, Yorkshire and are owned by Antin Infrastructure, a private equity firm. Documents were leaked to the BBC which show gross maltreatment of very vulnerable children in these homes and which were reported to police back in 2018 by a former support worker. She was told there was not enough evidence to proceed. But these documents show 104 reports of concern from 2018 to 2021. I describe these incidents but warn you that they make painful reading. If it is difficult for you to read about it, it is difficult for me to write about it, but obviously nothing like as difficult to experience it and we owe it to these children to record it so that no-one can make light of it.

Children were being kicked and punched resulting in one getting a black eye and another being swung round by the ankles. Another was reported to have been locked outside in freezing weather while naked. Several were not fed properly and some were not given medicine for days.

But in spite of Doncaster council receiving 66 warnings in a three year period and Ofsted receiving 44 alerts, the homes still kept their "good" rating. Amanda Spielman said that Ofsted needed new powers to regulate owners of children's homes so as to "join up information".

No, Ms. Spielman, I think you just need to employ people who can open their eyes, unblock their ears and work with compassion, competence and common sense, three qualities that are nowhere to be found in positions of authority at the moment.

These homes have at last been closed down.

****

The criminal justice system.

Lord Justice Edis, the senior presiding judge, warns that the criminal justice system is in "crisis mode." He talks about the issues I have previously discussed as he says that "First there are not enough courtrooms, then there are not enough judges, then when we've got the judges there are not enough advocates to do the cases." His comments coincide with warnings from the Criminal Bar Association who say that the system is "about to crack" due to a shortage of barristers.

Of the 60 circuit judges sought at the last recruitment drive 18 posts were left vacant.

Lord Edis goes on to say that "Conditions are also worse than before. The state of the buildings are such that people don't want to spend the rest of their lives working in them." **And of course we hear the same story that all the agencies which contribute to the system have been starved of resources.....staff and money.**

****

The Arts

Well the Arts, and especially the Opera, are not at the top of anyone's priorities and certainly the Arts Council England continues to make a complete pig's ear of it all. Glyndebourne has announced that it is cancelling its UK tour due to lack of funding and the ENO has just been told that it **can** stay in London for another year due to the noise and shouts of the backlash it has received. But quite where this leaves them is not at all clear. And then Richard Morrison in *The Times* writes that its Chief Executive, Stuart Murphy, says that maybe the ENO would not move to Manchester but to "another set of places who don't have much culture at all and we would be the main people in town." What is he talking about? He then does acknowledge what is absolutely obvious to everyone when he says that it would be hard to get "people who live and die for culture to move somewhere that has literally nothing."

Well Stuart Murphy is about to depart and there is, as yet, no successor. So as Richard Morrison says, "That crass comment only reinforces my feeling that it has to be the Arts Council that devises a sustainable future for ENO." **But, as he says, the cuts they have already made gives a clear impression "that it has people high up in its organisation with a real hatred of opera."** They deny this of course but the "the British opera scene hasn't looked this patchy since 1945."

It is just one more example of incompetence and lack of specialist and detailed knowledge from people who are supposed to know better. The ignorance everywhere you look is astounding and, to me at any-rate, alarming.

****

25TH JANUARY

The British Car Industry

Car production in Britain has plunged to new lows not seen since the 1950s, when Sir Anthony Eden was prime minister. This is just appalling to hear. I come from Coventry, which was at the centre of car manufacturing, and provided huge employment opportunities for those living in the area. We were very proud of all the car factories and the wealth they brought to the area.

There are various reasons for this collapse such as supply problems, the closure of Honda's Swindon factory, the declining market in China, Brexit of course, and then there is the collapse of Britishvolt the car battery factory supposedly being built in Northumberland. This is a huge shock as it was a flag-ship of Boris Johnson who said the plan would be part of the UK's green industrial revolution and in his own inimitable way he trumpeted the thousands of skilled jobs the Britishvolt gigafactory was expected to create. It was thought the Government put in around £100 million towards the £3.8 billion project last January but the firm could not secure funding to take the project on and has gone into administration with the loss of 300 jobs and it owed as much as £120m to creditors when it collapsed last week in a major blow to hopes of sustaining the British car industry.

Andy Palmer, the former boss of Aston Martin, believes this could be the beginning of the end for Britain's car industry unless some significant changes are made.

And here we go again. "The lack of government support, and therefore a lack of investor confidence in the sector, has made it near impossible for companies like BritishVolt to gain a foothold on the UK market" he says.

"Without a battery manufacturing base on UK shores the wider auto industry will collapse. Without a proper strategy to back-up the transition to EVs, the targets and lofty ambitions of politicians are not worth the House of Commons-headed paper they are written on".

However in *The Times* this morning we read that a battery company in Australia, called 'Recharge Industries', might save the day as they have just made a preliminary bid. They have said that they would want to secure support from the government "to understand the financial position" before potentially tapping the commercial market."

Yes well good luck with that one.

Come on Aussies sort out the poor and stupid Brits.

Time will tell what happens here.

****

Crumbling schools.

Ministers have abandoned an imminent publication of documents called the Buildings Conditions Survey in which data would show **which school buildings were judged to be a "threat to life."** Yes indeed there are thousands of dilapidated school buildings which are in need of urgent funding as some are at risk of collapse.

Labour is intending to use one of its opposition days in the Commons to force the government to release the papers by tabling a motion using a so-called "humble address".

Just more evidence of lack of transparency, no doubt due to lack of action, and a complete disregard for the safety of our children. There are over 700,000 children being educated in dangerous buildings. And we continue to hear about the threat to the lives of teachers and children by asbestos which is being dangerously exposed as the buildings deteriorate.

A headline in the *Daily Mail* states that "Classroom asbestos has reportedly killed 10,000 pupils and teachers in schools in the last four decades". These figures are produced by the Joint Union Asbestos Committee. The government has rejected recommendations to remove asbestos on the grounds of cost and, they say, insufficient evidence. Individual stories make tragic reading and I would suggest they start to read them.

****

26TH JANUARY

Home Secretary U-turns on Windrush reforms described as a "slap in the face" by campaigners.

Suella Braverman has quietly announced that she has ditched a commitment to establish a migrants' commissioner and also rowed back on calls to boost the powers of the independent chief inspector of borders and immigration.

"Our country's brave Windrush victims denied justice yet again," the shadow foreign secretary wrote in a tweet.

Former home secretary Priti Patel had originally accepted all 30 of the recommendations made by Ms. Williams, including the three ditched on Thursday.

Goodness. Suella Braverman makes Priti Patel look like Mother Theresa.

****

Then there is always Brexit.

There is an interesting article in *The Times* today by Simon Nixon. Whilst we all jump up and down and shout please rejoin the EU or at least the single market and the customs union he is saying that actually no, that is not going to happen and what we need to do is avoid the situation getting even worse.

In a long and detailed article he says "Top of the wish-list for many would be a wide-ranging mobility deal, both to allow British businesses to recruit from the EU to fill their labour shortages and to allow British citizens including professionals and performers to ply their trade more freely on the continent. Others would like to see a deal on food standards which would pave the way for a reduction in border checks. Universities are desperate for Britain to be readmitted to the Horizon research funding programme to prevent a brain drain of academic talent from these shores."

As he says, rejoining the EU is not an option at the moment, so maybe Sir Keir Starmer is correct when he rules this out. And it is very interesting to note that, when in Davos at the World Economic Forum, he spoke to many EU businesses and obviously made a good impression. He assured them that Britain "will be open for business" under a future Labour government. In the absence of the prime minister who had decided not to attend for reasons best known to himself, Sir Keir was the most senior British politician there. **EU officials welcomed his plans to rebuild ties with Brussels, saying the bloc is "aching" for a new relationship with the UK.**

Well we are all aching for a general election but whoever forms a government will have a long and difficult journey trying to mend broken Britain and return it to a country that we can be proud of once again.

****

NEWS IN BRIEF—JUST ONE DAY

27TH JANUARY 2023

Some headlines:-

HMRC boss says Zahawi tax mistake was not innocent.

Nadhim Zahawi has said that he paid a penalty but the head of HMRC has said "there are no penalties for innocent errors in your tax affairs."

****

£15bn written off on PPE and Covid drugs that can't be used.

The latest figures come amid continuing controversy about procurement failures during the pandemic. The Department for Health and Social Care estimates that storage and disposal costs for its excess and unusable PPE will be £319 million and that at the end of March last year the estimated monthly spending on storage was £24 million.

****

Raab told 'rights bill' is misconceived.

The president of the European Court of Human Rights has told Raab that his Bill of Rights would lead to **more** cases being taken to Strasbourg rather than fewer. His plan would not pull Britain out of the ECHR but would replace the Human Rights Act. This would implement a string of unnecessary constitutional reforms when actually the HRA was already doing a very good job in preventing cases reaching Strasbourg.

I think Raab 's understanding of all this is a bit limited actually and *The Times* revealed last month that the whole idea might be ditched by Sunak as he has decided to prioritise other legislation.

Actually I think Dominic Raab will be ditched very shortly.

****

Nadhim Zahawi has business ties connected to the brother of Matt Hancock.

I promise you I am not making this up.

Zahawi has been involved with a crowd-funding company his parents own with Matt Hancock's brother. 'Crowd2Fund' was launched in 2014 by Chris Hancock as an innovative platform for entrepreneurs to raise capital from investors. 'Balshore Investments', the Gibralter company at the centre of Zahawi's tax troubles, was listed as a founding investor, taking an initial share in the company. He has never stated an interest in the business in which his parents are now declared as persons of significant control for the firm. Money, money, money everywhere you look. That is the only concern of these people who pretend to be honest politicians.

****

Windsurfer quits UK in despair over sewage spills.

One of Britain's most successful windsurfers has moved to Spain after comparing training off England's south coast to "surfing in a sewer". Nicola Greaves of the 'Marine Conservation Society' said "Untreated sewage is being pumped into our seas for hundreds of thousands of hours each year".

And 265 MPs **voted down** an amendment to stop private water companies from dumping raw sewage into the UK's rivers and coastlines. At present, waste can be released from the sewage system and into the nation's rivers and coastal waters when there is heavy rainfall to avoid the sewage backing up into people's homes. Well obviously we don't want that but the Lords Amendment 45 to the Environment Bill would have placed a legal duty on water companies in England and Wales "to make improvements to their sewerage systems and demonstrate progressive reductions in the harm caused by discharges of untreated sewage". Just checking on the environment secretary. Who is it again? Oh yes, Therese Coffey.

****

Physiotherapists strike for the first time in their history.

****

No minister has been offered up to face a grilling on breakfast TV and radio.

This is the third time this week that no member of the government has appeared on shows such as BBC Breakfast, Good Morning Britain or Radio 4's '*Today*' programme. What are they afraid of? Mind you they have all just been to Chequers for an away day, or as Labour call it, a hideaway day.

****

Sir Rod Stewart backs striking NHS workers.

He says they "aren't asking for a great deal" and said it was time to "change the bloody Government".

Well this wonderful guy is all over the news today as he offers to pay for 20 or so scans for people stuck on waiting lists.

He said: "I personally have been a Tory for a long time, but I think this Government should stand down now and give the Labour Party a go at it because this is heart-breaking for the nurses, it really is heart-breaking. In all my years of living in this country I've never seen it so bad and anything I can do to help. Go on, the nurses. I'm on your side."

****

HS2: delayed AGAIN or scrapped for good? Government refuses to say if expensive project will ever terminate at London Euston.

HS2 has been dogged by criticism over its financial and environmental impact and it is in the news once again. This morning on the *Today* programme Lord Berkeley, a long-term sceptic of HS2, said billions of pounds would be 'much better spent on improving the railway lines in the north, east and west, than going to London a bit quicker'. And I must say that I agree with him.

But Jeremy Hunt said he did not see "any conceivable circumstance" the original plan would not be followed and that he was "incredibly proud" of the work going ahead. However it is being said that it might not be completed until 2038 which is a five year delay, it might have to terminate at Old Oak Common in the suburbs of West London and of course it will be vastly over budget.

****

Electric Shock.

I will just quote Martin Samuel in his *Times* notebook this morning when he says that "It will come as no surprise to any electric car owner that 300,000 chargers on the streets by 2030 is as about as likely to happen as a skiffle revival.

****

Stop dredging on River Tees until we solve crab deaths.

Yes this catastrophe will continue to be in the news until we get some sense from the environment department and that won't happen whilst Therese Coffey is in charge. Joe Redfern, a marine biologist who runs Whitby Lobster Fishery condemns the recent report from Defra and accuses them of having vested interests in shipping industries and in British ports.

****

Don't blow Britain's great life sciences chance.

The government's decision last year to halve the tax credit for research and development for small and medium sized companies has done real damage to the kind of companies the government wants to foster. According to Kate Bingham a partner in SV Health Investors, the start-ups in which her company invests "are moving jobs abroad and fewer clinical trials are being done in the UK" as a direct result. The fall in sterling has also made recruiting talent much harder. Clever post- doc researchers are in demand all over the world and a Home Secretary who makes it clear that foreigners are unwelcome in Britain will encourage them to take job offers elsewhere. Emma Duncan writes about this this morning in *The Times* and it makes distressing reading.

****

Ministers allow banned bee-killing pesticide to be used for third year running.

Bees are vitally important to the health of the country. Without their pollination many plants would die out. So it is important to look after them. So what does this government do? They allow sugar-beet farmers to use a banned bee-killing neonicotinoid pesticide this year – for the third year in a row. A single teaspoon of thiamethoxam, which is banned in both the UK and the EU, is toxic enough to kill

1.25 billion bees, according to Professor Dave Goulson, one of the UK's leading insect experts. The bee population is already struggling and of course if we were still in the EU this could not happen. "Oh but goodness how can we preserve our sugar beet crop if we can't use this pesticide?" sugar beet farmers are asking. Well the answer is to stop growing sugar beet and grow something healthier instead. Fruit and vegetables for example. Forget sugar and preserve the bees.

Well this is all in a day of the present Conservative government. We get used to it but we will never cease to be disgusted by it.

****

FREEPORTS

I think it is really important to understand what a Freeport is. They have been introduced to the UK by the present government and we know that they have a reputation for not thinking things through so I want to explore this in a bit more detail.

Here is the definition of a Freeport from the government website GOV.UK:-

Freeports are special areas within the UK's borders where different economic regulations apply. By delivering investment on specific sites benefiting from tax and customs incentives, Freeports will create thousands of high-quality jobs in some of our most disadvantaged communities. These sites have been carefully selected for their suitability for development by local authorities and key private partners and sit within an outer boundary, which represents the geographical location within which the benefits of Freeports are targeted and does not in itself confer any special tax, customs or other status.

In other words it is a free trade zone where goods imported into Freeports are exempt from taxes or tariffs that are normally paid to the British government.

It means manufacturers in Freeports can import raw materials tariff-free, only paying tariffs on finished products leaving the site for elsewhere in the UK.

Or, the goods can be re-exported overseas without UK duties being paid.

Firms also benefit from lower rates of national insurance if they take on new staff.

The idea is that this will stimulate economic growth like trade, investment and jobs near shipping ports or airports.

These were introduced by Boris Johnson following our exit from the EU to protect our trading links. He said they would bring in thousands of new jobs in some of the country's most disadvantaged communities. Well that all sounds fine and I am sure he thought it was a good idea. But as we know to our cost he was not a man of detail or joined up thinking, so we do need to delve a bit further.

These are the 8 English Freeport areas:-

- East Midlands, centering on the airport,
- Freeport East (Felixstowe and Harwich),
- Humber Freeport,
- Liverpool City region,
- Plymouth and South Devon Freeport,
- Thames Freeport,
- Solent Freeport (Southampton) and
- Teeside Freeport.

The 2 Scottish Green Freeports are:-

- Firth of Forth Green Freeport and
- Inverness and Cromarty Firth Green Freeport

However the whole scheme does have its critics.

The Office for Budgetary Responsibility has predicted that tax breaks in these Freeports will **cost the UK government £50million a year**. It says historical evidence suggests their "main effect" will be to move economic activity from one place to another.

But more concerning is the lack of scrutiny and fewer checks at border control which will, experts and insiders say, be a magnet for organised crime and could make it easier for gangsters to import drugs and guns into the UK.

Dr. Anna Sergi, an academic at the University of Essex who has carried out extensive research into Freeports around the world said that, "Freeports have a high risk for criminal exploitation for two reasons – money laundering and illicit trade."

She goes on to say that, "This means you can use businesses to smuggle in different forms of illicit goods, or goods that should be declared for duties.

"We already know this is a vulnerability of ports anyway – it's very difficult to check containers as it is, even more so if there is zero control over them."

A source at Border Force in the North West claimed that the agency would struggle to police the new regime. "We've got a massive gap in customs control, we're not really doing any of that work," they said. "The only work we're doing is on immigrations desks so that people can get through without there being any queues." **He also makes the chilling observation that the rise in gun crime in Liverpool could be due to the fact that there is no customs work happening there**. And of course we all know that there are strikes happening with the Border Force. It is not only about pay, it is also about the lack of sufficient training for new recruits. The source from the Border Force said that, "Whereas historically we trained them to do casework investigations into suspicious travellers or goods, now it's a three week course that doesn't cover casework. They're bringing them in just to do an immigration job."

He says that, "Organised crime gangs know exactly what we're doing and what we're not doing."

And yes there **are** around 80 Freeports in the **EU** but, guess what, in 2020 the Commission brought in new restrictions in response to concerns that they posed a risk of tax evasion, terrorist financing and money laundering.

Tony Saggers, former head of drugs investigations at the NCA, told the *i* that the UK is uniquely vulnerable to exploitation from international crime gangs and will present more opportunities for corruption. "Our drug market is high volume, we have the highest demand in Europe for cocaine and heroin," he said. **We've also got a 360 degree coastline**, many more ports than our neighbours and despite Brexit we are one of the most internationally connected countries. **Mr Saggers has been warning for several years that Brexit will alter the crime threats the country is facing**.

Absolutely I knew Brexit would be there somewhere.

So there we have it. Maybe they are a good thing but only if we do as the EU have done and have a more efficient border force. That will not happen in the present climate of course. It is actually very concerning.

****

THE DYING DAYS OF JANUARY

27TH JANUARY

Well I start with a close look at Jeremy Hunt.

I do feel that Chancellors these days need a bit of extra scrutiny.

He has just made a speech well ahead of his March budget.

I think there might have been the odd sensible statement in there but there was an enormous helping of complete rubbish. It was ignorant, insulting and patronising.

He said that there would be tax cuts at some time before the next election but businesses would take priority over workers. He suggested that government departments would not be given additional money to solve pay disputes meaning that it would have to be taken out of existing budgets.

He said "Our plan for growth is necessitated, energised and made possible by Brexit. The desire to move to a high-wage, high-skill economy is one shared on all sides. We need to make Brexit a catalyst for the bold choices that will take advantage of the nimbleness and flexibilities that it makes possible."

I promise you I am not making this up.

He also doesn't like the "declinism" that he is seeing everywhere and we all need to talk up Britain much more. "We are the sixth richest country in the world" he says, and we need to realise that we are doing so well and he really doesn't approve of people saying how dreadful everything is. "Declinism about Britain was wrong in the past - and it is wrong today. Some of the gloom is based on statistics that do not reflect the whole picture."

"The UK is poised to play a leading role in Europe and across the world in the growth sectors which will define this century."

What is he talking about? He is absolutely on a different planet. Where has he been these last thirteen years? Does he ever walk around his constituency, or anywhere for that matter, and listen to the people he is supposed to represent?

But that is not all. Just listen to this.

He said the four pillars of his vision to make the UK the most prosperous country in Europe are enterprise, education, employment and everywhere. Pardon?

He explains this very strange phrase as follows.

Enterprise--He said the attitude among Britons towards risk-taking must become bolder.

Education--He bemoaned the lack of literacy skills among parts of the population.

Employment--6.6 million working age adults, that is 20 per cent of the UK workforce, are economically inactive — five million of whom do not want to work.

Everywhere — he said it is "socially divisive" and "economically damaging" if young people feel they need to head to southern England to get ahead in their careers.

By this time my head is in my hands. Here is a Chancellor who has been in the Conservative government for thirteen years talking as if he has just descended from Mars.

But let us move on to the patronising bit. He has just noticed that we have a labour shortage. Now, at the risk of being a bit repetitive, why is that do you think? Anyway his answer to that is to tell the retired over 50s to get off the golf course and get back into work.

Well I think he has just lost the over 50s' vote.

And to finish he tells the teachers, who are about to strike, that, "It's not helping anyone to harm our children's education. Education is one of the most important things we can do if we want to improve our skills, improve our productivity, improve people's real wages in future."

"But no of course there is no money to pay you, there is no more money for specialist staff or for teaching assistants or for special needs. Goodness me no there is no money for free school meals or school trips and definitely not the sort of money that the education tsar Sir Kevan Collins asked for. Yes I know we have done an enormous amount of damage to children's education but please don't take a few days off by striking. It does not look good for a country trying to play a leading role in Europe and across the world".

OK, OK that last bit in bold was made up by me but I am extremely disgusted by his stupid speech. Actually so are many others.

Business groups have also criticised Hunt's speech for being "empty" and having "little meat on the bones of his vision"

Other remarks are 'a parallel universe', 'a lecture not a plan', 'a 'fluff' speech', 'a rigid approach'.

The ministers in this government are completely blinkered and devoid of common sense and reality. They go around in their chauffeured cars and sit in their tiny bubbles of privilege and excessive wealth. They

are not engaged with the people of this country.

They are not fit to govern.

****

So this is just a snapshot of our present Chancellor. Just in case some people think that maybe he is OK.

****

29TH JANUARY

Nadhim Zahawi has been sacked by the prime minister. The investigation by the ethics advisor was placed on the PM's desk this morning saying that it is clear that "there has been a serious breach of the ministerial code." And of course people are saying this should have happened weeks ago. In fact I got so angry that I dashed off another letter to *The Times*.

Sir, Nadhim Zahawi should have been sacked weeks ago. This has been the main running story for many weeks when we should have been talking about poverty, the cost of living, the strikes, the collapse of the NHS, the criminal justice system, the probation service, and many small businesses. Rishi Sunak has displayed weakness and indecisiveness as a leader. We need and deserve better.

Sue Wood

****

30TH JANUARY

The letter is published today.

And now we see that links between Boris Johnson and BBC chairman Richard Sharp are under fresh scrutiny, following a report that the

then-prime minister was told to stop asking Mr Sharp for financial advice. The leaked memo, reported by *The Sunday Times*, was sent on 22 December 2020 - about two weeks before his government announced Mr Sharp's appointment as the new BBC chairman and just weeks before Mr Sharp was appointed to the corporation.

Last week Mr Sharp said that he **had not** given advice to the former prime minister, and BBC News has been told Mr Sharp's position remains unchanged.

Well that is until it explodes. His appointment is to be investigated by the public appointments commissioner as well as an internal panel. He has also been asked to appear before the Department of Culture, Media and Sport's Select Committee to be grilled by MPs.

It really is all just a matter of time.

****

31ST JANUARY

Indeed it is! Last week William Shawcross was all set to investigate Richard Sharp and any connection he had had with a loan for Boris Johnson, but yesterday he decided to recuse himself from the investigation as he suddenly remembered that actually he had met Mr. Sharp on various occasions and thought it might be a conflict of interest. He says "As I have met Mr Sharp on previous occasions, I have decided to recuse myself from this particular investigation."

People seem to have such short memories; should they really be in positions such as this?

But **we** remember. We remember that his daughter Eleanor donated £20,000 to Sunak's leadership campaign and is now head of the policy unit at No 10. Now **that** could be a conflict of interest I would think.

****

Firefighters have just announced that they are going to take industrial action and will be going on strike for the first time in twenty years.

****

And here is more news about strikes. The Strikes (Minimum Services Levels) Bill cleared the Commons in a late-night sitting last night, with MPs voting 315 to 246, a majority of 69.

Under this bill, some employees, including in the rail industry and emergency services, would be required to work during industrial action - and could be sacked if they refuse. **Yes, this is the bill that would make it possible for nurses and doctors to be sacked if they go on strike.**

However it now has to clear the House of Lords, and Unions have threatened legal action if the new law is passed and they also say it is unworkable. Labour says it would repeal it if it wins the next election.

****

And just in case you were relaxing and thinking nothing worse can possibly be happening, the defence minister told the House of Commons yesterday that the British Army is in "urgent need of recapitalisation". I think he means it needs more money. He said that the military may not be able to protect the country against aggression from Russia. A senior US general had told Ben Wallace, the defence secretary, that the British Army was no longer a fighting force.

So there we have it. The first priority and duty of a government is to protect its citizens. They have failed. **Gross underfunding of the armed services have left it in a state of inadequacy at a time of serious instability in Europe.**

****

And so it goes on with no concern or innovative ideas from this government. **But then if you don't acknowledge the problem, and they don't, you cannot begin to solve it.**

****

100 DAYS AND BEYOND

So today, February 2nd, Rishi Sunak 'celebrates' his first 100 days in office which is twice as long as Liz Truss managed to achieve.

So how is it looking Rishi?

Hmmmm. I think he could be beginning to be a little bit worried. In fact I think he should be very concerned.

Yesterday was called '**Walkout Wednesday**' as up to half a million people went on strike in one of the biggest days of industrial action in more than a decade.

Teachers, university lecturers, civil servants, bus drivers, security guards and train drivers from two unions were out all day.

Teachers were getting the most attention as, of course, if they strike it affects parents everywhere. The majority of the population support their strike action but some were bemoaning the fact that for goodness sake they get long holidays and good pensions why do they need to strike? As someone on Twitter said **"If they can turn you against teachers and nurses they can turn you against anyone."**

And the government, true to form, said how dreadful it is to harm children's education in this way by closing so many schools. The hypocrisy of the government is staggering.

They have shown no concern whatsoever for the ongoing lack of funding and resources in schools, the difficulty in retaining teaching assistants or those supporting special needs, crumbling buildings, lack of staff for specialist subjects such as maths and science and the ever-increasing workload teachers are having to take on.

Schools are now expected to provide support for pupils suffering eating disorders, anxiety and depression. Many pupils now turn up hungry and unable to afford shoes. About one in six school-aged children have a diagnosed mental health problem up from one in nine in 2017. Teachers are providing so much more pastoral care than they have ever needed to do in the past. One school said that they were spending more than £250,000 a year on staff and services including buying uniforms and food for the poorer pupils. The Head said **"We are spending a huge amount on food. We have children stealing food from Sainsbury's. The system is broken."**

Yes they are striking because they need more money. Many are leaving because they can earn more elsewhere and they are being paid less than other professionals in similar professions.

So what does the government do under the leadership of Mr. Sunak?

They refuse to get round a table and negotiate about pay and they warn them that if they take part in further strikes they will be sacked.

Well that will sort out the problem.

****

Money Mr. Sunak? Well there is a lot swishing about if you know where to look.

Shell has just announced a record high of profits at £32.2 billion which is equivalent to just over £1,000 a second and is among the biggest ever made by a British company. So a higher windfall tax is being called for. You might remember that this government fought long and hard against imposing a windfall tax last year and even now are levying it at a lower rate than other countries.

It was great to hear Ed Miliband on *Radio 4* this morning talking such a lot of sense like a real grown-up and calling for it to be raised to 78%. He accused the government of letting the energy giants "off the hook" by leaving "billions on the table" because there is not a "proper windfall tax".

The other really concerning factor is that as Miliband says, "they have built in a massive loophole just for fossil fuel companies not for other energy companies, so that if they make so-called investments, they get massive tax breaks for that."

Well I think Rishi Sunak can do something about this.

****

And let us stay with heating and energy companies for the moment as I read about a really shocking story about British Gas. Paul Morgan–Bentley, a reporter on *The Times*, is to be congratulated for going undercover and working for 'Arvato', a service used by British Gas to pursue debts. Because of rocketing energy prices many people are falling behind with their payments and so prepayment meters are being installed. These are meters which can be used in domestic properties as a 'pay as you go' tariff. In other words, you pay for your energy before you use it - usually by adding money to a 'key' or smart card, which is then inserted into the meter. Energy is then credited to your account, and your meter will then use this credit until it runs out - the more energy you use, the quicker your credit will run down. But basically if they don't top up they self-disconnect. So, as an agent said "we don't actually disconnect them. It's a bit of a laughable loophole."

Debt agents are now forcing their way into people's homes in order to install these meters. They can apply for warrants in court. However they are supposed to check each customer for vulnerability first and obviously the courts presume they have done this. They are issuing warrants at top speed and have no time to check themselves.

The agents are taking no account of single mothers with young children, the disabled, elderly people, those with health conditions like heart problems or asthma. They shout through the door that if they don't open up they will fetch the police. But they take locksmiths and dog handlers with them and go in anyway if there is no-one at home.

These agents are actually taking delight in this aggressive approach and their team leader said "**Forcing our way in is exciting......I love it**".

Well of course they are all saying now that it must be stopped. Grant Shapps is on the case so I'm sure the forced fitting of these meters will stop very soon.

****

The Bank of England's Monetary Policy Committee is expected to lift interest rates again by 0.5 percentage points to 4 %, adding to the misery for millions of home owners who face a sharp rise in mortgage payments. Its base rate was already at a 14-year high.

****

Everyone was saying that a deal was about to be done with **the Northern Ireland protocol.** *The Times* reported yesterday that the two sides had reached a deal on customs checks. However Ursula von der Leyen said there would be no final agreement until "you give the final signature." Negotiations are still ongoing.

And Michel Barnier, the former ever- polite, courteous, and charming French Brexit negotiator has said that the door is open for Britain to rejoin the EU "any time",

His only advice is just on divergence. "If there is too large divergence, it will be more difficult." He was optimistic that the UK and EU would reach a deal to cut the number of Irish Sea border checks caused by the Northern Ireland Protocol. "It seems to me that there is a common will to progress to find operational solutions," he added. Indeed we live in hope.

****

The Environment. This is always a worry as we have to talk about the environment secretary who, as we know to our cost, is **Therese Coffey.**

Air pollution is causing great concern especially now, as the death of a nine year–old girl has been linked by a coroner to dirty air.

PM2.5 are tiny microns in diameter far thinner than human hair and they are mostly released into the air by burning fossil fuels and wood, including cars and stoves and the wear and tear of heavy vehicles releasing particles of brake pads, tyres and roads. They are extremely harmful as they can damaged the heart and lungs and even get into the bloodstream. Ms. Coffey has just announced that the initial target for reducing these microns by 2030 will be impossible to achieve and so it is being pushed back to 2040.

Well there has been one almighty backlash about this.

Campaigners, academics and politicians have said the delay is "ridiculous," "scandalous" and "frankly insulting." Frank Kelly a community health professor at Imperial College London said "we've published a report that 97% of the country can reach 10 (micrograms) by 2030. I don't accept the 2040 date." Sarah Woolnough head of 'Asthma + lung UK' said the delay would "cost lives."

And the government's response has been?????

No reply from either Sunak or Coffey to the little girl's mother when she wrote to them. And they broke a commitment to publish its modelling for scrutiny. Well we know that when Sunak promised transparency in his government he didn't mean quite yet. The Department for Environment, Food and Rural Affairs has promised that it would release the modelling. But too late. And will they now reply to the dead girl's mother?

****

The Criminal Justice System.

Rape and sexual offences are being prosecuted by junior barristers who lack the expertise to deal with complicated cases.

Defence counsel are getting better pay than prosecuting counsel ever since Brandon Lewis sorted out criminal defence barristers in the short time he was justice secretary when he gave them a 15% pay rise.

Andrew Cayley KC says "Once there is a solution to the pay, that problem will disappear. The current situation is not satisfactory."

Oh, how many times do we hear that?

****

The Cabinet.

So Gavin Williamson has gone. Nadhim Zahawi has gone, and the net is closing around Dominic Raab. His days are numbered believe you me. After him Suella Braverman anyone?

Mr. Sunak, I have to say that after 100 days in the highest office in the land, it is not looking good.

And in PMQs today, the Speaker mistakenly referred to Keir Starmer as Prime Minister. I think I would be very worried if I were you.

****

And the following days do not bring any better news.

I continue to be concerned and disgusted by a society which thinks it is acceptable to incarcerate vulnerable, abused and mentally ill women in prison. Over and over again, for years and years and years, we get reports and inspections of women's prisons which say they are unsafe and uninhabitable and that women are being further damaged and abused. My questions are:-

What are the prison charities doing?

Why is nothing ever done to improve things?

What sort of judge sends vulnerable women to places like these?

Why is this never reported in the main stream media?

****

3RD FEBRUARY

The report of the inspection of **Eastwood Park Prison for women,** which took place in October 2022 has just been released. It is utterly damning.

These are really vulnerable women and 83% of them spoke about suffering from mental health difficulties and many had been caught in a cycle of homelessness, drug or alcohol misuse and offending.

The conditions in the prison, particularly in the segregation units, were disgusting. Cells were dilapidated and had blood, scratch marks and graffiti on the walls. The women said they did not feel well cared for and the number of times force had been used against them had increased significantly since the previous inspection.

The report said that there were "very high rates of self-harm" and there had been two self-inflicted deaths since the last inspection in May 2019.

One experienced inspector described the conditions as the worst he had ever seen.

These women need highly skilled professionals to give the correct support but it was a struggle to recruit and retain enough staff.

These shortages were apparently set to worsen with the imminent withdrawal of detached duty staff who had been supporting the prison in recent months.

The inspection concluded by saying, **"We have given Eastwood Park our lowest grade for safety. This is very unusual for a women's prison, but the gaps in care and the lack of support for the most vulnerable and distressed women were concerning."**

And this is the way our society treats women in 2023.

The Conservative government treats the Ministry of Justice with contempt.

There have been 10 Lord Chancellors, (Justice Secretaries) since 2010 and most of them were in the post for just a year.

Now can we remember who the present Justice Secretary is? Oh yes. Dominic Raab. I need say no more.

****

6TH FEBRUARY

More headlines which should really concern you.

"Zero Chance" Tories will meet pledge of new hospitals"

Yes well we all know that one. Thank you *Observer*

Only 10 of the 40 projects have full planning permission. We'll be moderately lucky to have eight," said the boss of one of the NHS trusts waiting for a new hospital. "At the moment we are doing loads of maintenance work on ongoing basis, trying to sort out roofs and theatres and all those things. Some hospitals are literally falling down." As we have come to expect of this government there is "woefully insufficient funding" and the ever- rising costs will "completely scupper the plan and put NHS capacity at risk."

****

Oxbridge loses millions in EU funds as Brexit obstacles grow.

Oxford and Cambridge, once awarded more than £130 million a year for research programmes, now get only £1 million between them. With this of course the UK becomes less attractive to high-quality European researchers and students. Simon Marginson, a professor of higher education at Oxford, described Brexit as "a historic error of monumental proportions." Yes I think we can all agree on that.

****

Terrifying arts funding cuts are killing creativity, warns three-time Oscar winner.

Sandy Powell is an English costume designer and she will make film history this month when she accepts a prestigious Bafta fellowship. She is "terrified" by the lack of experimental live performance being staged in Britain just now. "A lot of the fringe theatre work is not out there anymore because the old funding routes have gone and that was always how you learned the value of taking artistic risks" she said when speaking to *The Observer.*

"What I would say to the government is that working in the arts really is a proper job and that, especially when times are hard, entertainment is what people want."

But we know what this government thinks of the arts. Funding cuts everywhere you look. Cuts in schools and universities, cuts in prestigious world famous opera companies, problems for touring companies getting visas to travel abroad and now we hear of this.

Cloth-eared ministers will not I'm afraid take any notice of this talented and elegant woman.

****

No wonder people don't read the papers or watch the news any more. There is no governance going on and even a third of all Tory voters are now saying that the government is mired in scandal and sleaze.

****

THE END IS NIGH

This might sound a bit dramatic but I am going to stick my neck out and say that I really am beginning to believe that we are into the final death throes of this government. It may still take some time but I just cannot see how they can survive for very much longer.

The date today is the 6th February and this is what is going on.

Away from the headlines apparently there is a 'secret' plot on a new WhatsApp group by back bench Tories wanting to oust the Prime Minister. Well not so secret as it is all over social media. And they are so frightened of the May local elections that the 1922 Committee is thinking of changing the rules in order to allow the possibility of a no-confidence vote in Sunak if the results are as dire as we know they are going to be. Normally he would be safe for 12 months before a vote would be allowed but these are not normal times.

And we just have to mention 'party-gate' and 'seat- belts' and 'tax avoidance' to realise that rule changes are no problem for the Conservative party. One rule for them.............or rather one rule for us and no rules whatsoever for them.

****

The prospect of leaving the **European Convention on Human Rights** is also causing some anguish in the Conservative government. The Prime Minister has been told that if we withdraw from this convention it would put us on a par with Russia and Belarus. But it is being said that Sunak is only threatening this because he is anxious to agree a customs deal with Northern Ireland. It is a bit of 'red meat' for the ERG. Oh goodness what a way to run a country.

But I do like the sound of one Tory MP. Jackie Doyle-Price a former minister said, "I have been a member of the Conservative Party for 36 years. This group leaves me cold. Upholding the law should never be a subject for debate for a Conservative. Our Home Office is crap. If the government wants to have a phoney war over the ECHR instead of sorting itself out it can do it without me." She accused Rishi Sunak of "willy-waving" over this threat.

We need to hear more from people like her.

However a senior Tory MP said he had been assured by No 10 that withdrawing from the ECHR was not a realistic prospect for Sunak. He just wants to placate Suella Braverman and keep her ideological purity intact to keep the right of the party onside.

****

Negotiations on the Northern Ireland customs deal are said to be nearing a conclusion. It is vital for many reasons that it does so very soon. One reason is that the EU have said that the UK could then rejoin the EU Horizon research programme. This would be very good news indeed which we are all in need of right now. The EU are saying that the absence of British researchers has damaged science across Europe. In a letter to *The Times* they say that "The sooner the UK fully rejoins the EU's international research programmes the better for everyone."

So Mr. Sunak, it is up to you.

****

9TH FEBRUARY

But Mr. Sunak has been busy playing musical chairs. There has been a mini-reshuffle going on. Well he had to appoint a new chairperson to replace Zahawi and so **Greg Hands**, a prominent remainer, has got the job.

Otherwise it is just a case of swopping people about. Labour compared it to "rearranging the deckchairs on the sinking Titanic".

Departments have been split up so we now have **Grant Shapps as minister for energy.** He, who has openly criticised the "vast increase" in onshore wind farms. And he, who also voted against supporting the reduction of the UK's net targeted greenhouse gas emissions to zero by 2050.

So that is an 'interesting' appointment.

Then we have **Michelle Donelan as minister of science.** She is 38 and held the post of culture secretary for all of five months. She was known for being the shortest-serving cabinet minister in British history after resigning from Boris Johnson's government just 36 hours after being appointed education secretary. Her background is politics, history and marketing and as Sir Jim Radcliffe (chairman and founder of INEOS) says in a letter to *The Times* this morning "The government surely has to be kidding."

Then we have **Lucy Frazer who is now secretary of state for culture, media and sport** replacing **Michelle Donelan.** She too has had a varied ministerial career, most recently serving as housing minister, and her departure from that role means the UK will soon have its **sixth housing minister in 12 months.**

Just to give you a flavour of the lack of longevity and therefore experience these ministers have here is a run-down of the dates of her previous ministerial positions.

- 10th September- 16th September 2021 Prisons and Probation.
- 16th September 2021-7th September 2022 Financial secretary to the Treasury.
- 8th September -26th October 2022 Transport.
- 26th October 2022- 7th February 2023 Housing.

She is now the new Culture Secretary and as Richard Morrison despairs in *The Times* the Tories have now had 12 Culture Secretaries in 13 years. She will be the fourth in 18 months.

The new housing minister replacing Lucy Frazer under Gove will be **Rachel Maclean**, the Member of Parliament for Redditch who will be the 15th housing minister since 2010 and the sixth in the past 12 months.

And there is fury in Whitehall about the Housing department spending, as the system has been changed following the reshuffle.

The Financial Times reported that the Department of Levelling Up, Housing and Communities had been "banned from making spending decisions on new capital projects" without an explicit green light from Her Majesty's Treasury because of questions over whether the ministry's policies deliver "value for money".

You may remember the story about the little boy who died because of long exposure to damp and mould in a council house in Rochdale. **Michael Gove the housing minister** announced he was allocating £30 million to improve social housing because of this tragic story.

Mr. Gove is widely regarded by housing experts as the only member of the government who has both understood the housing crisis and taken tangible action to fix it for almost a decade. During his time in the role, strides have been made on building safety and social housing reform.

Gove has his critics but he is actually the only member of the Conservative government with a functioning brain.

Apparently he was offered a new job in the reshuffle but he refused.

Oh my goodness, wait a minute, what am I hearing now? Lee Anderson MP has just been appointed deputy chairman of the Conservative party. This absolutely confirms my statement at the beginning of this chapter.

The Conservative government is imploding. They have just pressed the self-destruct button.

I will have to fill you in on some of the things this man has said. He became known as '30p Lee' when he told parliament in May last year that "you've got generation after generation who cannot cook properly. They can't cook a meal from scratch. They cannot budget." **He claimed that meals could be cooked from scratch "for about 30 pence a day".**

We need to remember of course that in the House of Commons he eats very nicely and where a £31 main meal costs just £3.45.

And just to be clear about the sort of person he is, he also sparked anger by posting on Facebook a video arguing that "nuisance tenants" should be forced to live in tents and pick potatoes.

"Let's have them in the field picking potatoes or any current seasonal vegetables, back in the tent, cold shower, lights out, six o'clock, same again the next day. That would be my solution," he said.

Then during the 2019 election campaign he forgot he was wearing a microphone when he got a friend of his to pretend to be an anti-Labour swing voter.

"Make out you know who I am... you know I'm the candidate, but not a friend, alright?" he was recorded as saying as he spelled out instructions to his friend minutes before bringing a journalist to his door.

One Tory has called Anderson a "walking embarrassment" and another said he was "everything wrong with the Tory brand".

He was also caught on camera physically attacking Steve Bray outside parliament, snatching his hat and saying he was dressed like a tramp.

Then I hear that he was suspended from the Labour party after receiving a community protection warning from Ashfield District Council for using a tractor to place boulders at the entrance of a car park in order to prevent travellers from setting up an encampment.

Following the suspension, he defected to the Tories.

And just when you think things can't go any lower we see in an interview with the Spectator that he said he thought **the death penalty should be re-introduced.** That should reduce crime he thinks. Well yes that has worked well in America hasn't it?

And this is horrifying. *The Canary* reports that Lee Anderson's support of the death penalty is straight from the **National Front's playbook.**

In 1970, the National Front put out one of its most infamous campaign posters. Along with the urging to "Put Britons First" and "Vote National Front", it stated six policies. These were:-

STOP immigration

REJECT common market

RESTORE capital punishment

MAKE Britain great again

SCRAP overseas aid

REBUILD our armed forces

Horrifyingly, each of these positions can be found in Tory policy or supported by individual Tory MPs right now. This is very, very frightening but we do need to know.

Well Rishi Sunak has dis-associated himself and his party with these views on the death penalty. Phew, that's a relief.

But if the Tory party think that this is the sort of man who can pull back the 'red wall' then they are more delusional than I thought.

As Tom Peck of *The Independent* says at the end of a long scathing article "it is not clear whether Sunak is himself even serious about winning the next election. One imagines he is. But it is hard not to conclude that it will not have been made easier, by hiring the least serious man in Westminster."

But this shuffle is mostly just musical chairs. Different posts, same inadequate faces.

****

The Conservative party is more politically divided than ever before. It doesn't help when Liz Truss and Boris Johnson make announcements to say that all their mistakes were someone else's fault and moan and moan and whine and whine and accuse everything of being unfair. It really is pathetic. William Hague writes a scathing article in *The Times* this morning. He says "If you became Prime Minister, with a majority behind you and a decent term in front of you, but were overthrown amid chaos, there is indeed someone to blame. It's you."

But there is a bit of good news. Liz Truss said she had no plans to be PM again.

We do need to find the good news wherever we can.

****

241

Therese Coffey has decided to stop any further investigation into the mystery of the dead and dying shellfish off the North East and North Yorkshire coast. "I have decided that it is very unlikely we will find the cause," she says so, "No further analysis will be undertaken by the government."

So complete abnegation of accountability and responsibility here then although acknowledgement that her intellect is completely inadequate for the task.

****

MONEY, MONEY, MONEY.

The way this government spent money in the past and continues to spend money now, and yet says there is no money to pay people's wages is just unbelievable. They waste it and they produce dis-incentives for people to invest here. But be in no doubt; this government is awash with money. And no longer can they be seen as the party to be trusted with the economy.

The boss of AstraZeneca has decided to build a £360 million manufacturing plant in Ireland rather than in the UK as he had originally planned.

"You need an environment that gives you good returns and incentive to invest" he says. "And just now that is not Brexit Britain."

The UK corporation tax is going up and the UK's voluntary scheme for branded medicines pricing and access is rising fast.

Britain is still renowned for its medical research but, as he says, **"If you want a life sciences sector you need more than research."**

"Ministers need to recognise the difference between their life sciences rhetoric and what's happening on the ground."

I'm afraid that will never happen with this government.

****

11TH FEBRUARY

We are indebted to the 'Good Law Project' who have managed to hold this government to account once again over its transparency claims. This is their email to me this morning.

"You may remember that back in March 2021, Boris Johnson told Parliament that details of all Covid contracts were now "on the record". A month later, Cabinet Minister Julia Lopez, claimed "all historical Covid-related contracts" had been published.

Neither statement was true.

Last month, we took the first formal step in legal proceedings against the Cabinet Office for its three-year failure to publish the 29 contracts awarded to suppliers as part of the Government's controversial 'Ventilator Challenge' programme.

In total, £277million was spent by the Cabinet Office procuring ventilators during the pandemic, with an eye-watering £143million going to waste.

Thanks to our challenge, the Government has now admitted it breached its own transparency policy in what it calls a "regrettable oversight". They say that the government will publish any outstanding information (subject to any redactions/exemptions that may apply) by 28th February 2023."

****

Unsafe meat is being allowed into the country, as we all thought would happen, because of a lack of post- Brexit border checks. It is being feared that African Swine Fever and other diseases will be introduced into the UK. But surely, you might ask, we have border checks and controls.

Well yes, a huge inspection site was built in Sevington, Kent at a cost of more than £100 million. It is a 230 acre site and has space for 1,700 goods vehicles. It has a 12 foot high perimeter fence which is guarded by security staff and inside are new state-of-the-art buildings and equipment for inspecting goods from Europe. However, six months after completion it lies almost deserted. The people who live nearby call it a great white elephant of Brexit.

Then there is the container terminal at Portsmouth International Port which is a new high-tech border control post and which cost the tax-payer and city council £25 million. Again still not in use.

Meanwhile the roads around Dover are still grid-locked with heavy lorries and so some levelling-up money, (originally supposed to help deprived parts of the UK) was re-routed to the port of Dover. £45 million in all.

Plenty of money to splash around there and all completely useless.

****

Then we are back to the NHS. Make no mistake, unless somebody acts fast we are heading towards its demise and replacement with an insurance scheme.

But the amount of money being donated to this Conservative government is astronomical. It comes from private health firms and individual donors. An investigation by openDemocracy reveals how Rishi Sunak's party has received at least £800,000 from more than 35 private health and social care businesses. The true figure could be even higher because donors do not have to declare their field of work, meaning some may have flown under the radar.

And this is on top of huge personal donations from some of the business moguls behind these private healthcare companies.

****

SUNDAY 12TH FEBRUARY

Well the word that dare not be spoken, is all over the front pages today. **BREXIT. There have been secret meetings.** Secret? But it is everywhere. What is this all about?

There has been a cross-party **summit**. Wow, that's an important word. And '**cross-party**' is even more exciting.

The Observer has obtained leaked documents (there are always some) which gives the title of the meeting as:

"How can we make Brexit work better with our neighbours in Europe?"

Oh my goodness, is common sense beginning to invade the Tory government? This is amazing. It was chaired by Peter Mandleson. David Lidington was there and many Labour MPs were there including David Lammy, also top chairs of pharmaceutical companies, business leaders and bankers, and Tom Scholar the former Treasury Permanent Secretary who was sacked by Liz Truss. It took place on Thursday and Friday.

The opening statement acknowledged there was a view amongst some that **"so far the UK has not found its way forward outside the EU"** with Brexit acting as a drag on our growth and inhibiting the UK's potential.

Agreed.

"The main thrust of the meeting was that Britain is losing out, that Brexit is not delivering, that our economy is in a weak position."

Agreed.

"There is also clear European as well as British strategic interest in a productive and closer relationship."

Agreed.

Concern is growing at the top of the Labour party that it poses a real threat to the success of any future Labour government unless problems such as increased trade friction can be addressed.

Agreed

They said that finding solutions is all the more urgent because of "global unrest, supply chain fragility and inflation."

Agreed.

Labour has already committed to using the 2025 Brexit trade and co-operation agreement to try to reduce barriers to trade.

Essential.

As *The Observer* says "The seniority of those who agreed to attend reflects a growing acceptance amongst politicians in the two main parties, as well as business leaders and civil servants, that Brexit in its current form is damaging the UK economy and reducing its strategic influence in the world."

Well they obviously haven't been reading my books, otherwise they would have realised all of this a long time ago.

But it seems to me as though panic is setting in, and I now have to go for a lie down as I have never before written the word 'agreed' so many times.

****

Sadly though, on my return, everyone else is continuing to destroy this country in every way they can.

We start with **Michelle Donelan**, our new science whizz kid, who has no scientific experience or knowledge whatsoever. As I reported earlier the EU has said we can re-join the Horizon programme if a deal can be reached between the UK and Northern Ireland. And there is mounting speculation at the moment that a deal is on the cards to reduce the red tape on trade between the two.

So what is Donelan's first announcement in her new role?

She says that, "if an agreement on 'associate' membership of the 100 billion euro (£88.6 billion) group cannot be struck the UK will look to create an alliance with the US, Japan and Switzerland." She declares the UK is "more than ready to go it alone".

Was she not at that very secret meeting?

Well, the president of the Royal Society, Sir Adrian Smith, responded to the news by saying Ms. Donelan's "first job" as Science Secretary "must be to secure association to Horizon Europe and other EU science programmes".

He said that, **"These schemes support outstanding international collaboration and without being part of them we are undermining the Prime Minister's stated ambition for the UK to be at the forefront of science and technology globally,"**

I think that meeting was all well and good but if you still have incompetent and inadequate persona at the helm we will remain stuck in a swamp of stagnation.

****

For we still have **Suella Braverman** as home secretary. On Friday evening there was a dreadful riot outside a hotel accommodating asylum seekers in a town called Knowsley in Merseyside. Initially there had been two peaceful protests and a counter protest. But then a group arrived who were only interested in causing trouble. They turned up armed with hammers and fireworks and set a police van alight. They caused violent disorder and terrified those in the hotel as well as those ln the other protests. Social media rumours had been circulating stating that a man had "made inappropriate advances towards a teenage girl." This was reported to the police but no victim was identified.

Fifteen people have been arrested including a 13 year old.

So Ms. Braverman eventually makes a statement in which she says she condemns the "appalling disorder" but added that the "alleged behaviour of some asylum seekers is never an excuse for violence and intimidation."

Oh my word, I cannot believe the depths to which this woman can descend.

****

Then I see a story about a political group called Patriotic Alternative. It makes my blood run cold.

Patriotic Alternative is a British far-right white nationalist group. It was founded in July 2019 by Mark Collett, who was the former director of publicity of the British National Party. He is an anti-Semitic conspiracy theorist who is inspired by Hitler's book Mein Kampf.

Patriotic Alternative promotes a white nationalist ideology and aims to combat the "replacement and displacement" of white British people by migrants who "have no right to these lands". Patriotic Alternative opposes all immigration unless one has a shared cultural and ethnic background or who can prove British ancestry.

In October 2020, counterterrorism experts reported that extremist far-right groups including Patriotic Alternative were using YouTube to try and recruit people, including children "as young as 12".

These were some of the people involved in Friday evening's riots.

****

Then we mustn't forget **Lee Anderson. He is now facing mounting questions over his links to alleged Nazi-supporting members of a scooter club.**

He regularly appears in photographs with a Skegby Scooter Club regular called Martin Dudley who supports white supremacist punk bands that reference Adolf Hitler. Dudley is also seen wearing a t-shirt which has an image of Odin's Cross, which the Anti-Defamation League says is "one of the most important and commonly used white supremacist symbols". They say it is "used by neo-Nazis, racist skinheads, Ku Klux Klan members and virtually every other type of white supremacist."

And Anderson's new job is to encourage people to sign up to the Conservative party.

He is being trashed by every decent thinking person in the country and I do not know how Rishi Sunak can possibly defend this appointment.

****

Oops here's Boris again.

In brief:

The Met are being urged to reopen the Party-gate inquiry as there have been fresh allegations.

He was paid £88,000 advance for a book on Shakespeare which should have come out in 2016 but Hodder and Stoughton confirmed that as yet there is no publication date. It is expected that his political memoirs will come out first. The advance, as you may remember, is £510,000.

BBC boss Richard Sharp is in trouble still as a cross- party committee has accused him of making "significant errors of judgement."

I say that you should never, never have anything to do with Boris Johnson. Everything he touches turns to dust.

****

Then in the wider world, the world of you and me, there is this:

In 2022 41% of year 6 pupils in England left primary school without meeting the expected targets in literacy and numeracy. That is 275,000 11-year olds which is 50,000 more than in 2019 according to the 'Centre for Social Justice Think-tank'.

Teachers are expressing concerns about their chances of reversing the slide given working conditions and resources. They point to the refusal by the Treasury in the summer of 2020 when it was being led by Sunak as the Chancellor to sanction the full programme of post- pandemic catch-up funding that was called for in a government backed review.

Lee Elliot Major, professor of social mobility at Exeter University, said the failure to equip all students with basic skills was "the biggest scandal of our educational system."

And the goal of our PM is to make it mandatory for all students to learn maths till they are 18. He doesn't have a clue.

****

Farmers received only 44% of post-Brexit payments last year. This year the cuts are set to be even more draconian with the government planning to slash payments by 36 %. Where, they ask, is the money going? Tin Farron, Lib-Dem says "They have rushed to cut basic payments and have failed to deliver the new schemes on time. This will lead to farmers going out of business, which means that we will fail to deliver vital environmental goals." He said "It's hard to know if this is incompetence or a deliberate betrayal of our rural communities, but they amount to the same thing."

****

So a very depressing day.

But then I see some news which restores my faith in humanity.

Another large group of people congregate outside the hotel which is housing refugees in Knowlsey. This time they consist of genuine locals.

There are Church of England vicars, pensioners, and residents of Merseyside holding up banners saying "refugees are welcome here".

These are the people who are the backbone of our country.

These are the people who give me hope for the future.

****

FINANCIAL EXCESS

13TH FEBRUARY

The Times is starting a new campaign called '**Clean It Up**' which is all about cleaning our rivers and making water companies responsible for the amount of sewage they are pouring into them. They want heavy fines, but the Environment Department has just announced that the maximum fines promised last year will now be cut as they say they were too high and disproportionate.

Well we have all been talking about this for a long time and every single river in the country is polluted. There are many charities trying desperately to get something done and now *The Times* is their unofficial figurehead. So congratulations to *the Times* for bringing this to everyone's attention.

But do the water companies have enough money or do we need to pay them more?

Let's see.

These are the current salaries of the water bosses.

Anglian Water: **£1.3 million**

Northumbrian Water: **£648,000**

Severn Trent Water: **£3.9million**

South West Water: **£1.6 million**

Southern Water: **unpublished**

Thames Water: **£2 million**

United Utilities: **£3.2 million**

Wessex Water: **£975,000**

Yorkshire Water: **unpublished.**

Keep remembering that this money is being paid by us to people who are quite happy to keep on pouring untreated sewage into our rivers and seas.

We must also keep remembering who the Secretary of the Environment is.

****

And I don't have to look far to see some more money being sloshed around. There are such things as procurement government credit cards which officials can spend on various expenses. Well it will come as no surprise to you that these expenses have risen enormously over the last few years, and by 71% since 2010.

A Labour dossier reveals nearly £150 million of purchases in a single year.

Holders of these cards can now spend £20,000 a transaction and up to £100,000 a month. I can't believe what I am writing here. This is **our** money.

It also won't surprise you to know that the Ministry of Justice and the Foreign Office have seen the biggest rises.

Liz Truss as FS spent £3,240 for access to a VIP lounge at Heathrow, £1,443 on lunch and dinner in Jakarta and £7,218 on a reception at a Sydney amusement park. The FO also spent £344,803 on restaurants and bars in 2021 as well as £23,457 on duty free wine and spirits rising to £95,834 in the first ten months of last year.

Rishi Sunak's Treasury spent £3,393 on 13 fine art photographs and was among several departments to see a splurge in spending at the end of the financial year.

The Department of Health spent £59,155 on stationery in March compared with just £1,470 the rest of the year.

They all love staying in 5 star hotels and eating in top class restaurants.

Well don't we all when we get the chance to use someone else's money?

****

Never let me hear someone say they don't have any money to give to nurses or teachers. They are practically drowning in it.

****

14TH FEBRUARY

They certainly are, for today we read this: Government spending on its consultants has reached a new high. This increase has come about because the government relaxed restrictions which had required central authorisation for contracts worth more than £20,000. This figure had increased to £60,000 and this year Cabinet Office approval was dropped altogether. So absolutely no control whatever on what is being spent. The Home Office and the Ministry of Defence are apparently the main culprits. At the time of writing that means Suella Braverman and Dominic Raab. No surprise there then. Although the Department of Health doesn't do very well either.

Let's look at the amount spent.

Defence:

£215 million to QuinetiQ

£31 million IT contract to Microsoft

£20 million to Newton Europe.

Home Office:

£4 million contract to Deloitte to handle small boat crossings.

£95 million police IT deal with CGI

£30 million on IT to PA consulting.

£62 million total to Deloitte for various contracts. In fact Deloitte does very well as the total estimated value of contracts with them last year is **£278 million**

Department of Health:

£42 million altogether last year including **£18 million** to develop an NHS Covid app.

And so it goes on.

This year already, consultancy contracts have continued with 73 contracts having been awarded to date, worth **£52 million**.

Nice work if you can get it and you can certainly get it under this government unless you are a hard-working teacher or NHS employee.

****

Chair of the Conservative Party

The Good Law Project has just revealed that Greg Hands, the new Conservative party chairman, helped Luxe Lifestyle Ltd, a company closely associated with the then Chair of his local constituency party, Mark Higton, land a £25m 'VIP' PPE deal. This is despite the company having no experience in providing protective equipment.

Following an FOI from 'Spotlight on Corruption', they say that Luxe Lifestyle supplied almost 10m items of PPE valued at £20m, which remains unused by the NHS.

They don't know how much profit Luxe made from the £25m deal, which was awarded without formal competition. The firm is a year late in publishing its annual accounts and has now applied to Companies House to be struck off the register.

****

And we are still getting more information about the deputy chairman.

Lee Anderson is being sued for libel after making comments about a man who runs a food bank in his constituency. Lawyers acting for Michael Hollis, who runs a food bank charity, said he was "outraged" after the Ashfield MP made claims about money in "brown envelopes" changing hands in relation to a planning application. This was put up on Twitter. When Anderson refused to remove the post Mr. Hollis instructed a legal firm to sue him for libel.

****

Not surprising that a business man called Iain Anderson, founder of the 'Cicero' public relations group, has just claimed the Conservatives are 'not the party it used to be' and revealed his backing for Sir Keir Starmer.

He is quitting after 39 years as a Tory party member.

"The first thing is the party's approach with business," Mr. Anderson told *The Financial Times*.

He said the Tories' approach seemed to reflect Mr. Johnson's claimed 'f*** business' attitude over Brexit.

Mr. Anderson was scathing of what he claimed would be the Tories' approach to the next election. **"It was made pretty clear the plan is to run a culture war to distract from fundamental economic failings," he added. "'It's not something I want any part of'"**

****

And there is another blow for the Tories as a top businessman who worked for David Cameron showered praise on Labour.

Former CBI President Paul Drechsler says Labour leader Sir Keir Starmer is "winning" the economic argument against Rishi Sunak among Britain's bosses thanks to a "seismic" change in the party's image.

Writing in *The Independent*, former CBI president, Mr. Drechsler says high street giants and other top firms now talk with "warmth and optimism" about Labour.

Yes well it isn't all that difficult to spot that the intelligence, vision and brain power of Starmer is light years ahead of Sunak.

"Labour" he says "is now the party of business."

This is a seismic change.

****

INCOMPETENCE AND NEGLIGENCE

15TH FEBRUARY

Just more incompetence and negligence. This time from the Prime Minister.

We keep hearing that the Northern Ireland protocol deal is about to be agreed. Apparently official negotiations were concluded at the end of last month. The outline of the agreement was presented to Rishi Sunak. They are now waiting for him to sign it off but he has done absolutely nothing about it. He is being accused of "sitting on it". Well we know why he is prevaricating. He knows it will stir up the Tory infighting over Brexit. So the non-governing goes on.

We hear that it could all be announced as early as next week but then we hear that, no probably not, because we will be concentrating on the anniversary of the invasion of Ukraine.

Dither, delay, and running scared.

****

"Cancer is the single largest cause of death in the UK and one of the most serious healthcare burdens for societies." I think nearly every one of us will have experienced cancer in one way or another.

But now we hear of a report in *The Independent* which completely beggars belief.

This month, the Government have announced that it would create a single strategy in England to tackle major illnesses such as cancer, mental health and dementia.

This seems absolutely crazy and irresponsible. Experts writing in the British Medical Journal have expressed dismay at the move, arguing a dedicated cancer plan is needed now more than ever. The move was also criticised by leading charities, with Macmillan saying the 10-year cancer plan promised by ministers had "been discarded", while the 'CatchUpWithCancer' campaign said it was "deeply concerned".

This is outrageous.

Professor Richard Sullivan, from the 'Institute of Cancer Policy' at King's College London, and Dr. Ajay Aggarwal, from the London School of Hygiene and Tropical Medicine, said the Government decision "jettisons decades of global consensus that, to deliver affordable, equitable and high quality cancer care, dedicated cancer plans are required".

They added: "Subsuming cancer into an overall non-communicable disease agenda simply signals that cancer is no longer a political priority or reflects a Government not willing to deal with its complexity and escalating costs."

We know only too well that this government is not willing to pay for anything which benefits us, the public, in any way whatever.

The experts said a long-term plan for cancer "is more critical than ever" after more than a "decade of declining funding for cancer services compounded by the Covid-19 pandemic

They added: "Such a plan needs to deal with the post-pandemic realities of backlogs for care: sicker patients with more advanced cancers and huge deficits in the cancer specific workforce."

The pair said that, without a dedicated long-term plan for cancer, services "will fracture, costs will increase, inequalities widen, and patients will experience even greater delays leading directly to lost lives".

Then I see a headline saying:-

"Could PM Rishi Sunak be gone before the next election?"

Well if he doesn't go very soon and take his disgusting ministers with him we might as well all say goodbye to any health care for us, for our children, for our friends, or for anyone.

Will this appalling cancer-care strategy make the main news? I doubt it.

****

18TH FEBRUARY

The Northern Ireland Protocol is in the news again. Sunak has actually gone to Belfast and they are saying talks have been "productive." Wow, he has actually moved at last. Today he flies to Germany to talk to the EU. He says there is more work to do but a deal could be announced as soon as next week. This would indeed be a feather in his cap and I would be forced to say 'well done Prime Minister' but the ERG, and other Brexiteers, would go ballistic.

We wait to see what happens.

****

Meanwhile the government is concerned over Britain's increased economic inactivity and the increase in long term sick leave since the pandemic. So they are thinking of asking GPs to sign fewer sick notes and to encourage sick people to realise the 'benefits of work.' Just when you think this government cannot get more despicable they come up with something like this. It really is unbelievable. I don't think this is what people had in mind when they voted for Brexit

****

Thinking of emigrating? Well I wouldn't blame you, and here we go.

A delegation from Western Australia will visit the UK later this month in a bid to recruit doctors, police officers and teachers.

It sounds very tempting. They promise high wages and a lower cost of living.

The state's economy is booming thanks to its mining and fossil fuel extraction industries, with the territory producing nearly half of Australia's exports.

Well Perth is a bit isolated but it has a Mediterranean climate, plenty of sport, rugby, football and cricket, a symphony orchestra, ballet, festivals, beaches, jobs and careers and a good education system.

They are looking for 31,000 British workers. Doctors, nurses, police and also plumbers, electricians and builders. 'You will be taken care of' they say. Well that would be novel.

I don't think they will have a problem but yes, then the rest of us will have to keep working until we are 70, and even, of course, if we are unwell.

****

Just when we thought that Liz Truss had disappeared without trace we hear about a speech she has just given in Japan. Japan? What is she doing there? Well according to Simon Tisdall of *The Guardian* she is stoking the flames of a second cold war. This is the first time we have heard from her since she resigned as Prime Minister and she thinks it is a good idea to use inflammatory language when talking about China.

As Mr. Tisdall says "there is a serious, calm and thoughtful discussion to be had about the western democracies' future security and economic relationship with China, and it is under way in Washington and European capitals. Judging by her confrontational, attention-seeking speech in Tokyo today, Britain's disgraced former Prime Minister Liz Truss is not part of it".

Apparently she thinks that Britain is still a global power with influence, and with sufficient financial and military firepower to scare Xi into submission. Well if she had stayed in the UK she would realise, like all of us, that this is not the case.

Simon Tisdall calls her "delusional."

"Alone and adrift in a post-Brexit vacuum she helped create, Britain's ability to influence world events is diminishing rapidly," he says.

"Empty threats do not make good foreign policy."

How is it possible for people to be so lacking in self-awareness? How can she be so ignorant? Hasn't she got advisers or minders to tell her to shut up?

****

Next week sees the two-day conference of the National Farmers' Union in Birmingham, and their president, Minette Batters, has been speaking out about the scandal of the appallingly inefficient border controls since Brexit. She accused ministers of a 'dereliction of duty' by failing to uphold safety standards.

Yes everywhere we look the story is the same. No care, no responsibility, no knowledge, no accountability, no interest, no presence.

For we hear that Sunak can't be bothered to attend the conference. He will send a video. Of course no-one can ask any awkward questions or throw tomatoes. Mind you farmers wouldn't chuck food at anyone, it's too precious.

But our future prime minister Keir Starmer is going and really wants to engage with farmers.

Ms. Batters is very concerned about the lack of checks on imports that are coming in from the EU. "We have the massive risk of African Swine Fever in Europe, and to not be investing in our defences for keeping our biosecurity and animal and plant health safe, I think is just a dereliction of duty."

She said, "If there was a food scare from Europe, it would be very difficult to trace it right now."

She is also concerned about the impact of Brexit policies on farmers.

Food supply chains were turned upside down overnight after Brexit, and farmers are now beset by rampant inflation that has sent the prices of fuel, fertiliser and animal feed rocketing.

But they also face additional concerns about disease. The African Swine Fever virus has killed more than 100 million pigs globally and our pig farmers will be extremely worried.

Then with some scientists warning of a likely spring outbreak among wild birds, and infections found in species from minks, otters and seals to foxes she said the poultry sector was already in a weakened state, having shrunk by about 12%, mainly under the impact of inflationary pressures.

"If the government failed to provide sufficient support to farmers, the 'social infrastructure' that farming provided to the countryside would be lost and some of the most isolated and vulnerable communities in the UK would be devastated," Ms. Batters said.

"I think that's the bit that the government doesn't understand, because without the people we can't deliver for the environment, we can't deliver for food production," she said. "When I say to members of the government, when they talk about taking land out of production,

I say 'what about the people?'

And nobody answers that question."

****

19TH FEBRUARY

And of course Mr. Sunak is very busy at the moment as he tries to get a deal with the EU over Northern Ireland.

But look who has just crawled out of the woodwork to try to mess it all up. Yes, you guessed correctly, former has-been PM, Boris Johnson.

He has just threatened to derail Rishi Sunak's efforts to thrash out a new Brexit deal after warning that ditching the Northern Ireland Protocol bill would be a "great mistake".

For goodness sake this man just cannot resist continuously contributing to the downfall of the UK.

A government official told *The Sunday Times* that "Boris is being a bloody nuisance, winding up the DUP. He is causing mischief."

Peter Mandelson told Sky news that "There is nothing that Boris Johnson is doing now or indeed throughout recent history with the EU that could possibly be described as helpful." He went on to say that, "He and his supporters want to undermine the Prime Minister, just as a continuation of the fratricidal war in the Tory party."

The Government has indicated that a successful outcome would mean the Protocol Bill would no longer be required. But the bill is still seen by Brexiteers as a key bargaining chip with the EU.

However Mr. Sunak can rely on Labour's support in a Commons vote, as Sir Keir Starmer took the unusual step of offering it. He told *The Observer:* "My offer to the Prime Minister stands. If a deal is on the table, and it delivers for the UK, Labour will back it. He doesn't need to go scrambling around to appease an intransigent rump of his own backbenchers who will never be satisfied with anything."

But, Mr Sunak would likely face a backlash from within his own ranks if he tries to get a deal over the line on the back of the Labour party's support.

Simon Hoare, Tory chair of the Norther Ireland affairs select committee, told *The Independent* this week that a deal would be "the return of grown-ups doing politics in a sensible way", adding: "Let's just get the bloody thing sorted and done."

We won't hold our breath. There are no grown-ups in this present government which is why we are waiting so impatiently for Starmer and Co. The shadow front bench consists of grown–ups, each and every one.

****

20TH FEBRUARY

But it is back to the NHS and I am so appalled that this crisis has not yet been addressed by this government. People are now telling the PM that he will not be able to keep his pledge of cutting the waiting list if he continues to ignore this catastrophe. Just how stupid and unintelligent is this man?

I read a report in *The Independent* by Rebecca Thomas, health correspondent, about the backlog for children's surgery which chills me to the bone.

The backlog for children's surgery has increased by almost 50% in two years and hundreds and thousands of children are having to cope with unacceptable delays in treatment of all kinds.

Mike McKean, vice-president of policy at the Royal College of Paediatrics and Child Health, said that intensive care capacity was being "pushed to the limits".

He said "Lengthy waits are unacceptable for any patient, but for children and young people, waits can be catastrophic, as many treatments need to be given by a specific age or developmental stage. It is not the same as for adults. If you miss the right window to treat a child, or wait too long, the consequences can be irrevocable."

But surely everyone realises that?

Dr Michael Absoud, clinical academic at the Department of Women and Children's Health at Kings College London said, "Despite the fact that children were not very impacted by Covid, these services were disproportionately impacted. As a paediatrician, I find it remarkable it is not a priority topic."

Remarkable but, as I keep having to say, not surprising.

The Royal College of Paediatrics and Child Health expressed fears that children's services would not feature in the government's forthcoming major long-term plan for the NHS.

After every sentence my jaw drops further towards the ground.

The College has called for the government to launch a strategy for managing children's health conditions.

Dr Absoud said there had been a "lack of urgency" about helping children's services to catch up on delays caused by Covid.

He added: "It's always been a Cinderella service, but when you're teetering and get a big shock to the system like the pandemic, then you get this hit [to services]. There needs to be new thinking with regard to integrating physical and mental healthcare delivery, multidisciplinary workforce planning, and capital investment."

But we know this government can't think like that so we turn to Labour for some sense.

Shadow health secretary Wes Streeting said: "Every child matters. But the Conservatives have failed to train the staff the NHS needs, leaving more children than ever before waiting to be treated. Labour will give every child a healthy start to life. We will scrap the non-dom tax status to train 7,500 more doctors, 10,000 more nurses a year, and 5,000 new health visitors."

Well that sounds positive but there is going to be much more than that to do I think.

****

Over the weekend a two day forum was held in Bristol for junior doctors.

Professor Philip Banfield, the chair of the BMA, has said that the Prime Minister Rishi Sunak and Health Secretary Steve Barclay are standing on the precipice of a historic mistake by failing to stop the strike action of those working for the NHS.

He hit out at a "conveyor belt of prime ministers with empty promises to the people" over the NHS, who have been "cutting it to the bone and sucking out the marrow to boot."

He concluded by saying: "All the levers to reverse the exodus of staff and the underfunding and chronic decline of the NHS are within the gift of the----------

- Health Secretary, who can make pay review bodies properly independent and fit for purpose;
- the Chancellor, who as chair of the health select committee wrote a book about fixing the NHS and improving patient safety but seems to have forgotten that now he's in a position to make things right;

- and the Prime Minister, who has money to ignore billions wasted in dodgy PPE, so should have the money to rescue the NHS from the brink."

He said that junior doctors deserve better pay, and the government is letting patients down.

And later today we will know the outcome of a ballot by 45,000 junior doctors about taking industrial action.

Not hard to guess what the outcome will be.

And we have just heard that they have voted to strike. They will take part in a 72-hour walkout possibly as early as mid-March. BMA doctors' committee co-chair Dr. Ruth Laurenson said, "The government has only itself to blame standing by in silent indifference as our members are forced to take this difficult decision."

****

The incompetence and waste goes on.

We have a very small fleet of five Border Force boats which were originally designed only to be used by customs officials. These boats need to be replaced urgently as the Borders security experts say that they are regularly being taken out of service for emergency repairs and these are the boats that the Home Office are planning to use to stop the small boat crossings.

They were due to be updated in April 2022, then planned for April 2023 but it is all now delayed yet again until April 2024.

And of course the cost has increased. It has gone up from £200 million to £224 million. But when it was first costed in 2020 it was £50 million.

I hope you are keeping tabs on all this wasted money of yours.

But as Tony Smith, former director of Border Force said these boats "aren't really equipped to pick up migrants."

The whole asylum system as we see over and over again is completely broken.

****

Meanwhile food banks are struggling to meet record demand not just from families who are out of work, but also from people who are in work – including NHS staff and teachers. Some are pleading for more food in order to be able to cope.

****

We need to lighten this load a bit.

The name **Boris Johnson** is coming up yet again and I think you might like this.

The Met police are being urged to reopen its investigation into the Partygate scandal following the release of a podcast that raised questions about the force's initial inquiry. The deputy chair of the London Assembly's police and crime committee has written to the Met commissioner, Mark Rowley, asking if he was "taking new information into account when making a decision regarding the reopening of the investigation" into the Downing Street lockdown parties.

One of its focuses is the so-called "Abba party" held in Johnson's flat above 11 Downing Street on 13 November 2020. Apparently the music was so loud that it could be heard downstairs in the press office. There was also food and alcohol and Boris attended the fun and games for at least part of the evening.

His constant denial that rules were broken in the flat that evening is a key to the Privileges Committee's work on whether MPs were misled.

Well the Partygate investigation has been going on for nine months, would you believe? And the deadline for submissions was passed at the beginning of this month. That means that very soon Johnson could be called in to face questioning. This part of the investigation will be televised! Johnson could be accompanied by a legal adviser but the rule is he must attend in person.

Just suppose he decides not to (for some reason or other!) he could be suspended from parliament for contempt of court.

And yes I do have a large grin on my face.

****

Good news, good news, good news, good news, good news, good news, but not from the Tories.

Please excuse my excitement but the Labour mayor of London, Sadiq Khan, has just announced that he is planning to give free school meals to every primary school child in London, for one year, starting in September.

I have been writing to my MP about this for so long that Oliver Dowden has black-listed me and refuses to answer my emails.

Surely the government will now be shamed into extending this throughout the country?

Mr.Khan said his scheme would be funded out of higher-than-expected collections of business rates and council tax, and would be for the 2023-24 academic year only.

He heavily criticised the government for its "inaction" and made it clear that it would be up to the government to step in after the scheme came to an end.

Don't worry Mr. Khan, this government will have disappeared in a cloud of smoke well before then.

****

So I end this chapter on incompetence and waste with a bit of hope.

****

DANGER

The hope does not last long.

Danger from the right.

The long awaited report on the government's counter-extremism programme called **'Prevent' by William Shawcross has just been published.**

Its controversial conclusion was that the programme had focused disproportionately on the far right and not enough on Islamist extremism. The report has caused a huge backlash and some harsh criticism, and an open letter, sent to the government, says that they have failed to address the threat of the far-right in the UK while tacitly endorsing the violence that asylum seekers are facing.

We have witnessed this violence outside the hotel in Knowsley recently and we have heard the inflammatory language from the Home Secretary. We have watched Lee Anderson spouting fascist language and I have seen people from Patriotic Alternative talking on Twitter and it is so inflammatory that it brings to mind Nazi Germany.

This letter, addressed to the Prime Minister, Home Secretary and other cabinet and shadow cabinet ministers, has been signed by prominent charities and equalities organisations including the 'Community Policy Forum,' 'Refugee Council,' and the 'Joint Council for the Welfare of Immigrants.'

It claims that the government has continually failed to "adequately address the dangers posed by Islamophobia and racism against vulnerable people seeking protection, and radicalised communities in the UK".

The letter added: "With government ministers continuing to promote incendiary language, labelling asylum seekers with harmful stereotypes and painting them as unworthy of sanctuary, there must be accountability for their role in normalising and tacitly endorsing the threats that asylum seekers now face. As such, the government must immediately disown such language and pledge to tackle far right rhetoric inciting hatred against minority groups."

The letter argues that the report made use of "incomplete and skewed evidence to minimise the threat of the far right," and called on the government to reject the recommendations of the Shawcross review.

They mention the dreadful riots at Knowsley. They say that, "The response to the violence and intimidation directed at refugees in Knowsley has highlighted the normalised far-right hatred in the UK,"

Isobel Ingham-Barrow, chief executive of 'Community Policy Forum' said that accepting the recommendations of the Shawcross review would only increase the challenges posed by the far right.

She added: "Instead, the government must urgently develop a strategy to combat the far right and pledge to protect human rights, rather than attempting to eradicate them when they are inconvenient."

I find this the most frightening aspect of this country and this government today.

****

25TH FEBRUARY

But then I make more and more frightening discoveries.

I come across a group called 'Hope not Hate.' How have I missed them before? They are an adversary group whose mission is to expose and oppose far-right extremism. And it would appear that they certainly have a huge task.

They have come to my notice now because Mark Townsend, Home Affairs Editor of *The Guardian,* has written an article about a secret organisation operating out of the House of Lords would you believe?

Actually its existence emerged after an email was sent to 235 people but – instead of blind copying them it was accidentally sent so that everyone could see the entire list. That in itself is worrying!

But it is all quite astonishing and deeply concerning in equal measure.

This organisation is called **New Issues Group** or NIG for short and they have been collaborating with known far-right and anti-Muslim extremists and opening doors to them in the corridors of power otherwise known as the House of Lords.

The 'New Issues Group' was founded in 2012 and has continued to meet in secret every few months since then. The primary objective of the NIG is to raise awareness around what its core supporters perceive to be the dangers of Islam and Muslims within the UK. The defence offered by many of those involved in the NIG is that they are against Islam but are not "anti-Muslim.

But judge for yourselves. These are some of the people involved. They include the former UKIP leader Malcolm Pearson and the Tory former deputy speaker of the House of Lords Baroness Cox. Some of its online "guests" include Tommy Robinson, founder of the 'Anti-Muslim English Defence League'(EDL) and among the documents seen by 'Hope not Hate' is a 2015 "memorandum" created by another NIG member, Magnus Nielson – a known anti-Muslim activist with links to the EDL. And Alan Craig, who is a former UKIP spokesperson and who launched the far-right group 'Hearts of Oak' in 2020 is also involved.

The findings of this investigation show that many of them sometimes make no distinction between Islam and Muslims or between radical Islamists and the wider Muslim community. Thus, the NIG may target issues that are ostensibly laudable, such as women's rights in the Muslim community, but the other comments and histories of those involved (some of whom have freely associated with far-right extremists) reveals more worrying motivations.

This goes some way towards explaining the fact that when you look them up some of their aims seem OK.

Then I see that the most important Christian group represented within the NIG is '**Christian Concern**,' which is a prominent evangelical organisation in the UK.

'Christian Concern' includes three "specialist ministries. Together, these groups campaign around a series of issues including opposing Islam, abortion, adultery, premarital sex, pornography, homosexuality, polygamy and "other harmful sexual practices". Goodness me what on earth are those? The mind boggles! But it just re-affirms to me the fact that certain elements of every religion are obsessed with sex.

But of course the real danger presented by this group concerns the lack of transparency in British politics today and the House of Lords in particular. How on earth has it been allowed to exist at such a high level?

****

It leads me to delve further into other organisations of course.

We have:

- Hearts of Oak
- Christian People's Alliance
- Equal and Free LTD
- The Counter-Jihad movement
- English Defence League
- Sharia Watch UK
- Christian Concern

All extremely concerning. Do look them up.

****

So the Northern Ireland Protocol negotiations drag dangerously on.

Rishi Sunak finds himself between a rock and a hard place. If he drives forward with his plans there will be one almighty explosion from the right wingers and he will be out of his job before you can say 'general election.' If he caves in to the right wingers then the country will be in uproar and he will be out of his job sooner than you can say 'general election'.

Meanwhile Labour pulls further ahead in the polls.

Watch this space.

****

Money, Science and Betrayal.

I will just quote from an article I have found written by **Boris Johnson** in June 2021 and available on Gov. UK.

In it he says:

"We want the UK to regain its status as a science superpower, and in so doing to level up.

What we are offering now is record funding combined with the strongest possible political support and backing for science and a clear indication of where government sees greatest need.

Of course we must generously fund pure science. We must allow for serendipity. You cannot plot or plan every breakthrough.

But you can certainly set out to restore Britain's place as a scientific superpower – while simultaneously driving economic prosperity and addressing the great challenges we face – and that is the plan of the government."

Hmmm. I don't think anyone else can have read this. For now we hear that the Treasury has taken back £1.6bn that it had allocated to research, and especially earmarked for UK involvement in the EU's Horizon Europe £100bn research programme. This move has prompted angry reactions from the research community, with the president of the Royal Society, which represents the UK's leading scientists, questioning the government's commitment to boosting research.

Prof James Wilsdon, who specialises in research policy at University College London told BBC News that the move by the Treasury makes a "mockery" of the Prime Minister's stated commitment to science.

"If the government has indeed ploughed £1.6bn of unspent Research and Development funding back into Treasury coffers, this is a complete betrayal of assurances that ministers repeatedly gave to the research community.

"This government has already abandoned its 2019 commitments to double R&D spending to £22bn a year. Any further cuts blow another hole in the credibility of its commitments to science and research."

This whole debacle is because of the dispute with the Northern Ireland Protocol.

But to withdraw funds already promised to science is disgraceful and a complete betrayal of all those fine words.

So many talented scientists have already left the UK. Superpower? What planet are they on?

****

Well the **National Farmers' Union Conference** which took place on 21st and 22nd February will be remembered for all the wrong reasons. **The words tomatoes and turnips spring to mind.**

As the shelves in our supermarkets are empty of salad items the bad weather in Spain is being blamed. However we see markets in Europe absolutely bulging with produce and so we have to conclude that it is Brexit that is the problem.

Indeed the 'Save British Farming' group blamed Brexit and the "disastrous" Tory government for the shortages – describing the idea of only the weather in Spain being to blame as "absolute nonsense". "The reason that we have food shortages in Britain and that we don't have food shortages in Spain – or anywhere else in the EU – is because of Brexit, and also because of this disastrous Conservative government that has no interest in food production, farming or even food supply," said chair Liz Webster.

Minette Batters, the president of the NFU, said farms were struggling with labour shortages and soaring energy prices, with the poultry industry "reeling from avian influenza".

We have seen progress", she said, but then: "More often than not – it has been incredibly hard getting government to back up its rhetoric with concrete actions."

Gracious how many times do we hear that. All talk and no action.

Ms. Batters also said costs in agriculture have risen almost 50% since 2019 and UK egg production has fallen to its lowest level in nine years.

Then the Environment Secretary steps in with both feet.

Therese Coffey (yes she is still here), contradicts Ms. Batters as she refused to accept that Britain's supply chain had seen market failure. She rejected responsibility for the current supermarket rationing of fruit and vegetables, saying: "We can't control the weather in Spain."

Well she got roundly booed by the farmers.

How dare she think that she knows better than Minette Batters, or anyone else for that matter.

Later, in the Commons, she said that people should only eat seasonal fruit and vegetables and should be eating turnips instead of tomatoes.

So of course the headlines are all saying "**Let them eat turnips**" and she is being roundly ridiculed for this.

The trouble is that a turnip farmer called Richard Parry who used to produce 30 million turnips every year has said that his business collapsed since the Tories came to power due to rising energy prices and labour shortages, partly caused by Brexit, which made his turnip business financially unviable.

Also the turnip harvest, if you are lucky enough to have one, is in the autumn.

So, sorry Ms. Coffey, but turnips are not the answer and your government is responsible and you have no idea.

She also went on to say that the best way for people to boost their incomes is by either getting into work if they are unemployed or "potentially to work some more hours" or "get upskilled" in a bid to secure a higher wage.

Keir Starmer was at the conference and he said that, "food security is national security" and that his party would commit to "buying, making and selling more in Britain".

And Sunak? Where was he?

Well he made the brief appearance by video link and pretended to be the farmer's best friends when he jokingly said that his participation in "the early morning milking in Wensleydale" had left him with a greater empathy for the plight of Britain's farmers." What? That's it?

As Ben Marlow says in *The Telegraph*, **"If the Tories lose the support of the countryside, they can kiss goodbye to the next election."**

****

26TH FEBRUARY

Well they are also losing businesses.

You might remember that when **Boris Johnson** was Foreign Secretary he made the now infamous remark **"fuck business"**. He said this in June 2018 to Belgium's ambassador to the EU during a reception at the Foreign Office.

Well congratulations Boris because that is exactly what is happening. In fact I would say this is "**world beating**."

I have already said that business leaders are longing for Starmer to take over and we hear today that Lord Sainsbury has returned to the Labour fold and given the Labour party a donation of £2million. He had moved to the Conservatives after Corbyn.

But there is a report just published by the 'Purposeful Company Think Tank' called 'Advancing Purpose' and Will Hutton who is their co-chair mentions it in today's *Observer*.

Wow, it makes interesting reading.

As he says, we are all desperately wanting growth but nothing tangible is happening at the moment and this is causing low wages, increased poverty and has unacceptable social consequences.

Leading City figures are very concerned and this report says that top insurance companies want to create a £50 billion private sector national wealth fund to invest in British business. It would be better still, of course, if the government would work in partnership with their own £50 billion fund but I can't see that happening. However Keir Starmer and Rachel Reeves have already proposed such a fund.

Companies are exiting Britain at an alarming rate as they have no backing or funding here and they are going to the States or are being bought out by foreign companies.

Many leading figures are realising that the City must play its part in re-vitalising the area not least because it will prove beneficial to all in so many ways. But they feel abandoned by this Tory government (don't we all?) and therefore, they feel, it is up to them to do something.

Will Hutton ends his article by saying that this is an extraordinary moment. We have "a City of London that wants to back and invest in business with a social purpose on an unprecedented scale, a Labour party that wants to do the same and a potential vehicle to make it happen. A cause for optimism in hard times."

As I said, 'Wow'. This does make re-assuring reading.

****

27TH FEBRUARY

And more cause for cautious optimism.

I have just been watching the news conference with Rishi Sunak and Ursula von der Leyen about the new Brexit deal which they have just signed which will resolve the issues with the Northern Ireland protocol.

My word, the body language was as interesting as the actual words. The eye contact and smiles and nods and warm glances between them was wonderful to behold. I think after Cameron and May and Boris and Truss, Sunak at least was a sensible, polite and trustworthy breath of fresh air. (I don't say this sort of thing very often).

This really does sound like good news for everyone but particularly for the people of Northern Ireland.

Ms. von der Leyen said she was looking forward "to turning a page and opening a new chapter with our partner and friend".

Highlighting two key examples, she said the new framework "will ensure that the same food will be available on supermarket shelves in Northern Ireland as in the rest of the UK", and "will permanently enable all medicines, including novel ones, to be available in Northern Ireland at the same time, under the same conditions, across the UK".

Also of course it will drop the barrier to the Horizon programme which will be amazing.

"We knew it was not going to be easy" she said. "We knew we needed to listen to each other's concerns very carefully, above all we had to listen to the concerns of the people of Northern Ireland." As she said we have so much in common with the war in Ukraine, and climate change and we stand shoulder to shoulder.

She was so upbeat and so charming.

Sunak too was eloquent and positive. Today's agreement is about "stability", "real people" and "real businesses", he said. It is about "breaking down the barriers between us, setting aside the arguments that for too long have divided us, and remembering that fellow feeling that defines us, this family of nations, this United Kingdom."

My word this is novel. We haven't heard words like these from our politicians for years.

Of course he has to get it through the Commons now and there are people such as Boris Johnson, Steve Baker and Suella Braverman lurking in the wings. Boris will be furious as he has been criticising Sunak over these last few weeks as of course this is the protocol he signed and said there would be no border down the Irish Sea and all would be wonderful. He wants to derail Sunak, but hopefully now, this will be the end of Johnson. The DUP and the ERG will be watched very closely to see how they respond.

Then of course Rees-Mogg raises his head and warns Mr. Sunak of a possible Tory revolt if the DUP does not support the deal.

He told GB News: "It will all depend on the DUP. If the DUP are against it, I think there will be quite a significant number of Conservatives who are unhappy."

He said that the position of Mr. Johnson, who he described as the "biggest figure in UK politics", will be "fundamental".

The arrogance and self-importance of these people never fails to astound me.

But Sunak is 'over the moon'. He is literally jumping up and down in his excitement. This is unique, he says. No-one else has access to the huge global market of the UK as well as the EU market. Everyone will want to come here to invest. Northern Ireland is in an 'unbelievably special position.' The best in the 'whole world'.

So, apparently to 'get Brexit done' it means joining the single market. The irony of this is certainly unbelievable. I think we would all like some of this Mr. Sunak. Northern Ireland is now a favoured state and why can this not apply to the rest of the UK?

Be in no doubt here. What we are celebrating is the reclaiming of some of what we had before Brexit.

The fact that we all think this is so good just confirms the fact that we are still well and truly down the rabbit hole.

****

And then it is always, always back to the NHS. These are still dangerous times.

28TH FEBRUARY

A headline today reads "**How many will I kill today?**" Ambulance call staff are facing appalling conditions. So often they literally have no ambulances available to send out and they describe having to listen to patients dying on the end of the phone. Long waits in A & E are causing thousands of avoidable deaths and the level of stress and burnout amongst the staff everywhere is unprecedented. The Royal College of Emergency Medicine said that there were 23,000 excess patient deaths in 2022 linked to long A&E waits.

And the government, especially the health minister Steve Barclay, sits and does nothing.

****

Then we hear that the drug Evushed will not be recommended for people with weakened immunes systems. 'Nice' says there is not sufficient evidence that this drug, made by AstraZeneca, protects against existing coronavirus variants or those variants expected to circulate in the next six months.

But the speed of the 'Nice' analysis has been widely criticised. This drug has been used safely and effectively in over 30 countries world-wide. Fiona Loud, policy director of Kidney Care UK, said that "an opportunity has been wasted due to failure to act quickly and decisively." She believed it could have helped many vulnerable people to return to a normal life.

Yes but "quickly" and "decisively" are not adverbs we associate with anyone in the present government.

****

So we limp towards the end of February surrounded by danger and no sign of any vision, wisdom or practical action to resolve any immediate problems.

We still have an unprecedented number of strikes, crumbling public buildings with the legal courts, schools, hospitals and prisons, sewage in our rivers, hungry children, abject poverty, a huge cost of living crisis, a shortage of labour, a cruel asylum system, corruption in our police forces, climate-change disinterest, a broken supply chain, increasing homelessness, a disregard for the European Court of Human Rights and some draconian bills going through parliament.

Yes Mr. Sunak you might have found a bit of backbone to face down the ERG and the DUP over your new deal with the EU on Northern Ireland but do not think for a moment that you are the right man for the job of PM.

The calibre of your ministers reflects the complete disdain in which you hold the electorate. You, and they, insult our intelligence every single day. We are appalled by your lack of concern and your lack of interest in the privations of the majority in the UK today.

One bit of advice. Instead of travelling by private jet or helicopter or chauffeured car around the UK, just take the tube or the train. You will be surprised by what you see. Not pleasantly surprised I'm afraid but your eyes might just open a fraction.

It would be a welcome, Mr Sunak, to the real world.

****

MARCH

"As mad as a March hare" is an expression that comes to mind as we enter the third month of the year.

Looking this expression up on *Wikipedia* it says that the "phrase is an allusion that can be used to refer to any other animal or human who behaves in the excitable and unpredictable manner of a March hare." Well it would seem that some of this excitability is running around Westminster at the moment.

Certainly Sunak is still jumping up and down with excitement at his new deal with the EU. In fact the video of him on Twitter has been taken down by Downing Street, maybe because it is causing too many people to say hang on a bit isn't this what we had before Brexit?

But then we see that more than 100,000 WhatsApp messages which were sent between Matt Hancock and other ministers at the height of the pandemic have just been leaked to a journalist. Actually Hancock **gave** them to the journalist who **was** a friend and it is the journalist who has leaked them to *The Telegraph*.

The journalist, Isabel Oakeshott, worked with Hancock on his book called 'Pandemic Diaries' which is a sort of memoir and she got hold of these messages at that time.

Well some of them look like dynamite!

- Toby Young, the general secretary of the 'Free Speech Union', wrote that: "It confirms our worst suspicions. They weren't 'following the science'. It was a clown show."
- Sam Tarry, the Labour MP, wrote: "The lockdown files proves what we already knew that this govt's claim that they put a "protective ring" around care homes was a barefaced lie. Hancock ignored the Chief Medical Officer's advice, and as a result, people died. Shameful."
- Paul Brand, the UK editor of ITV News, said: "This appears to be pretty damning for Matt Hancock. Care homes have always said they felt the Government acted recklessly."
- Carol Vorderman wrote: "It makes for shocking reading. The many thousands of care home deaths which might easily have been prevented, the school closures, face masks, the casual nature of it all."

But I wrote about this in my book *Beneath the Bluster*. On May 30th 2021 I quote Sam Monaghan who was the chief executive of MHA the largest charitable provider of care homes in the UK who said, "On the 20th April 2020 rules on discharge to care homes from hospitals clarified that negative tests were not required before discharge. By that time" he said, "nobody was talking to us. Some of the managers have described it as feeling abandoned by everyone around them."

Then we hear messages concerning lockdowns and schools. Hancock wanted to lock schools down but Gavin Williamson wanted to try to keep them open. However when it was announced that schools would be closing **Hancock writes:-**

"Cracking announcement today. What a bunch of absolute arses the teaching unions are."

And Sir Gavin responds with: "I know they really, really do just hate work."

I had decided that this must be fake news when I first saw it, but no, there it is, all over *The Telegraph*.

Then there is more talk about maybe Johnson returning as leader.

So Jacob Rees-Mogg, long-time supporter of Mr. Johnson, urges his fellow Tory MPs to "calm down and live with the leader we've got". He told ITV news that "If we're a grown-up party, we cannot change leader again between now and an election."

And even staunch Johnsonites admit that he will have to get through a parliamentary investigation into Partygate first.

Well we are all waiting for that day.

So this is where we are at the beginning of March. Surely, surely it can only get better.

****

Err, no I'm afraid it can't.

It's official. This government is going bonkers.

This is not a normal political term but we do not live in normal political times. So many familiar names keep coming up in the news.

****

2ND MARCH

Sue Gray. Now where have we heard of that name before? Yes Partygate and the Sue Gray report.

Well she has just resigned as the Second Permanent Secretary to the cabinet office and has accepted a role as Chief of Staff for Sir Keir Starmer.

Oooh my word, they are not happy about that.

You may remember that Sue Gray was called in to investigate Partygate because the civil servant first called upon to do so had to recuse himself when he suddenly remembered that actually he had attended one of these so-called parties that actually weren't parties. Sue Gray was described then as unimpeachable, honest, dedicated, straight and absolutely trustworthy.

Well how they have changed their tune. They are now saying that she was entirely responsible for the 'Partygate' fiasco. It was obviously a left wing stitch-up. Rees- Mogg calls her a "conniving friend of the socialists." They say she was obviously in cahoots with Keir Starmer all along. They say she orchestrated the whole 'Partygate' to entrap liar Johnson and she corrupted the entire civil service along the way. I mean these are the people who are meant to be running the country. They cannot perceive how certain people can't bear to work for or with them anymore.

But others have pointed out that she would have had to persuade the party-goers to vomit up the walls, bring in loads of wine, break Wilfred's swing etc. etc. As this quote from the UK civil service twitter account says "Arrogant and offensive. Can you imagine having to work with these truth twisters?"

In actual fact Sue Gray took the Labour job after being blocked from a senior Whitehall role.

But they can't leave it there.

On the **6th March** they call for an urgent question about it all in the House of Commons.

The Speaker indicates that he had an unprecedented number of requests for this urgent question and every single request had the exact same wording.

The debate was farcical. Johnson of course was not there at all. None of them could believe that Sue Gray could possibly go over to the opposition. They say that she will now tell Labour all their dirty secrets. What? Surely they don't have any of those.

Lee Anderson said that she had crossed the line and she should resign. But that is what she has just done for goodness sake. Oh ye of little brain.

John Crace writes in *The Guardian* a complete endorsement of my remark when he says that "it goes without saying that MPs present (at the debate) were some of the stupidest ever to have been elected."

Sir Keir Starmer is not saying much. He is just enjoying the 'give them enough rope and Tories will find new ways to self-destruct' scenario.

Then Angela Rayner makes an impassioned speech and Jeremy Quinn (Tory MP) tells her to "mind her tone." I leave that one with you.

****

Boris Johnson. Well this is a name that keeps popping up from no-where. Although may be not for much longer. The cross-party Privileges Committee investigating Johnson has just released an interim report which is pretty damning. They have found that there **was** significant evidence that he misled MPs over lockdown parties, and that he and his aides almost certainly knew at the time that they were breaking rules.

One witness said that the then Prime Minister told a packed No 10 gathering in November 2020, when strict Covid restrictions were in force, that "this is probably the most unsocially distanced gathering in the UK right now".

Other new evidence includes a message from a No 10 official in April 2021, six months before the first reports of parties emerged, saying a colleague was "worried about leaks of PM having a piss-up – and to be fair I don't think it's unwarranted".

In response to a suggestion they described an event as "reasonably necessary for work purposes", Johnson's then Director of Communications said: "I'm struggling to come up with a way this one is in the rules in my head."

A huge amount of material asked for by the committee had been redacted and many months went by before they got anything.

When Johnson was asked personally to submit evidence he said he "held no relevant material". Six months later, in response to another request, his solicitors supplied the committee with 46 WhatsApp messages between Johnson and five other people.

So we are all looking forward to 2pm on Wednesday 22nd March when we will see Boris Johnson being interviewed by this committee for four hours on television. If found guilty he will face a suspension from parliament.

****

6TH MARCH

Sadly no few days can pass without the name Suella Braverman raising its head. So here we go again.

She is facing a legal challenge by the 'Black Equity Organisation' who is seeking a judicial review over her decision to ignore many of the key recommendations from the Windrush inquiry of 2018.

Campaigners are due to hand a petition in to Downing Street today, signed by more than 53,000 people.

They are calling on the government to do more to recompense survivors and act on the lessons of the scandal.

The recommendations dropped by Suella Braverman, which had been accepted by her predecessor Priti Patel, included a commitment to establish a migrant's commissioner, to increase the powers of the independent chief inspector of borders and immigration and to holding reconciliation events with the Windrush community.

The role of the migrants' commissioner was due to see someone appointed who would be responsible for speaking up for migrants and flagging systemic problems within the UK immigration system.

The reconciliation events were proposed meetings between ministers, Home Office staff and those targeted during the scandal. All now ignored.

After five years there are still many victims waiting for justice.

****

7TH MARCH

Suella Braverman. I am really sorry but this name keeps cropping up and not in a good way. The government has just introduced its new 'Illegal Migration Bill' in the House of Commons and it makes my blood run cold.

The 'Illegal Migration Bill' will change the law so that those who arrive in the UK illegally will not be able to stay here and will instead be detained and then promptly removed, either to their home country or a 'safe' third country. The new law would also deny anti-slavery protections to anyone who entered the country illegally, which is the normal route for those who are smuggled by traffickers.

In other words they are saying that all asylum seekers who arrive here in a small boat across the Channel will be treated as criminals. This includes unaccompanied children. And they will never be allowed to enter the UK at any time in the future. In the statement at the beginning of this bill she says:" I am unable to make a statement that in my view the provisions of the Illegal Migration Bill are compatible with the Convention rights, but the government nevertheless wishes the House to proceed with the Bill." In other words it is against the law but vote for it anyway.

In the debate today I watched Suella Braverman give her speech in the House of Commons. In it she said that police chiefs have been telling her that these migrants were bringing in illegal drugs. She does take us all for fools.

Yvette Cooper gave an impassioned response saying that "there is no point in ministers trying to blame anyone else for it, they have been in power for 13 years. The asylum system is broken and they broke it."

As Rafael Behr says in *The Guardian*, "**the Illegal Migration Bill represents a new stage of constitutional degradation**. It takes the most dysfunctional elements of Westminster process and applies them as the deliberate instrument of government policy."

He also points out that there is "no mechanism for dealing with all those who will have their claims to sanctuary automatically and irreversibly invalidated (in breach of the UK's commitments under international conventions on refugee rights). They will end up in legal limbo, pending removal to Rwanda, or some as yet unidentified country. Without mass deportations, the bill condemns asylum seekers to internment or destitution. The cost will rise; the boats will still come."

Rishi Sunak gives a press conference, in the Downing Street press room, the first of his premiership. The picture is abhorrent. He stands behind a brand new lectern with the message "Stop the boats" engraved on it. Who on earth thought that one up? Remember each new lectern costs the tax-payer between £2,000 and £4,000.

350 charities, businesses legal groups and unions have said this bill is "cruel and unworkable." They also say that some of the language used by ministers could draw "frightening parallels from history."

The Archbishop of York says it is "immoral and inept."

'Save the Children' , 'Refugee Action',' Friends of the Earth,' and 'Doctors of the World,' say that this bill " proposes we lock up families, children and other refugees simply for asking for protection and fundamentally undermines this principle and makes a mockery of our international commitments."

"The glaring racism at the heart of government, whilst pulling the ladder of refuge from Africa the Middle East, Afghanistan and most of Asia must be called out."

Paul Butler, the Bishop of Durham, who speaks for the Church of England on refugees, said the proposed legislation was "likely to push thousands of people, including children, into a prolonged legal limbo and imprisonment, and does nothing to support timely and effective consideration of asylum requests."

Rose Hudson-Wilkin, the Bishop of Dover, said the bill lacked "in basic human compassion", and was "dehumanising". Migration was often "the only option between life and death". Deporting asylum-seekers without a hearing was "a brutal response given that there is currently no fit asylum application process in place here. There has to be a better way."

Leaders from the **Baptist, Methodist and United Reformed churches** issued a joint statement last week which said "Instead of dignity, these plans will foster discrimination and distrust, and cause immeasurable harm to people already made vulnerable by conflict and persecution. If ever there was a contemporary example of ignoring our neighbour and walking by on the other side, this is it."

Lord Alf Dubbs who fled Nazi Germany as a child, was talking on LBC about Lineker's right to call out dangerous language by the Home Secretary and others. **"Germany in the thirties started off with vilifying a minority,"** he said.

The bill has been voted through and now goes to the House of Lords.

There was a massive demonstration in London starting in Whitehall which stretched for miles.

Never reported on the BBC or in the main stream media but helicopter photos were shown on Twitter.

****

Then the very next day we hear from Dave Penman who is the general secretary of the FDA, a trade union for civil servants in the United Kingdom. He accuses Suella Braverman of insulting civil servants. What did she say? She accused civil servants of blocking efforts to stop small boat crossings of being part of a "left-wing activist blob" with the Labour Party. Dave Penman says she should withdraw this insulting message and apologise to her staff. He said she had broken the ministerial code (what again?) which states that "ministers must uphold the political impartiality of the civil service."

We wait for that apology.

****

So we come to hear the name, Gary Lineker.

Who is he? Well he is a sports presenter on BBC and a former professional footballer. He presents 'Match of the Day' every Saturday and is a hugely popular and respected TV presenter.

However he sparked a huge BBC impartiality row last week after criticising the Government's new legislation on small boats and comparing language used to launch the policy to that of 1930s. He did not do this on the BBC, he did it on his private twitter account.

But the BBC and the government went into meltdown.

In his tweet, he commented on a video of Suella Braverman unveiling the government's plan to stop migrants crossing the Channel on small boats and saying the UK is being "overwhelmed". In fact she said that there are 100,000 million displaced people all over the world and they are all coming here.

So Gary Lineker tweeted: "There is no huge influx. We take far fewer refugees than other major European countries.

"This is just an immeasurably cruel policy directed at the most vulnerable people in language that is not dissimilar to that used by Germany in the '30s."

And the BBC pulls him off the upcoming flagship programme of 'Match of the Day.'

Oh my goodness this was **not** a good move. The backlash was enormous. People were furious at this ridiculous over re-action by the BBC. They were saying what a thoroughly decent guy he is. Then all his fellow sports presenters walked out of the BBC in support.

Of course we hear comments from the right-wing which are appalling. They accused him of saying that red-wall voters were Nazis and they said he was a holocaust denier.

But by the following week the BBC had re-instated Lineker on 'Match of the Day'.

He tweets "Well it has been an interesting couple of days. Happy that this ridiculous out of proportion story seems to be abating and very much looking forward to presenting 'Match of the Day' on Saturday. Thanks again for all your incredible support. It's been overwhelming."

Then he puts up a new profile on Twitter. Behind him he has the engraving which stands at the entrance to the BBC in London. It is a quote by George Orwell and it says: **"If liberty means anything at all it means the right to tell people what they do not want to hear."**

So interesting that the BBC tried to silence him, thereby proving his point.

****

Snippets you might have missed.

James Cleverly MP Foreign Secretary, speaking about an increase in funding for defence, states that "on every continent of the world, the UK walks taller today than it has done for many years."

But Mr Cleverly, **this** is what the French are saying on their 'culture' radio about the state of the UK.

"Essentially the UK is dysfunctional, unhappy, divided, hopeless with no direction or realistic aspiration."

Yes to all of that.

****

'Private Eye' magazine has been banned from the House of Commons. This just happens to be the only main news outlet where you get the unvarnished truth.

****

The new **'Wild Life' series for the BBC by David Attenborough** which consists of six episodes has had the sixth episode removed from the main channel and will now be shown on BBC iPlayer. Apparently this episode takes a stark look at the losses of nature in the UK and at what has caused the declines. They are worried about a right-wing backlash. As you will know by now we are governed by the extreme right wing.

The Telegraph actually attacked the BBC for creating the series and for taking funding from "two charities previously criticised for their political lobbying" – the WWF and RSPB.

I do have to pinch myself continuously at the moment to make sure that I am not dreaming all of this.

****

Sunak meets up with Macron in Paris and gives him nearly £500 million to build a detention centre in northern France.

I say that it should be an assessment centre.

Macron says that "the consequences of Brexit were underestimated."

****

Sunak has had to upgrade the local electricity network in his constituency of Richmond in order to heat his private 12 metre swimming pool at his manor house there.

This, at a time when over 350 public pools have had to close or reduce their hours due to increased energy costs.

In fact only last month, the operators of a swimming pool near the PM's home said it would reduce public access because of the increased cost of energy.

****

Sunak has been reprimanded by police in Hyde Park for letting his dog off the lead. The notices are very clear and say "When walking your dog in the Royal Parks, please respect the wildlife as well as the other park users by keeping your dog under control." I think he would have understood a three word slogan more easily actually.

****

Junior doctors are on strike for three days. **A meeting was called by Steve Barclay but he didn't turn up.**

****

Not one new onshore wind turbine has been installed this year so far. There are none under construction. There are no planning consents and there are none being submitted into the planning system. There is no governing going on.

****

Many Tory MPs are being deselected all of a sudden. This is extremely concerning. **A fringe group, the 'Conservative Democratic Organisation', is actively attempting to unseat MPs that it considers are insufficiently right-wing.** It has prominent support. Priti Patel, Nadine Dorries and Jacob Rees-Mogg will attend the CDO's "Take Back Control" conference and gala dinner on the night of the Eurovision final. Lord Cruddas is leading this group and apparently there as many as 60 MPs on the target list.

The Conservative Party as we knew it, is dead.

****

THE BUDGET

15TH MARCH

Well Jeremy Hunt was very excited by his budget and so were most of the cabinet and the back benches. But others were not so keen. So far as I can see it looked as though the budget was on course to rob the poor to give to the already rich. But let's see what others, more qualified than I am, have to say.

The Institute for Fiscal Studies said that all households face 'continuing pain' amid a 'lost decade for living standards' as they are hammered by high prices and low wage growth. The IFS calculated that if the salary threshold at which workers start paying the 40p rate of income tax – currently £50,270 – had risen in line with inflation since 2010, it would now be £56,680 and next month would go to £62,410.

Paul Johnson director of the Research Institute said the stealth tax raid will raise £120 billion for the Treasury over the next five years by taking up to six million more people into higher brackets, in a process known as fiscal drag.

The freeze on fuel duty was also criticised by Paul Johnson as he said that the decision to spend £6 billion to freeze fuel duty is a "political choice" and that the money could be spent elsewhere.

Yes that is a political choice. Money for motorists, but not for nurses, doctors and teachers.

The Official OBR forecasts suggest that the next two years will be the "worst on record" for household incomes. The increase in the income tax bill is equivalent to raising the basic rate by 4p. They say that business investment is 20% lower than its estimates at the time of the referendum vote in 2016.

The **Resolution Foundation** Think Tank says a combination of weak economic growth, high inflation and modest salary increases means the average pay packet is not expected to return to its 2008 level in real terms until 2026.

Hunt is also facing criticism over his surprise decision to remove the lifetime allowance on pensions – the amount that can be saved in a pension scheme before being taxed. This one has really got people going. Concerns have been raised over the fact that the policy, which will cost £1.1bn a year by 2028, is only expected to help around 15,000 high earners.

By 2028, the Government's tax take will amount to 37.7% of GDP – almost 5 percentage points higher than its pre-pandemic level.

Housing experts have criticised the Chancellor for not offering any measures to tackle the UK's housing crisis in his Budget.

A new report featuring research from the **University of Southampton** says rural homelessness is on the rise and has been worsened by the pandemic and the cost-of-living-crisis.

There has been a "24 % increase in the number of people sleeping rough in rural areas from 2021 to 2022." they report.

The disability benefits are also subject to change and we all need to keep an eye on this one. **Basically Hunt wants everyone to work no matter how old or how disabled you are**. When interviewed on the Laura Kuenssberg programme last Sunday he said "the government won't use immigration to fill labour shortages because that was the decision in the Brexit referendum."

Just when I think I have discovered the most un-intelligent comment by a Tory MP I find another even worse.

But the one that concerns me is childcare. Great drum rolls greeted this statement but as with everything this government does you need to look at the small print. The staff ratio will change from 4 toddlers per adult to five per adult. This is detrimental to children's progress. It is being said that unless there is much more funding the whole scheme will collapse.

But then I see something much more disturbing. This government is desperate to get more people into work because of labour shortages caused by Brexit, long waits for routine NHS procedures and an exodus of older workers since the pandemic.

So they are going to introduce sanctions relating to universal benefits for parents who do not comply with certain conditions.

When their children turn three they will be pushed into near-full-time work or have their benefits docked.

Parents, which includes single mothers, will now have to be available to work for up to 30 hours a week once their youngest child turns three, which is nearly double the current requirement of 16 hours.

They have to meet with a job coach every three months – up from every six months – as soon as their child turns one. Parents of two-year-olds will have to attend coaching monthly.

And they have to seek employment if their partner is in paid work but their wages are topped up with universal credit. These individuals previously had no obligation to work.

I find this absolutely abhorrent. A problem caused solely by this government is being exploited at the expense of mainly women and young children.

David Webster of Glasgow University said, "It's a complete disregard of children's needs and will have drastic effects on lone parents."

Ben Harrison, the director of the 'Work Foundation' think tank at Lancaster University, said that "research indicates sanctions impoverish claimants and damage mental health. Even employers themselves say pushing people to take any job, regardless of whether it is suitable to an individual's skills or ambitions, is not helpful and can actually end up causing more issues for organisations than it solves," he said.

Becca Lyon, the head of child poverty at 'Save the Children UK', said the move risked making children poorer.

I am disgusted by this treatment of parents of young children. Never ever believe any Tory MP who says they are only concerned with the well- being of children. Not only do they not improve their life chances, they actively destroy them.

So this budget all looks very much as though it is give it away with one hand and take it back with another. And a poll has just shown that more people are concerned than reassured by this budget.

****

THE DOWNWARD SPIRAL

16TH MARCH

The UK has been downgraded by an annual index of civic freedoms from 'narrowed to 'obstructed'.

The Civicus Monitor tracks the democratic and civic health of 197 countries and it stated that the UK government was creating a 'hostile environment' towards campaigners, charities and other civil society bodies and was becoming 'increasingly authoritarian.'

Well we have absolutely already seen that with their anger towards the WWF and the RSPB for goodness sake. We are now alongside countries such as Poland, Hungary and South Africa.

We have seen it in the draconian new laws they have passed already or are in the process of passing.

****

19TH MARCH

Children.

A forthcoming Refugee Council report reveals that the government's migration plan 'would bar 45,000 children'. And at the moment Afghan child refugees who are here and in school and about to sit their GCSEs are being shunted around the country like cattle by the Home Office. A report in *The Observer* by Anna Fazackerley describes the plight of many Afghan children who are doing really well at school but are being compulsorily relocated out of London to areas without school places or which are doing a different syllabus and so they will be unable to sit their exams which take place in under a month's time.

And along with all of that we have photos of Suella Braverman in Rwanda. This is a publicity stunt where she is seen standing in front of the buildings which will be used for refugees deported from the UK. However she only invited reporters from *The Telegraph*, *The Express* and *The Daily Mail*, banning the BBC and *The Guardian*. But that doesn't stop her being photographed laughing her head off in front of these buildings being posted all over Twitter. My word, she says "these are lovely. I need to get the name of the interior designer. Refugees will be so well looked after here." So what will the new slogan be? Come to the UK for a wonderful new life in Rwanda. And transform from 'illegal migrants' into 'refugees.'

****

20TH MARCH

There is a long and very concerning article by Nesrine Malik of *The Guardian* today. I quote it at some length because it is so important and so relevant. I know that many do not read the news or watch the news at the moment because it is all so depressing but if we don't keep our eyes and ears open then we will sleepwalk into a nightmare of corruption and authoritarianism. Indeed that is the direction of travel with this government.

She writes that, "The leave campaign was a masterclass in how the flapping of butterfly wings end in a storm – we cannot let the country become captured by broadly unchallenged immigration hysteria, no matter how sheltered we are from it, without paying for it somehow further down the line. And so we sacrificed our freedom of movement, along with so many other losses, cultural and economic, which continue to be revealed."

She goes on to say that we need to remember that, "shortly after writing an article imploring people to recognise the good that immigration does for the country and not to "fall for the spin" of Brexiters, Jo Cox was murdered by a man who hoarded Nazi memorabilia, and in court gave his name as "Death to traitors, freedom for Britain". The links between state propaganda and violence are inescapable."

She ends her article by saying that, **"An immigrant shivering on the beach or languishing in detention may be a long way from your life, but the government has sketched a line, long and winding, that connects you. When you speak up for them, you speak up for yourself."**

We need to wake up, and we need to wake up NOW.

****

Meanwhile the Sunday papers are all looking forward to the trial of **Boris Johnson** on Wednesday 22nd. He and his allies are going absolutely bonkers (sorry that word again) as we get nearer and nearer to the day when he is finally held to account. As Andrew Rawnsley writes at the end of a long article in *The Observer*, **"It is not just the fate of a disgraced prime minister that is at stake. It is the credibility of parliament, the trustworthiness of our political culture and the health of our democracy"**

****

BORIS JOHNSON

23RD MARCH

And so it came to pass that yesterday, we were witness to the spectacle of Boris Johnson digging his own political and moral grave.

Yes it was all there on television for everyone to see.

The Privileges Committee was made up of four Conservative MPs, two Labour MPs and one from the Scottish National Party.

Well millions of words have been written about this in the media this morning but this is just my review.

First of all, the politeness and the calm demeanour of the members of the committee were in stark contrast to the attitude of Johnson. The whole interrogation lasted just over three hours and as time progressed, Johnson got more and more shouty and blustery and aggressive.

He gave long, rambling answers often repeating himself. He consistently interrupted the questioner before he had finished asking the question.

He started to bang the table with his fist to drive home a point he was trying to make, he pointed a finger, he said people did not know what they were talking about and he accused people of talking absolute nonsense. He became more and more agitated and at one point Lord

Pannick, his barrister who was sitting next to him, could be seen rolling his eyes.

His main defence though, about the fact that he didn't think any rules were broken, completely astonished me and I think many others as well. Many of the 'parties' were leaving gatherings to say a thank-you to someone for all their hard work. He said that he felt it was absolutely essential for him to be there for morale purposes and of course you always give a toast so alcohol would be there. Yes there were many people there but we have to understand that 10 Downing Street is a small and cramped space and people might have "inadvertently drifted into other people's orbit". There is no "invisible electrifying fence" there and the guidance said that social distancing at work events should be adhered to "to the best of your ability".

Really? I didn't hear that being said anywhere.

When asked if there were any special measures taken he said yes, we didn't touch each other's pens. "But you did pass drinks around?" "Er yes."

He kept saying that the guidance was that it was OK to have these gatherings all for morale purposes. And he said that yes he would have told others that it was perfectly OK and absolutely up to them if they wanted to hold unsocially-distanced farewell gatherings in the work place.

Well I never heard a message like that.

He kept saying that 10 Downing Street is such a small building that it really is impossible to keep your distance. But it has 100 rooms and is nearly 4,000 sq. ft.

And of course everyone is describing how they were fined for much milder transgressions of the lockdown rules than this. We couldn't sit on a park bench if there was someone else there. An elderly lonely man invited a friend to his garden on his birthday. They sat well apart and he was fined by the police. And of course there were thousands of people unable to say goodbye to their dying loved ones. Well the stories are legion. You will all have one of your own. And yet Johnson thinks what he was doing was perfectly OK.

Then there were some interesting questions about his 'assurances'. "Who exactly assured you that you hadn't broken the rules?" he was asked.

Well not a senior civil servant. Simon Case said that he hadn't. No legal advice whatever. Oh yes it was his senior communications advisers: Jack Doyle and James Slack and an unnamed No 10 official. No he didn't want to give her name. Perhaps you could put it in writing, he was asked and send it to us.

As Harriet Harman, who was the brilliant chair, said these were very "flimsy assurances". And when Tory MP Bernard Jenkin said "You did not take proper advice" that was when Johnson exploded and said "This is complete nonsense".

But the part that really made me laugh (although believe me I do know how serious this all is) is when he was asked about the fact that some of his allies had tried to criticise the Committee by calling it a witch-hunt or a kangaroo court. He replied by saying in effect that, no he doesn't even want to repeat those words and of course if their findings completely exonerate him which obviously they absolutely should, then they will have been seen to be completely fair. When pushed to say if he would say the same thing if they found him guilty he said, and I paraphrase, no of course not!

But midway through proceedings, I see a tweet from Jacob Rees-Mogg which says "Boris is doing very well against the marsupials."

So there we have it. Completing the interrogation Harman gave him the opportunity to change his assertion that all rules were followed but he said "no absolutely not. That is what I firmly believe."

The Committee will take many weeks to mull over the evidence before giving their verdict. But **we** have already made up our minds!

We saw. We heard. And also we paid. Yes Johnson's legal fees were paid for by the tax-payer. All £220,000 of it.

****

At one point during the interrogation Johnson had to go to the Commons to vote on the Windsor Framework Bill on the Northern Ireland Protocol. This didn't go well for him either. All the usual suspects shouted loud and clear that they were going to vote it down. Boris Johnson, Liz Truss, Rees-Mogg, Jonathan Gullis, Andrea Jenkins, Ian Duncan-Smith and members of the ERG and the DUP. This was not what Brexit was all about and they were going to give Sunak a bloody nose. But it was guaranteed to go through anyway because Labour was voting for it. In the end it was passed by 515 to 29. This means that it could have got through without the Labour vote which means that enough Tories voted it through.

This is a good result and it could possibly signal the decline of the ERG.

****

But any smattering of good news does not last.

Inflation has gone up and so have interest rates.

Talks have broken down with junior doctors who have just announced they will be going on strike for FOUR days from the 11th April. Actually this will take them quite close to the council elections so I think it might get resolved fairly soon.

Then there is this disturbing article in *The Times* today by Emma Yeomans. A report by the Centre of Social Justice has disclosed that more than 140,000 children were "severely absent from school last summer. "Severe absence" is defined as spending more time out of school than in school.

There are many reasons for this of course, and it has got worse since the pandemic. They are being called the "ghost children" of the pandemic. The report call for 2,000 attendance monitors to be hired nationally across the UK and for the government to invest in youth work and family support.

But we know that this government does not care about families or children so I can tell you now that this will not happen.

****

24TH MARCH

But what on earth is this? I'm afraid we have to go back to Boris Johnson.

Adam Forrest of *The Independent* has reported that the 'leaving work event' for Mark Sedwill was the 'bring your own booze' occasion in the garden, on **May 20th 2020.**

However it is interesting to note that Mark Sedwill did not announce his retirement until **June 2020** and did not actually retire until **September** of that year. How will he explain that one? Well I'm afraid that it is impossible.

****

END OF TERM REPORT

26TH MARCH

So just a summary of where the UK is this Sunday and in the last week of March before the Easter recess.

The campaign group 'Led by Donkeys' has entrapped some top Tory MPs by putting up a fake South Korean website and then asking the MPs who got in touch if they would like to work for them. Matt Hancock, Kwasi Kwarteng and Sir Graham Brady were among those who said that yes, maybe they would be interested, and yes **£10,000 a day would be about right**. I have just had to double check the veracity of this statement but there it is all over the media.

****

NHS managers in south-west England have imposed new rules that could deny autism assessments to thousands of children. These are effective immediately with no notice or consultation. Children and teenagers will only be referred if they meet one of six criteria. Jame Breitnauer who has an autistic son said that, "We believe that the changes to the criteria are naïve and irresponsible. We believe that it puts children at genuine risk."

****

A headteacher committed suicide after an Ofsted report on her primary school downgraded it to 'inadequate'. Since then there has been a huge debate about the inadequacies of Ofsted and about the stress they cause and how they are not fit for purpose. Many inspectors have had no experience of primary school teaching and do not seem to take into account any difficulties the teachers faced. There are so many stories of teachers suffering ill-health and leaving the profession due to appalling inspections. And many inspectors have resigned as they say the system is so flawed.

****

Social care services are still at distressing level of inadequacy. Nuffield Trust researcher Laura Schlepper said that "Broken, complicated and fragmented services, demoralised staff in short supply and the increasing strain on friends, family and informal carers to pick up the pieces all create a sobering reality. These are yet another reason for politicians to replace words with action on social care reform." There were 165,000 unfilled vacancies in social care last year.

****

HS2 is going to be delayed by two years, the transport secretary Mark Harper announced recently. So the area around Euston is devastated. All work has stopped and locals are left with a huge mess and a mile-long hole in the ground. Hundreds of homes have been demolished, a school, a pub and other businesses have been knocked down as it is being said that the high-speed line linking Birmingham to London will now terminate at Old Oak Common nearly five miles away. This is due to rising costs. So the high speed stops abruptly before you get to central London. But just after this announcement we see a photograph of a tree stump on the Euston Rd just outside Euston station. It is the stump of an ancient tree which was probably about 200 years old. Removed with hundreds of other trees to make way for the HS2 enlargement of the station for a line that never comes. State vandalism.

****

Pregnant women are still being sent to prison in England in the year 2023. In a freedom of information request by *The Observer*, it was discovered that women in prison were seven times more likely to suffer stillbirth. The Sentencing Council is due to review whether there is a need for new guidance on sentencing pregnant women. If you have read my previous books you will not be surprised when I say that words fail me.

****

A report into the Metropolitan police force by Dame Louise Casey has accused it of being institutionally misogynistic, racist and homophobic. This is a shocking report and she makes it absolutely clear that it must be acted upon, unlike the MacPherson report of 20 years ago.

****

27TH MARCH

60 Conservative MPs are voting on an amendment of the Illegal Migration Bill in order to make it harsher and even more cruel than it already is. They would take us out of the ECHR. And Suella Braverman is accused of secretly backing them. Well not so secretly as it turns out.

****

In a report today the head of the National Infrastructure Commission said Net Zero targets look to be increasingly threatened by failures of ministers to act. Sir John Armitt the chairman said "The government comes forward with these big ideas but what you don't see is the necessary detail to back that up." But Sir John, that is this government in a nutshell.

****

Rishi Sunak is unveiling powers which will allow the police to move on rough sleepers deemed to be causing "public distress". Where exactly will they be moved on to? As Matt Downie, Chief executive of 'Crisis' says in a letter to *The Times* "If we had the housing and support services we need we would not have people on the streets in the first place. Crisis has long campaigned for the cruel and outdated Vagrancy Act to be scrapped. It must not be replaced by measures that criminalise and punish the very poorest in society."

****

The Office for Budget Responsibility has warned that Brexit has been as bad for the economy as the pandemic and as the invasion of Ukraine.

****

Britain's ambition to be a science super-power is at risk unless promises to fund maths research are fulfilled. Professor Ulrike Tillman, president of the London Mathematic Society said "without proper funding in maths, the chancellor's plans for a future built on technology and driven by AI will turn to dust."

****

Rishi Sunak has been discovered to have lied about asylum backlog figures when speaking in a debate in the House of Commons on December 13th. He tried to compare the numbers in the backlog to when Labour was in power and his exact words were that it is "half the size than it was when Labour was in office." This was in answer to Labour MP Alison McGovern who argued that the backlog was "now 14 times bigger" than when her party left office.

Sunak told her to "get her numbers right."

Oh dear. Stephen Kinnock shadow immigration minister was very concerned about this and wrote to Sir Robert Chote, the chair of the UK Statistics Authority, about what he believed to be a factual inaccuracy by the prime minister.

And yes, would you believe, the UK's statistics watchdog has now confirmed that for every one person who was waiting for an asylum claim in 2010, eight people are waiting today, with a staggering 166,000 currently awaiting decisions. Sir Robert Chote has written to the immigration minister, Robert Jenrick, to point out the inaccuracy.

18,954 asylum seekers awaiting decisions in June 2010 and **166,261** awaiting decisions in December 2022. Yes, that looks like a significant increase to me.

Stephen Kinnock said: "The Tories are making so many false and misleading claims about Labour's record in office because they want to deflect attention away from their own failures".

So we wait to see if Sunak apologises to the House as indeed he should as he has broken the ministerial code.

It is also interesting to note that the organisation 'Full Fact' has identified other factually inaccurate claims made about immigration matters including the claim by the Home Secretary, Suella Braverman, that 100 million refugees could come to the UK and the claim that asylum-seekers get £175 a week from the government. All lies.

And watching the second day of the committee stage debate on the Illegal Migration Bill it is disheartening to see the empty benches.

Later at the Liaison Committee I heard Rishi Sunak say the most appalling thing I have ever heard. When questioned about the Illegal Migration Bill and why he thought it was necessary to detain children indefinitely before deporting them he said that not detaining children would be a "pull factor".

"It's important that we don't inadvertently create a policy that incentivises people to bring children who wouldn't otherwise come here," he said.

This bill breaks international law and every moral code.

****

30TH MARCH

The cruelty continues as we hear that they are planning to move asylum seekers out of hotels into military bases and unused barges because they think this will save money.

Charles Dickens would be horrified.

In a statement to the House Robert Jenrick, the Immigration Minister, said that the accommodation will be as basic as possible in order to deter people from coming in the first place. "We will ensue that those who arrived were not made "destitute", he said "but nothing more."

"We must not elevate the wellbeing of illegal migrants above those of the British people," he told MPs. How many times do we have to say there is no such thing as an illegal immigrant?

The crassness, stupidity and ongoing cruelty never fails to astound me. But I should be used to it by now as they are indeed world beating at it.

Responding to this statement, the 'Refugee Council' said the plans were unworkable and "not who we are as a country". Enver Solomon, its Chief Executive, said: "We should be providing accommodation which treats people with humanity, dignity and compassion, not barges and shipping containers."

Well definitely unworkable I would say as some of the army barracks to be used are in Conservative constituencies and their MPs are saying not in my back-yard! But the words "humanity, dignity and compassion" never appear in what passes for the Conservative party at the moment.

As Diane Taylor of *The Guardian* says "If the government does not engage with the truth about who asylum seekers are and what propels them towards the UK they will never solve this issue." Asylum seekers do not come here in order to be put up in hotels. To say it could be a pull factor is complete nonsense and they have probably never heard of them. **As Ms. Taylor says she has interviewed hundreds of asylum seekers and the reasons for coming to the UK "can be summed up in two words: seeking safety."**

****

Then I hear about two further items about this bill. **Suella Braverman has got into another ugly row, this time with the 'Board of Deputies', which is the largest Jewish community organisation in the UK.** They have criticised potential breaches of the UN refugee convention in the Home Secretary's Illegal Migration Bill. She responded by calling them "misinformed" and suggesting it wasn't an "appropriate intervention". How dare she?

There is a letter in *The Observer* from the director of the Wiener Holocaust Library and the Chief Executive of the 'Association of Jewish Refugees'. They say that they are "increasingly concerned about the impact of the proposed Illegal Migration Bill and the discourse and language surrounding its formulation." The long letter finishes by saying "We urge this and all governments to demonstrate compassion and give safe harbour to those in danger."

And official documents just published claimed that using force against refugee children could be "necessary".

The Home Office said children travelling irregularly to the UK to join loved ones would not be exempt from the unprecedented measures, adding: 'This approach equally applies to those unaccompanied children who may have family or relatives already in the UK.'

They say that, 'using force on children would be an absolute last resort and would only be used if completely necessary. Using force on children in family groups may unfortunately be necessary if a family is resisting removal.'

Steve Valdez-Symonds, Amnesty International UK's refugee and migrant rights director, called the plans "terrifying".

I call them child abuse.

****

Well this is not looking good Mr. Sunak. Our Prime Minister is facing questions over a possible conflict of interest after it emerged his wife is a shareholder in a childcare agency that will directly benefit from policies announced in the Budget.

Well I missed this one, but apparently, under the childcare reform plans announced in the budget, Jeremy Hunt said that the Government will pilot incentive payments of £600 for childminders joining the profession and £1,200 if they join through an agency. It so happens that the PM's wife has financial interests in an agency called Koru Kids which can expect to see a major increase in business as a result of the pilot, as it will drive prospective childminders to sign up via agencies.

When asked whether Mr. Sunak wanted to declare an interest about the policy at the liaison committee he replied: "No, all my disclosures are declared in the normal way."

At no point did Mr Sunak state that his wife is a shareholder in Koru Kids. His latest register of ministerial interests dating from May 2022 does not declare that his wife owns shares in Koru Kids, despite Companies House records showing she is listed as a shareholder from March 2021. This is gaining momentum in the news so I think Sunak should be feeling rather uncomfortable.

****

We then get a 1,000 page new energy plan from Grant Shapps our energy and net zero secretary. If you scan it quickly you might be forgiven for thinking that it sounds reasonably OK. But of course we have learnt never to do that with this government. It includes support for carbon capture projects, nuclear energy, offshore windfarms, electric vehicles, home heat pumps and hydrogen power. However most of these plans are based on existing commitments and there is no new extra funding.

No-one is happy.

Mark Maslin, a professor of climatology at University College London, said: "At the moment the government announcement is more of the same, lacks insight to the energy issues and invests money in dead-end technology such as hydrogen. Yet again the UK government has missed the opportunity to radically change the UK energy production and market. This is the time that innovative business-led initiatives are needed."

Many green business groups are saying that the UK's new energy plan is a missed opportunity full of "half-baked, half-hearted" policies that do not go far enough to power Britain's climate goals.

They fear the country could surrender its leading role in climate action because of the government's "business as usual" approach to delivering green investments.

Then, on the very same day, new data is released which reports that Rishi Sunak has apparently spent more than £500,000 of taxpayer cash on private jet hire in the space of two weeks.

And protesters are queuing up outside his Richmond mansion, dressed in bathing costumes, asking to have a swim in his newly heated private swimming pool!

Have a good Easter Mr Sunak.

****

And just as they all depart for their holidays they become very excited about a new trade deal which has just been signed off with 11 Asia and Pacific nations.

But why did we leave the one on our doorstep? We already have free trade agreements with all these members except two and the gains for the UK from joining are expected to be modest. The government's own estimate show it will only add 0.08% to the size of the UK's economy in 10 years.

Whereas, if we remember, the Office for Budget Responsibility has previously said that Brexit would reduce the UK's potential economic growth by about 4% in the long term. It was just Brunei and Malaysia left that the UK didn't have a deal with and between them those two account for less than 0.5% of the total of UK trade.

Hmmm, a bit difficult to see the benefits here.

And unions are worried as to how we keep standards at a sufficiently high safety level. Some, including Members of a House of Lords Committee, want to know how the UK intends, for example, to ensure standards on environmental and animal welfare standards will be met.

In fact in an article on *The Guardian* by Nick Dearden, he writes that "Britain has ditched environmental standards, signed up to terms that will undermine British farmers, and left us open to being sued by multinational corporations in secretive courts. And all for no real economic benefit."

In just one example he says that "European tariffs on palm oil aim to stop deforestation, but the UK is understood to have agreed to scrap the tariffs as a condition for entry into the Pacific deal, in effect reneging on deforestation pledges made at the UN climate conference in Glasgow." The immorality of this government is indeed 'world beating'.

There will be pressure for the UK to import food containing pesticides that have been outlawed here, antibiotics in livestock farming or hormone-treated beef.

And surprise, surprise, the parliamentary committee able to properly scrutinise treaties like the CPTPP was abolished last week.

But we have the trade secretary, Kemi Badenoch, saying that the deal reflected newly acquired "post-Brexit freedoms to reach out to new markets around the world and grow our economy".

It just might mean that we will all die of food poisoning.

****

So there we are. They all now break up for the Easter recess and we await their return with trepidation. But, Mr. Sunak, I have to say that I think you are failing in every single department and you need to take a long hard look at yourself over Easter and work out why it is that you are continually attacking the most vulnerable in society.

****

A DANGEROUS MONTH

2ND APRIL

There is now just one month until we have the local elections and April starts off with lie after lie after lie by, and I am very sorry about this but I have to say it, Suella Braverman.

She is on the media circuit this Sunday morning and I find it really difficult to understand how she thinks she can get away with so many lies and so much ignorance. I have already said many times that she is totally unsuited to any ministerial post, as she is completely incompetent and highly dangerous. But this is something else entirely.

Lie number one: Rwanda will accept thousands of refugees from the UK.

No, they have said they will accept 200.

Lie number two: No we won't have to accept any refugees from Rwanda.

The reciprocal clause in the Bill which says that the UK will have to accept Rwandan refugees in return and which I, Suella Braverman have signed, really doesn't mean what it says. She was asked about this four times.

Lie number three: We already have over 7 million unemployed in this country.

This was not challenged by Laura Kuenssberg and in actual fact the unemployment number so far this year is 1.25 million.

Lie number four: Rwanda is a safe country.

When told that in 2018 twelve refugees were shot and killed by the government for protesting about food rationing, she didn't blink an eye. 'I didn't know about that and that was 2018 and it is now 2023.' Well Yvette Cooper was talking about it in the Commons when Patel was Home Secretary.

Lie number five: The fifteen to 40 hour delay of vehicles trying to cross the channel at Dover is nothing to do with Brexit.

It is because every single passport has to be looked at and stamped since we came out of the EU whereas before we were all waved through. In November it will be even worse because everyone in every coach and elsewhere will have to step out-side to be finger-printed and to have biometric testing. When Sunak said 'Stop the Boats' we didn't think he meant stop the boats going **out** of the country. Number 10 has just agreed that actually yes it is mainly because of Brexit.

Why is this woman still in a job?

****

And I am sorry to have to say this but the Suella show goes on. Ms. Braverman recently criticised a "Benefits Street Culture" as she thinks there are too many people claiming welfare. "We have got a lot of carrots to get people into work but we have got to add more conditionality and a bit more stick," she said.

But what is this we see? We hear that she has claimed £25,000 in expenses over five years whilst she was living rent-free in her parent's home when her parents were not there.

She has been accused of exploiting a loophole in the system. One MP has said that although it is within the rules, it is not "in the spirit" of them.

And Sir Alistair Graham, former Committee on Standards in Public Life chairman said: "This looks like an attempt to game the rules to maximise benefit."

Well to me it is just more of the same. Greed and corruption at the highest level and no-one ever being held to account.

****

And if that is not enough we hear this. Braverman was talking about new laws and announcing plans to end child sexual abuse which is always a good thing of course. She announced plans to introduce mandatory reporting of suspected sexual offences against children following the seven-year Independent Inquiry into Child Sexual abuse investigating institutional failings in England and Wales. However despite previous Home Office-commissioned research stating the majority of grooming gangs involve white men aged under 30, the home secretary described 'vulnerable white English girls' being harmed by 'gangs of British Pakistani men'. She said that it was "mainly British Pakistani men who are members of grooming gangs that 'pursue, rape, drug, and harm vulnerable English girls'."

Again, as she so often does, she has caused a storm. These remarks have sparked outrage.

Robina Qureshi, CEO of 'Positive Action in Housing,' a refugee and migrant homelessness charity, said: "The Home Secretary, Suella Braverman, has reached a new low. Her remarks are in direct contradiction to her own department's research. She is openly parroting far right myths about racial groups and amplifying them into national trends. Her commentary is unacceptable, and I call on her to apologise for her gross misrepresentations of our communities."

A review found that most group-based child sexual exploitation offenders are commonly white.

Sir Peter Wanless, NSPCC chief executive, welcomed the Government's focus on tackling child abuse but also stressed that race should not be the sole focus on the issue.

"Child sexual exploitation by organised networks is one pernicious form of abuse and it's welcome to see the Government focus on disrupting perpetrators and protecting victims. This must be backed up with funding for services to help child victims recover and support for a justice system that is struggling to cope."

But this is always the problem. Words, words, words, but no funding so no action.

I repeat: why is Suella Braverman still in her job?

****

Therese Coffey has announced new plans to deal with water pollution. Well there is a headline to fill your hearts with apprehension. As so it turns out. She has been accused of rehashing old policies, lacking ambition and just shuffling the deckchairs.

They want to banish wet-wipes. This is the third time in the past five years that this government has said they will ban them.

They will bring forward £1.6 million in investment to stop 1,000 sewage dumps a year. But there are 300,000 sewage dumps a year so that is just 3%.

Then there are fines for water companies. Well Ofwat already has the power to impose a fine that is 10% of a company's annual turnover. It has done this precisely once in the last 30 years. The £250 million fine which was said to be crazy and disproportionate just before Christmas and so not implemented has now become an unlimited fine.

As Feargal Sharkey says in *The Times*, this is not a plan. It's desperation.

"What is required" he says, "is a properly managed, costed and deliverable 10 or 15 year plan—along with people who can be held accountable for delivering it.

None of that exists and, until it does, none of it is going to stop."

****

6TH APRIL

And who is this all over Twitter? A Conservative MP called Scott Benton. An undercover investigation by *The Times* has secretly filmed him talking to reporters who pretended to be investors with an interest in the betting and gaming industry and were looking for an adviser.

So there he is, the chairman of the all-party parliamentary group for betting and gaming, outlining how he could help and use his position to try to water down proposed gambling reforms.

He said he could leak a copy of the forthcoming white paper on gambling reforms at least 48 hours before general publication.

He could submit parliamentary questions. He had done this on behalf of companies before apparently.

He boasted of his "easy access to ministers". Very easy to speak to them when in the lobby between votes.

He could "call in favours" from colleagues who would be happy to support the company's interests and offered to host a dinner at the Commons.

Hang on who would be paying for that?

Interesting that when asked how much he would be expecting to earn he said between £2,000 and £4,000. Er, this would be for about two days a week.

All of these actions are in breach of the longstanding rules prohibiting "paid advocacy" as well as flouting the new restriction on providing parliamentary advice, which came into effect a few days before this meeting. You really couldn't make it up.

As I said, Twitter went into overdrive, and we have just heard that he has had the whip removed.

Any more for any more?

****

Well I think we need more police patrolling the lobby in the House of Commons.

Oh wait a minute I think there is a problem with that idea. The Met has failed to meet the targets of hiring 4,557 new officers which were set by Boris Johnson in 2019. Now there's a surprise.

When the last set of statistics were published at the end of December, the Met was more than 1,300 officers short, meaning it needed to recruit almost 450 people a month between January and March.

The number of officers recruited by the Met on average over the previous two years has been around 250 a month.

So just more words and very little action.

****

17TH APRIL

So we come back after Easter to the most disruptive strike in the history of the NHS. And where is the government? Where is the Department of Health? Where is the health secretary Steve Barclay? Absolutely no-where to be seen. A complete abdication of responsibility.

Junior doctors are striking for four successive days. So on the 'Today' programme on Radio 4 this morning we hear from the BMA, and from a doctor, but no-one from the government although they were invited.

We hear stupid questions such as "surely a lot of people will be harmed by this strike?" But it is **because** a lot of people are already being harmed by the lack of investment in the NHS that they are going on strike. You shouldn't have to wait 6 months for an appointment to just get a diagnosis about a serious sounding disease. Wards are so drastically understaffed that patient safety is at risk on a daily basis. You shouldn't be paying doctors who are performing complicated surgery and intricate examinations £14 per hour. They are asking for £19 per hour. Your plumber gets that much.

So we have all been told to be really careful this week but don't worry our prime minister will be OK. He has a private GP and he and his family will go to a private hospital if needs be.

****

And a few snippets you might have missed.

The Worker Protection Bill which was introduced by a LibDem politician is set to be blocked by Conservative MPs. This Bill is designed to introduce a requirement for companies and work places to take "all reasonable steps" to prevent harassment of staff. This of course includes sexual harassment of women. Tory MPs, having initially backed this Bill are now saying things like "Oh dear this would have "a chilling effect on every conversation in a workplace.".

And guess who is speaking out the loudest against this Bill? Jacob Ress- Mogg.

Angela Rayner says that the Tory ministers who originally backed this Bill are now "turning their backs on women experiencing sexual assault at work. Yet another Tory broken promise."

****

But there is good news about another Bill and it does need reporting.

The retained EU law bill which was going to be completely destroyed, mainly at the behest of (and I am sorry to mention him again so soon) Jacob Rees- Mogg, looks as though it might be saved. There was going to be a mass rebellion in the House of Lords and this would not look good in the run-up to the local elections.

In a speech at the second reading of the bill, Lord Cormack described it as a "constitutional monstrosity". Indeed it is.

One idea being mooted is to extend the "sunset clause" under which laws would cease to apply by at least another year, taking them beyond the likely date of the next general election, meaning the Bill would in effect never come into force. Within the civil service, officials say it is inevitable that most of the EU laws will be retained. That would be a huge relief for every worker in the country. So fingers crossed.

****

And then there is this from the Good Law Project.

'**A year on since the invasion of Ukraine by Russia, we can reveal that the Conservative Party is still receiving large donations from individuals and companies with links to Russia**. Our investigation shows that, since the start of the war in 2022, the Conservatives have accepted at least £243,000 from Russia-associated donors -including at least £61,000 into Tory coffers in 2023 alone.'

'Lubov Chernukhin, a British and Russian citizen, is married to Vladimir Chernukhin, a former deputy finance minister under Vladimir Putin and chairman of Russian state corporation VEB.RF, which has previously been sanctioned by the UK.' She has continued to donate large sums of money to the party. Since the onset of war, Mrs Chernukhin has handed £175,000 to the Tories. Overall she has donated more than £2m to the Conservative party.

'Aquind', a British cabling company controlled by Russian oil tycoon Viktor Fedotov, has donated £42,000 to the Conservative party in the past 14 months, including a £10,000 cash donation to Liam Fox MP reported in January this year.'

'Alexander Temerko, a major Tory donor and 'Aquind' director has donated a further £10,000 to the Tories during the same period. Temerko has donated over £700,000 in total.'

Well this is all over Twitter and my word we are indebted to the Good Law Project for unearthing this. Corruption and secrecy at the highest level allowed to go unchecked.

****

The international Monetary Fund forecasts UK GDP will shrink by 0.3% in 2023, worse than other G7 countries.

****

Nothing and no-one is exempt from Brexit madness.

A punk band from Germany was allegedly refused entry into the UK due to post-Brexit rule changes. The Stuttgart-based band called 'Trigger Cut' was due to play at seven UK venues this week but was refused entry into the country.

"Today we got refused at the UK border for weird reasons," the band wrote in a Facebook post. "We would have needed a special certificate of sponsorship but no one knew before, not even the venues, promoters, or the German customs authority."

"Brexit bureaucracy??? A post-Brexit nightmare."

The band, which consists of three members, also said that the whole experience "at the UK border was humiliating and sad".

Well this sort of experience means that it won't be worth any bands trying to get into the UK from the EU.

****

Then we hear this from openDemocracy.

During the pandemic loans of more than £157 million were handed out to at least 171 private schools and colleges, including, surprise, surprise, schools which had been attended by government ministers. This, I believe, is because of their charitable status.

But none of them were in financial difficulties, unlike state schools who were specifically barred from applying for any government subsidised loans at this time. As one school leader has warned "In under three years we will be bankrupt. No one is in a position to keep going for very long eating their reserves." And as budgets tighten in state schools, head-teachers have been forced to cut staff numbers and watch equipment falling into disrepair.

But we see that £5million was given to Charterhouse the old school of Chancellor Jeremy Hunt. £2million was given to Gordonstoun the King's old school.

Robert Gordon's College, old school of Michael Gove, Levelling –up Secretary, Reading Blue Coat, old school of Steve Barclay, Health Secretary and Eastbourne College, old school of Johnny Mercer, Armed ForcesMminister, all received tax-payer subsidised loans.

So who was chancellor at the time? Rishi Sunak.

And who was education secretary at the time? Gavin Williamson.

Just another example of how this government is actively downgrading our education system and has zero interest in the welfare of our children. Do they even know what state schools are?

****

But it goes on. Last month the United Nations launched the **Freshwater Challenge** which is a project that calls on all countries to commit to clear targets to restore freshwater ecosystems. Well what a brilliant project you might think and you would be right. But then ask yourself this question. Why has the UK not signed up to it?

Many conservationists have criticised the lack of commitment by the UK when other countries such as the US, Finland, the Netherlands. Canada, France and Germany have already signed up.

An RSPB spokeswoman said "The lack of support for this scheme highlights the real lack of a strategic approach from Westminster to tackle water quality and water use."

Mark Lloyd, chief executive of River Trust said "the UK is one of the most nature-depleted countries on earth and restoring our freshwater environment is the best way to turn that around."

Charles Watson, chairman of River Action said "This cowardly decision only highlights the failure of government to commit to ambitious targets to reverse the terrible ecological state of the UK's rivers, which have been so severely degraded by unmitigated sewage and agricultural pollution in recent years."

A Defra spokesman said "We were recently made aware of the 'Freshwater Challenge' and are carefully considering any potential role the UK could play in helping achieve its objective."

So yes, absolutely no rush, no idea and no action. Sums up this government perfectly.

****

And at the same time we read that a pipe dumped sewage into a Welsh river for more than 7,800 hours. In total, there were 194,900 sewage dumps from "high frequency spill overflows" in 2022, lasting a total of 1.3 million hours. Public outrage against sewage being dumped in our seas and rivers has unsurprisingly increased in recent years. The Lib-Dems have been strong critics of the government's inaction and singled out for criticism United Utilities in the Lake District, South West Water in Devon and Cornwall and Severn Trent, which supplies the Midlands and Wales.

But never fear, Therese Coffey is here. She has warned that sewage dumping in rivers could take 25 years to fix and obviously very sorry and all that but it could put water bills up by around £800 by 2049.

Two words to you Ms Coffey. (No not those!!) 'Freshwater Challenge.'

****

We are in the middle of the four day strike (April 11th-14th) by doctors in the NHS and there has been no action from the government whatsoever. Steve Barclay has refused to negotiate. The BMA have called for ACAS to get involved but as yet nothing. The NHS waiting list in England stood at a record 7.2 million people in March this year, with 2.6 million waiting longer than 18 weeks. More and more people are resorting to crowdfunding in order to pay for their treatment.

But this government is intent on privatising the NHS and we are grateful to openDemocracy for getting answers through a Freedom of Information request.

The government handed almost half a billion pounds to private healthcare companies to fix the NHS backlog last year. And now, NHS bosses in England have been given the green light to spend up to £10bn on private health companies as part of the government's plan to reduce the record number of patients waiting for care. However they are still not treating as many patients as before the pandemic.

The BMA calculates that the net cost of the pay rise for doctors by the government would be £1.03bn – a tenth of the potential spending on private healthcare companies. Even the £500m spent last year could have funded an 8% uplift in junior doctor wages for the year in question.

The biggest beneficiary of the outsourcing has been the Australian healthcare multinational 'Ramsay', which received £134m to offer non-emergency care to NHS patients between 2021 and 2022. 'Spire Healthcare', which operates 38 private hospitals formerly owned by Bupa, has been handed a further £108m over the same period. 'Circle', which is owned by 'Centene', one of the biggest US healthcare corporations, was paid £50m.

And the diagnostic centres run by 'Inhealth' at a cost to the individual or the National Health Service has had questions raised about the value of their tests.

The consumer group *Which?* has argued that some tests "are likely to cause more harm than good, some give widely inconsistent results and little useful information, and some detect disease when it's not really there." They add that "false results cause worry, more investigations, and even unnecessary treatment."

So a lot of money swishing around but none of it going to those working so hard in the NHS.

****

But I spoke too soon because this is worse. I have written in all of my books about child abuse in children's homes and yet on it goes.

The BBC have obtained confidential reports from the Hesley Group of children's homes which describe shocking treatment and abuse of children. Three homes have now been closed but Hesley still continues to run a school, and placements for adults with complex needs.

The education secretary, Gillian Keegan has repeatedly declined to be interviewed about Hesley or to comment on the excessive remuneration received by its chief executive. Hesley's latest accounts recorded a 16% profit of £12 million for all the sites it runs.

Kevin Stolz, a social worker who ran Doncaster Council's investigation team says that "lessons have not been learned. The 2010 report doesn't seem to have had any impact at all. Local authorities just continue to feed people into this system and Hesley continues to make these massive profits."

Many staff who faced allegations of physical abuse were able to leave Hesley and work with vulnerable children at different providers. The government says it is "horrified" by events at Hesley and plans to strengthen standards in children's social care. But just remind yourself of the date of that initial report. **2010.**

****

14TH APRIL 5PM:

The RCN have rejected the government's latest pay offer and announced a 48 hour strike from 8pm on Sunday 30th April to 8pm on Tuesday 2nd May. The right-wing media and the government are saying this is very disappointing and say that the BMA needs to sort out its militant members.

I say this government is responsible for this industrial action. They had nothing to say about the many, many unnecessary deaths happening **before** any strike action took place, nothing to say about the continued under-funding and under-staffing of the NHS, nothing to say about the lack of maintenance of hospital buildings, nothing to say about the disappearance of the promised 40 new hospitals, nothing to say about corridor care and they still have nothing to say now as they continue to refuse to negotiate or to bring in ACAS.

We are a country with no governing going on. There is a complete vacuum where there should be men and women of wisdom, vision, intelligence and compassion.

****

And we have a prime minister who is living in a parallel universe. He thinks that the answer to all our problems is that we need to understand basic maths. Yes you read that correctly. He feels that it is the "anti-mathsmindset" of us all that is damaging the economy.

So we are all responsible and it is nothing to do with him. Well we are used to this government blaming others for their inadequacies but this is on a completely different scale.

He is being asked how exactly he is going to accomplish his goal of every child learning maths up to the age of 18 when there are not enough maths teachers at the moment and almost half of all secondary schools rely on non-specialist teachers for maths lessons and actually many children leave school at 16. Retention and recruitment targets have not been met since 2012/2013. Schools are crumbling, teachers are buying food to feed hungry children and head-teachers are in tears as they have to sack teaching-assistants because they are out of funds.

And the School Rebuilding Programme, launched by Boris Johnson more than three years ago, and which you might have missed, and which had the aim of transforming 500 schools by 2030, has only managed to complete four. They should be doing 50 per year.

The government continues to be locked in a bitter dispute over pay as average real-term salaries fell 11% between 2010 and 2022. These statistics are from an analysis by the Institute for Fiscal Studies.

And teachers in England are about to start a new series of strikes next week on April 21st. But oh no, the government will not even consider raising their pay or even negotiating with them.

****

And then we hear about the post-code lottery with children's and young adult's mental health.

Research by the 'House' magazine which has been shared with *The Guardian*, states that a quarter of a million children in the UK with mental health problems have been denied help by the NHS as it struggles to manage surging case-loads. They also revealed that spending per child is four times higher in some parts of the country than others, whilst average waits for a first appointment vary by trust from 10 days to three years. Apparently the threshold of how ill a patient must be before seeking medical help has been raised to absolutely ridiculous levels. Even those under 18 who are seriously ill and have self-harmed or attempted suicide are being denied care because they are not "deemed ill enough."

Olly Parker, head of external affairs at 'YoungMinds,' said the FOI findings showed the "system is in total shutdown" with "no clear government plan to rescue it", after the 10-year mental health plan was scrapped.

And Dame Rachel de Souza, the children's commissioner urged the government to roll out mental health support teams in every school by the end of 2025, and for any mental health investment to target children.

So the Department of Health and Social Care says that "Support in school is vital and that's why we are increasing the number of school mental health teams to almost 400 by April 2023, providing support to 3 million children and young people." So why did you scrap the 10 year plan just three months ago?

I also say to Mr. Sunak, surely this should have far more priority than the teaching of maths. Our children need care. We have lack of affordable child-care in the early years, ghost children who are out of the school system completely, children being abused in residential homes, mentally ill children being denied treatment, children going to school hungry and being denied free school meals, and all you can say is 'give them more maths.'

****

Latest news on Dominic Raab and Rishi Sunak.

As we await the results of the bullying investigation against Raab we now hear about a legal action launched against him by ex-prisoners from Young Offenders Institutes in the 1960s to the 1980s.

A group of survivors are furious about Raab's refusal to mount a public inquiry to examine alleged claims of cover-ups and collusion.

More than 2,000 victims have come forward from just one Institute, Medomsley in County Durham. They are accusing prison guards of rape and sexual abuse, and although several men have been prosecuted, survivors say the full extent of the horrors they suffered has not been properly investigated.

Claimants argue that Mr. Raab's decision to scrap any investigation was legally "irrational" and violates obligations under human rights laws, including the freedom from torture and inhuman or degrading treatment. They are saying that there are reports that this level of abuse happened elsewhere and not just in the one centre.

Mr. Greenwood, the head of child abuse at Switalskis Solicitors, said he had been contacted by 160 people held at the former Eastwood

Park youth detention centre in Gloucestershire, but believes the true number of victims there will be more than 1,000. "A large number of men are still tormented by their memories of painful abuse in detention centres," he said.

And then we have this from the government as justice minister Damian Hinds said: "The government has the deepest sympathy for the men who suffered sexual or physical abuse while detained at Medomsley Detention Centre. A judicial review claim has been launched in regard to the government's decision not to hold a public inquiry into Medomsley. It would be inappropriate to comment further while legal proceedings are ongoing." Their usual answer to everything.

I hope you can keep up with all of this.

I am actually finding it difficult to keep up with the number of judicial reviews and investigations and legal actions against all our ministers at the moment

****

18TH APRIL

Well the maths project is not going well. Sunak has acknowledged that there are not enough maths teachers and has said it won't be instigated before the end of the year. But here we go again. The incompetence is on a world -beating level. Having left it until the last minute to obtain endorsements from people in various British industries to support this project, they only managed to recruit one person. Unfortunately they forgot to ask him whether he thought it was a good idea. His name is Stephen Fellows who is a leading film data analyst. Well he accepted the invitation from No.10 because he wanted to speak out **against** the idea of compulsory maths until 18!

He stopped maths at 16 and he said that "forcing students to study maths until the age of 18 risks stifling the passions and interests of individual students, the very qualities that education should be cultivating."

He also said that their recruitment might have been more successful if they had approached people earlier. Today is Tuesday the 18th April. He was approached last Friday.

Of course this is just distraction on the hoof politics.

I say that one in seven primary schools have no school library, rising to one in four in more socially deprived areas, and this is the big scandal at the moment.

The Primary School Library Alliance published a report on the 15th November 2022 and said that "over three-quarters of a million children in the UK do not have access to books that we know enable better educational outcomes and greater well-being." Of course a certain level of basic maths is necessary but it is just as important, if not more, so for all children to leave school with a good level of literacy.

My question to the secretary of state for education is: **Why is there not a library in every school?**

****

19TH APRIL

In a report today by Phoebe Dampare Osei of LBC we hear from Sir Michael Marmot.

Now, if, like me, you used to think that when some people said that the NHS is on the way to being dismantled and privatised, you thought that was nonsense, then I suggest you read the following very carefully. I changed my mind a while ago but still find it difficult to persuade others to follow suit.

Sir Michael Marmot is the Professor of Epidemiology and Public Health at University College London. He is currently the Director of The UCL Institute of Health Equity and he was also an advisor to the Director-General of the World Health Organisation. He was speaking on 'Tonight with Andrew Marr', and this is what he had to say:-

"If you had the hypothesis that the government was seeking to destroy the National Health Service...all the data that we're seeing are consistent with that hypothesis.

"They may say 'no, no, no, no, that's not what we're seeking to do', but if you look from 2010, waiting lists started to increase - not just the pandemic, not just the war in Ukraine - from 2010".

He explained how pre-2010 "waiting lists came down, satisfaction with the NHS was high, spending on the NHS went up at about 3.8% every year".

He contrasted it with the post-2010 drop in funding of around a "1% increase per year".

"Waiting lists started to climb and climb and climb, 150,000 vacancies for doctors and nurses, failure to pay doctors and nurses properly - it's a recipe for making the NHS fall over", he stated.

"That's why I say if you have the hypothesis that this was a sort of malicious undermining of the NHS, the data we're seeing are consistent with the hypothesis.

"I have no special insight into what motivates ministers, but they're not behaving as if they want to preserve our NHS."

He also explained how the Commonwealth Fund's regular comparisons of health care systems in 11 countries showed that "the NHS always used to be number 1, and equity of access, number 1 - the best performer".

"We're slipping down the rankings. It's a tragedy", he concluded.

It **is** a tragedy and we are sleep-walking towards a disaster of unprecedented proportions. Some of us are clear-sighted but many close their eyes and prefer not to know. And who can blame them?

****

For, on the same day, (19th April,) we hear that inflation remains above 10 percent, whilst food and drink prices rose by 19.1 percent which is the fastest annual rate since 1977. Everyone is worried that this will add to the pressure on the Bank of England to raise interest rates. Higher priced mortgages, higher food and energy costs, wages not keeping up with inflation, these are the issues at the front of everyone's minds at the moment.

****

20TH APRIL

My hero Simon Rattle has lambasted Sir Nicholas Serota, the chairman of the Arts Council England, as being clueless about the classical music world. Well yes I think we can all agree about that. He gives an interview in *The Times* today. At the end of this season he will leave his six year tenancy of the London Symphony Orchestra and will become the conductor of the Bavarian Radio Symphony Orchestra in Munich.

In his long interview with Richard Morrison he says "The BBC and Arts Council England, the two largest funders of musicians in the country seem to be operating a pincer movement against our art form."

What is so disgraceful though is that there has been no consultation and no discussion whatsoever. Whilst the musicians do understand the present economic situation and know that some people have to make the decision as to whether to buy food or heat their homes, they do want to talk. "Please talk to us" says Rattle. "At the moment it just looks like a demolition free for all."

It is interesting to note of course that the cuts to the BBC singers have been reversed possibly because they were worried about protests at the Albert Hall. And Rattle says he is worried about the future of the Proms. He fears they may be next in line for a savage cut. "You presumably know" he says "that the idea of considerably shortening the Proms season has been seriously discussed inside the BBC. Will this be the next big battle we have to fight?"

So yet another important aspect of our lives continues to be under threat by this government.

****

Also today, the BMA have contacted ACAS to be an independent arbitrator to help solve the doctor's restoration pay dilemma. The NHS is extremely concerned about the effect that any more strikes would have on patient care. The government have refused to call in ACAS. The chairman of the BMA said this morning that in the last 9 months he has not had a single face to face meeting with Steve Barclay.

****

The report of the bullying investigation into Dominic Raab has landed on the Prime Minister's desk this morning. Apparently he is studying it closely and will give his verdict later today. To sack or not to sack, that is the question.

****

Well that is still the question. We are hearing that there will be no decision today. Dither and delay. Weak and feeble. Of course if the report had exonerated him we would have heard by now.

****

21ST APRIL

Raab has resigned! Well that has saved Sunak from having to make a decision. The report has not yet been made public but Raab's resignation letter is very revealing.

To paraphrase, he says: I will go but for goodness sake the whole thing is completely ridiculous and everyone else is to blame but me.

Part of what he **actually** wrote was: "While I feel duty bound to accept the outcome of the inquiry, it dismissed all but two of the claims levelled against me. I also believe that its two adverse findings are flawed and set a dangerous precedent for the conduct of good government." He goes on to say that basically high standards need to be set which was what he was doing. "In setting the threshold for bullying so low," he goes on to say, "this inquiry has set a dangerous precedent. It will encourage spurious complaints against ministers, and have a chilling effect on those driving change on behalf of our government- and ultimately the British people." He finishes by accusing the inquiry of having been leaked to the media amongst other improprieties and hopes they will also be investigated.

Actually quite a bullying tone in the letter. But Sunak is still being accused of not making the decision to sack him yesterday.

We await the publishing of the report with interest.

****

Well it has been published late this morning and is 48 pages long so it is still being poured over.

But it does say that Raab acted in an "intimidating and "insulting" manner. He described some work as being "utterly useless" and "woeful" and complained about the absence of "basic information" from officials, whom he perceived to be resistant to his policies.

The report also looks at his conduct as Foreign Secretary and concludes that "he acted in a way which was intimidating, in the sense of unreasonably and persistently aggressive conduct in the context of a work meeting." His conduct also involved an abuse or misuse of power in a way that undermines or humiliates. He introduced an unwarranted punitive element."

Well there will be a lot more to come but that is the essence of it all.

Meanwhile this, to me, is the real scandal. The next Justice Secretary will be the tenth in ten years.

Here they are:-

Chris Grayling. 6th September 2012 - 8th May 2015

Michael Gove. 8th May 2015 – 14th July 2016

Liz Truss. 14th July 2016 – 11th June 2017

David Lidington. 11th June 2017 – 8th January 2018

David Gauke. 8th January 2018 – 24th July 2019

Robert Buckland. 24th July 2019 – 15th September 2021

Dominic Raab. 15th September 2021 – 6th September 2022

Brandon Lewis. 6th September 2022 – 25th October 2022

Dominic Raab. 25th October 2022 – 21st April 2023

One of the interesting things here is that it was Brandon Lewis who sorted out the strike of criminal barristers to everyone's agreement. Just check the length of time he was in this post.

****

The new Justice Secretary is Alex Chalk KC.

The new Deputy Prime Minister is Oliver Dowden.

****

22ND APRIL

Well Dominic Raab does not go quietly. Since his resignation letter he has given an interview for the BBC, written an article for *The Daily Telegraph* and said that it is all the fault of the passive aggression of a few civil servants who wanted to block him. In other words he displays his bullying technique very clearly.

From the Prime Minister, we haven't heard a word.

****

And the scandal with our maternity services continues. It really is unbelievable that after the Ockenden report which was published last year and which I wrote about in both of my previous books, the NHS has not geared up to overhaul every maternity service in England.

On January 14th 2022 Channel 4 News sent out a tweet which read, 'An NHS England spokesperson said the NHS "remains one of the safest places in the world to give birth," and they have invested an additional £95 million "to boost maternity workforce numbers, training and leadership development programmes."

Fine words as usual but not sufficient action.

And certainly not the safest place if you live in Shrewsbury, Morecombe Bay, East Kent and now Nottingham.

We hear today that Donna Ockenden has been asked to lead another inquiry by families in Nottingham where dozens of babies have died or been injured in their city hospitals.

Although Ms. Ockenden insists that many maternity units are doing an excellent job, she says a concerning number are failing to deliver a good level of care.

"Maternity care has too often been treated as the Cinderella service" she says.

"We weren't listened to".

She is reluctant to use the word crisis but she warns, "I think that without urgent and rapid action from central government downwards – on funding and workforce and training – mothers and their babies are not going to be able to receive safe, personalised maternity care that they deserve and should expect."

Well we know that the words 'urgent' and 'rapid' do not go together with 'Conservative government' so we do not hold our breath.

But Michelle Rhodes, chief nurse at Nottingham University Hospitals NHS Trust said "The trust are 100% committed to making the necessary and sustainable improvements that are required to provide the best possible care for women, babies and families who use our maternity services." But then she goes on to say that "Six hundred and sixty families have thus far been accepted onto (an independent review}".

660 families? I really do despair. Why is this necessary in the first place? Why have their maternity services not been offering the "best possible care" up until now? **How many babies and mothers have to die or be severely injured before action is taken?**

****

Then we hear this from Steve Barclay. Do you remember him? He is the Health Secretary presiding over the worst series of strikes in the history of the NHS. He has been notably absent for the last few weeks as he refuses to negotiate.

But look everyone. He has suddenly surfaced. Ah, maybe he is planning a meeting with the doctors and the nurses.

Well this is what he has said:

"Following a request from NHS Employers I have regretfully provided notice of my intent to pursue legal action to ask the courts to declare the Royal College of Nursing's upcoming strike action planned for 30 April to 2 May to be unlawful.

"The government firmly believes in the right to strike, but it is vital that any industrial action is lawful and I have no choice but to take action. Strike action with no national exemptions agreed, including for emergency and cancer care, will also put patient safety at risk. "This legal action also seeks to protect nurses who could otherwise be asked to take part in unlawful activity that could in turn put their professional registration at risk and would breach the requirements set out in the nursing code of conduct."

So there we have it. Instead of agreeing to sit down and talk he is about to turn nurses into criminals and is presumably going to use tax-payers money in order to do so.

Oh dear. Poor Mr. Barclay. He really doesn't want to do it. He is taking this action regretfully and he is trying to protect nurses from their own actions.

But what I want to know is, **what will happen to those nurses who are perceived to have broken the law?**

****

Oh my goodness me I think we have a Tory politician talking some sense. In an interview with *The Guardian*, Mr. James Cleverly our Foreign Secretary no less, has said that he thinks the UK should remain a signatory of the European Convention on Human Rights.

Well he needs a round of applause for saying this. Many right-wing Tories have called for us to leave the ECHR so that we can ignore their rulings on the deporting of asylum seekers.

It really is not a good idea to join up with Belarus and Russia as the only European countries outside the ECHR.

Indeed. Absolutely not.

****

And..................another bit of good news from the Tories. A senior Tory said that too much time has been spent on **Dominic Raab's Bill of Rights** already and with him gone hopefully this Bill will go too.

****

23RD APRIL

The Sunday Papers.

Well there is a lot more about the Raab debacle as you would expect. The government are talking about maybe having to politicise the civil service a bit more. You see they don't like it when anyone disagrees with them. They say that perhaps ministers should get more say as to who is appointed.

The civil servants are saying that the report on Raab was watered down a bit because the anonymity of the complainants had to be protected. And there is anger at the fact that the report was not published for two hours after Raab announced his resignation. This was a deliberate decision from Sunak and gave Raab time to commandeer the headlines.

Sunak is being criticised for weakness and it is being emphasised that this is the third minister who has been forced out of his cabinet in the first six months of his premiership.

****

So we are awaiting the results of at least three further investigations.

Sunak for the budget announcement on child care agencies and the involvement of his wife, Johnson for Partygate, and Richard Sharp for his involvement in procuring an £800,000 loan for Johnson.

There is the Covid inquiry of course but this book will be finished well before the conclusion of that.

Well there are some interesting details emerging about the Richard Sharp case. He is defying calls to resign as he says he followed correct procedure. But if you remember it was he who discussed with a distant cousin of Johnson's, Sam Blyth, who had offered Johnson financial assistance. He is denying this in spite of a Cabinet Office memo addressed to Johnson explicitly telling him "Given the imminent announcement of Richard Sharp as the new BBC chair, it is important that you no longer ask his advice about your personal financial matters." Sources are saying that the findings of the report will be "grim".

At the time of all this **Oliver Dowden** was the Culture Secretary and it was he who signed off Richard Sharp's appointment for the BBC.

And we mustn't forget that, according to the Electoral Commission, **Mr. Sharp has donated £400,000 to the Conservative Party since 2001.**

****

So where is Boris I wonder? Well it won't surprise you to know that he is on holiday again.

And where is that lovely holiday taking place? Well he is staying at his aforementioned distant cousin Sam Blyth's villa in the Dominican

Republic. This is the fourth holiday in the six months since he retired as PM and the second one in the Dominican Republic.

A report in *The Mirror* states that this villa usually costs £4,100 a night. But he has not declared any hospitality provided by Mr. Blyth, and did not do so after a previous stay as a guest of his cousin. It is understood he does not believe it is necessary because he is staying with family.

So that's OK then. So long as his constituents are OK with that.

****

Then it is back to the Home Office and to the chaos, confusion, incompetence and possible future law-breaking that is happening there.

I read a long article in *The Independent* by Lizzie Dearden. She is *The Independent's* Home Affairs Editor. She received a commendation in the crime and legal affairs category of the 2020 British Journalism Awards, for "a range of high-quality exclusive stories on huge matters of public interest".

Well this story is of huge public interest.

She writes that, '"The Home Office is facing an "exodus" of asylum caseworkers who fear being forced to act illegally under the Illegal Migration Bill.'

A case- worker, who remains anonymous, said "colleagues had raised concerns in meetings and on government message boards that plans to detain and deport asylum seekers without considering their claims would break international law.

"You cannot enforce a law if you're not willing to play by the law. You cannot strip human rights from people in a country in which we have the Human Rights Act and have signed the

Refugee Convention. Being elected doesn't give you the right to break the law."

Indeed it doesn't and our ministers would do well to remember that.

The other main problem is lack of training for them all, and the setting of impossible targets.

In December, Suella Braverman was very critical and accused asylum caseworkers of making decisions too slowly, telling a parliamentary committee: "Frankly their productivity is too low, the average decision-making rate of a decision-maker per week is one. We need to increase that considerably."

This, of course, is in accordance with the government's edict of "always blame others when it is you who is at fault."

Ms. Deardon goes on to write that 'David, (not his real name), said it was "impossible" for more than two decisions to be made a week because of the exhaustive process required. He said that when caseworkers receive a claim they must review and read all associated documents, but that material is regularly missing and hard to find because of backlogs meaning he is frequently considering applications made in 2019.

"You have to contact the person that wrote that note by the phone, e-mail, whatever." David added. "You hope that they are online and they're not on annual leave and whatnot to ask: What about this document? Where is this? Where is this thing?" Following that stage, a series of security and immigration checks are made and substantive interviews must be arranged, which can take up to eight hours each and involve translators.'

He says that the Home Office is not trying to improve the assessment rate they are just trying to stop as many asylum seekers as possible.

He goes on to accuse 'the Home Office of "inadequate" training to deal with traumatised people giving accounts of "rape, torture, imprisonment, beatings" on a regular basis.

'He said that after conducting his first interview with a female asylum seeker who had been sobbing while giving a graphic account of abuse, managers "laughed" and told him to "get used to it".

The annual attrition rate for asylum decision-makers hit 46% last year and, he says, "There's going to be a big exodus if this bill gets passed."

This is a damning article and whilst we are pretty sure that this unlawful Bill will not get passed it just shows the dangerous extent of the inadequacies of the Home Office.

****

10 days until the local elections.

24TH APRIL

There is fighting in Sudan. Hundreds of British nationals are stranded in Sudan caught between warring factions and they are complaining that they are being ignored and abandoned by the British Foreign Office. They have had no contact from anyone and have no power and limited supplies of food and water. It is now into the second week of the violence.

The interesting thing here is that all the diplomatic staff from the embassy, and their families, were evacuated extremely quickly and are safely home.

But James Cleverly our Foreign Secretary said on the radio this morning that without an end to the fighting, ministers are "severely limited in our ability to provide assistance to British nationals". In other words he said that his advice to everyone is to stay indoors until the fighting is over.

How much do we pay him for this sort of help and advice?

Then in the next breath he says that never-the-less he knows that people out there are creative and resilient and knowing the situation on the ground as they do they could find ways of getting out themselves. But of course that would be entirely at their own risk.

Gosh yes don't even think of blaming us if you get into trouble of any kind.

But we do hear from a Conservative MP, Alice Kearns, who is chair of the Foreign Affairs Select Committee and seems to have a little more grasp of the situation when she says:

"The reality is we have to get British nationals out." She acknowledges that evacuation is "enormously difficult" because there are thousands of British nationals in Sudan.

She says that even if it cannot be done because it's too dangerous, "we have a moral obligation to tell British nationals as soon as possible because they then need to make their own decisions".

And she suggests that lack of proper and regular communication with the British nationals in Sudan suggests that no lessons have been learned since evacuation efforts from Afghanistan.

Well why does that not surprise me? And if you have read this far it won't surprise you either.

****

Yesterday we all had a 'terror alert' on our phones. I say all but actually many people did not receive it.

It was at 3pm. I say 3pm but many people received it at one minute before or one minute after with some being woken at 2am by the alarm despite the fact it was supposed to arrive the day before.

It was a 10 second beep and actually you could easily have missed it. In fact many people did because they had got, or put, their phone on silence. And of course if you didn't have a smart phone you would not have got it at all.

It was a trial run so that if successful we can all be alerted to any imminent disaster.

So what do we do when we hear it?

Well if it is anything like the advice from the Foreign Office in a state of war I expect it will be 'stay indoors'.

Or maybe if it is a flood warning it could be 'look outside'. I think it would be unlikely to be an avalanche or a tsunami or an earthquake or a volcano eruption.

If a real terrorist attack, it would probably be 'hide under the bed'.

Yes. Yes I am being flippant here I know. But this is how this government makes me feel.

And, in fact, is it any wonder?

Becky Morton, political editor of the BBC, has exposed the fact that at least part of the contract for this terror alert was awarded to Fujitsu who were paid £1.6 million to work on this project. The rumours are that it was sub-contracted out to Infosys which is of course owned by the PM's father-in-law and Twitter is horrified.

Speaking to some journalists they say they can find no evidence of this.

But in a press release issued by Infosys on October 17th in 2003 they say that, **"Infosys will partner with Fujitsu in the area of middleware product development. The Infosys-Fujitsu relationship started in February 2002 and is expected to grow in the coming years. Fujitsu hopes to use Infosys' global experience and presence to roll out its products to new geographies across the globe."**

So maybe Fujitsu are no longer associated with Infosys but they have certainly been very close in the past.

But it is nevertheless scandalous that they awarded even part of the contract to Fujitsu in the first place. They were the firm who were also at the centre of the Horizon Post Office scandal which caused so much unnecessary stress to so many post office workers. This decision has been criticised as "immoral" by peers.

Conservative peer **Lord Arbuthnot**, a longstanding campaigner for the victims of the Horizon scandal, questioned why Fujitsu had been granted the contract.

"Fujitsu's Horizon system caused sub-postmasters of this country to be shamefully accused of things they had not done," he said.

Fellow Tory peer **Lord Cormack** said awarding the contract to Fujitsu was "completely wrong" and "immoral".

Labour peer **Baroness Chakrabarti** also said there were "basic decency and morality concerns" about the contract being granted while a public inquiry into the Horizon scandal was ongoing.

Meanwhile, Labour's **Lord Harris** said the involvement of Fujitsu could undermine public trust in the alert system.

Every single statement that comes out of this government needs very careful analytical probing.

****

In *The Times* today there is a very concerning and worrying article by Edward Lucas, who is a non-resident Senior Fellow at the Centre for European Policy Analysis and has a regular column in *The Times*.

He writes about a friend of his who has to remain anonymous. He describes his friend in the most glowing terms. He has written a best-selling book and "makes a comfortable living consulting and lecturing."

He is also a strong voice on social media and he has harsh criticism for the government on migration, Brexit, corruption and other issues and frankly, he sounds a guy after my own heart.

However, he was due to speak at a conference recently when he gets an email from the organisers. This is what it says and it is extremely frightening: -

"Rules introduced by the Cabinet Office in 2022 specify that the social media accounts of potential speakers must be vetted.... to check whether these people have ever criticised government officials or government policy. The vetting process is impartial and purely evidence-based. The check on your social media has identified material that criticises government officials and policy. It is for this reason ....that I am afraid that we have no choice and must cancel your invitation."

As Mr. Lucas says these rules were never debated in parliament nor publicly announced. The only way they got to hear about then was through an anonymous briefing to *The Financial Times* last summer. They quoted "friends of" the then Cabinet Office Minister Jacob Rees-Mogg. Oh yes I knew his name would be there somewhere.

Lucas's friend cannot complain publicly and if this blacklist becomes known others will refuse him and he could be professionally ruined.

Mr. Lucas says "He is one of the most insightful and admirable people I know.

This is not a political page-turner. This is Britain right now."

He ends this article with these chilling words:-

"Decision–makers who cut themselves off from the best sources of information for political reasons are unlikely to find their work improves. **That mistake spelt disaster for the communist bureaucrats of eastern Europe. It may do the same for their modern heirs in Whitehall.**"

So there we are. We are officially a police state.

****

25TH APRIL

I hope you don't live near a reservoir. A worrying report appears today which discloses serious investment failings in dams and reservoir infrastructure. The Environment Agency has been forced to reveal a serious lack of maintenance by the transparency regulator and it is written about in *The Times* by George Greenwood, Investigations reporter. Freedom of Information disclosures show that the EA has, in numerous cases, ignored engineers' orders to start repair work.

Two reservoirs have been awaiting repair work for eight years, and 18 have been waiting for at least five years, whilst 93 have been waiting for two years. It all seems to be about keeping costs low rather than securing good service. There is insufficient supervision and poor reporting of statuary inspections by reservoir engineers.

I really do not have to point out how dangerous this is. It was brought home in 2019 when there was the partial collapse of the Toddbrook reservoir near the town of Whaley Bridge in Derbyshire. 1,500 people had to be evacuated.

****

Boris again.

There is a new book out by Anthony Seldon and Raymond Newell called "Johnson at 10: The Inside Story."

The one quote to pick out is the one about the Brexit vote. He actually thought, along with most people, that the Remain vote would win. He positions himself so that whatever the outcome, he would become the next prime minister. That was the only thing that matters to him. It always was and it always would be.

"He reckoned it was win-win. 'If I come out for Brexit and we lose, I position myself as a hero Eurosceptic, from which I can win the leadership at the next contest. If we win, then I'll be clear favourite for prime minister.' "

But when he realised that the vote had gone for leave, albeit by a small margin, he went into complete and utter panic.

"What the hell is happening?" he kept saying, before it hit him: **"Oh shit, we've got no plan. We haven't thought about it. "I didn't think it would happen. Holy crap, what will we do?"**

So began the most self- destructive action ever taken in the history of these islands.

****

26TH APRIL

Well, well this rocketing inflation is all our fault. Why on earth did we not know this before? We have been told by some-one in the Bank of England, who goes by the name of Huw Pill, that for goodness sake we must all stop asking for pay increases and just get used to being poorer. He was speaking on the podcast "Beyond Unprecedented."

Oh I have just seen that Andrew Bailey the governor of the Bank of England did actually say last year that workers would need to stop asking for pay rises.

So who are these 'workers' then?

I presume all bankers, and hedge fund managers, and politicians are working very hard. So how much poorer will they be? Huw Pill who has only been at the B of E for six months has a salary of £ 88,154 and benefits of £7,029 already. Benefits? What benefits? Andrew Bailey 'earns' £597,592 with salary plus benefits.

How dare they tell the rest of us to just get used to being poorer.

We then see this.

Almost three million emergency food parcels have been handed out at food banks in the last year - with the number provided for children topping a million for the first time.

More than the entire population of Sheffield used a Trussell Trust food bank for the first time in the last year (around 760,000 people). That is a 38% rise in first-time users compared to the same period last year.

Exactly how much poorer do they want us to be?

****

27TH APRIL

James Cleverly says evacuation flights from Sudan cannot last for much longer unless there is a cease fire. British citizens have to make their own way to the airport facing heavy gun fire, unlike other countries who arranged pick up points with coaches. Security checks for the British once there could take up to ten hours. There is some controversy around the fact that some elderly relatives do not have visas and are being refused an airlift. One British cardiac surgeon who had just visited Sudan for Eid refused to leave without his 86 year old mother.

Suella Braverman says there will not be any safe and legal routes up and running any time soon for refugees from Sudan.

And now NHS doctors are being turned away at the airport in Sudan.

The Sudanese Junior Doctors Association UK has criticised the UK government for stopping NHS doctors from getting on the evacuation flights.

"They went through a dangerous journey to get to Wadi Saeedna amid a fragile ceasefire and queued for hours just to be thrown out and left with no hope to be able to return to their home and job," they tweeted.

This whole evacuation process has been a shambles.

****

BREAKING NEWS 1.15pm

The strike by nurses on Tuesday 2nd May has been declared illegal by the High Court.

Yes, if you remember, our Health Secretary, who refuses to negotiate with our nurses over their pay dispute never-the-less found time and money to take the case to court.

And yes legally speaking that is correct. A ballot result only lasts for 6 months and 2nd May is the first day of the seventh month.

So now they will have to cut their walkout short by a day.

Speaking outside the Royal Courts of Justice following the ruling, Royal College of Nursing general secretary Pat Cullen said it was the "darkest day" of the dispute so far. She said: "They (the government) have won their legal action today. But what this has led to is they have lost nursing and they've lost the public. They've taken the most trusted profession through the courts, by the least trusted people. Nurses will continue to strike on Sunday evening and again on Monday, but no strike action will happen on Tuesday 2 May."

And then we read in the paper today that our Health Secretary, Steve Barclay, denies claims that civil servants have complained about his behaviour. Hmm well his behaviour to our nurses is completely despicable. I think we can all see that.

But this treatment of the medical profession is unprecedented.

And the nurses' union, the RCN has been ordered to pay the government's legal costs of £35,000.

****

28TH APRIL

BREAKING NEWS! Richard Sharp, chairman of the BBC, resigns.

The report on his appointment is due out any minute and it was said to be damning. So another one bites the dust. Who is next I wonder?

****

The PM was at the Scottish Conservative conference when this news exploded and boy, was he worried.

He angered every journalist there as he and his minions tried to block the media and tried to silence them. Word had been sent around to say that a select few, hand-picked outlets would be allowed to speak to the Prime Minister. Other than news agency PA, these were almost exclusively papers which lean right, such as *The Express* and *The Telegraph*. *The Scotsman, The Herald, The Independent* and *The National* were all excluded.

There was a clash in the hall-way when some were pushed back but eventually they were all allowed inside. Then they were told that they could only ask one question about Richard Sharp's resignation or ask nothing at all.

Some 30 journalists in the room put the offer to a ballot, and not one voted to accept it.

Eventually, Tory press officers said that Sunak would be doing one question to one broadcast camera on the topic of former BBC chair Richard Sharp. Everyone would have to share that and be happy.

Well happy they certainly weren't. They were furious with Sunak's attempt to evade the press and decided that this was clearly the top story.

A spokesperson from the Scottish Parliamentary Journalists' Association said: "Journalists expect to be able to hold the Prime Minister to account when he is in Scotland as a vital part of the democratic process. Today's actions to restrict access are unprecedented and undermine that important principle."

What is he frightened of? He does not dare to come out to face the public or the media because he is not up to the job.

****

He likes being secretive our Prime Minister.

Sophie Huskisson, political editor of *The Mirror*, writes in an article today about a "culture of concealment" at the Treasury when he was Chancellor. Labour said the now PM had tried to "cover up the evidence of his incompetent management of the economy and his flagrant waste of public money" during the pandemic.

Research shows that the number of Freedom of Information requests it responded to dropped to the worst level in Whitehall during his time there.

"Over Mr. Sunak's tenure, the Treasury granted just 21% of all FOI requests in full in 2021 and just 17% in 2022 - a drop from 36% in 2019 before he was Chancellor."

There is an internal review going on at the moment because the Treasury has fully withheld information asked for by Angela Rayner last July when she asked for details of questions used in focus groups and polls that cost the taxpayer £287,280.

They really should know not to mess with Angela.

Well it has not been 'Dishy Rishi' for a long time and now it seems to be 'Fishy Rishi'. It honestly looks to me as though we are seeing the dying embers of this Conservative Party. They really are a shambolic mess for which we are all paying the price. I know I do keep saying this but one day it must be true.

****

Oh my word we are now hearing that Sunak has flown from Glasgow to Cardiff for the Welsh Tory conference and is refusing to take any questions from journalists there.

****

29TH APRIL

Teachers were on strike yesterday and I have just seen something which I have never seen before. All four teaching unions have just given a news conference televised by the BBC to announce that they are getting together to initiate coordinated strike action. This is unprecedented. The four union heads were serious, articulate and absolutely scathing about this government. They have not yet formulated the details of any industrial action but are giving the government a window of opportunity to get round the table and talk. They are wanting it to be possible for them to be able to call off any strikes this autumn.

As they say though, the government are in a parallel universe. Gillian Keegan, Education Secretary needs to speak to them or face the consequences. They have asked for ACAS to come and mediate but the government refuses to do so. So all four teaching unions are in formal dispute with the government. The ball is in the government's court. If they continue to do nothing and ignore the cries for help then between 300,000 and 400,000 teachers will be on strike next term.

****

SUNDAY 30TH APRIL

I have written about the asylum seekers and the way they are treated by the Home Office so often, but today we hear about more incompetence, more under-funding and more under-resourcing that has led directly to the deaths by drowning of at least 27 people in the Channel.

This information is taken from a report in *The Observer* by Aaron Walawalkar, Eleanor Rose, and Mark Townsend.

International maritime law dictates that States take initial responsibility for any incident reported to them even if it is not in their waters. They take control until it can be handed over to the country concerned. Well this is a good law and I am surprised it even needs saying. I would have thought that this would be the obvious and humane thing to do. Nevertheless it is enshrined in law. Under a 1979 convention all States are responsible for the search and rescue of vessels in distress, regardless of who they are or why they are there.

But there appears to have been many instances of emergency calls to the police who have passed them onto the local Coastguards who have not taken action.

On the 3rd November 2021 there was a distress call but no action was taken for more than three hours when eventually a mission coordinator concluded the incident was happening in French waters. But there is no evidence in the logs obtained under the FOI requests that the UK operators ever tried to contact the French.

It was just three weeks later that a dinghy sank in the same stretch of water killing at least 27 people, which was the worst tragedy in the Channel for decades. Records disclosed to French lawyers show that calls for assistance had been made to both countries. No help arrived.

Documents obtained by *The Observer* and 'Liberty Investigates' suggest that 440 people were left to their fates on four separate days. And an internal data base, cross checked with ship-tracking data and analysed by experts, say that HM Coastguard "effectively ignored" at least 14 more boats carrying 328 people on 11th, 16th and 20th November.

But what we are also seeing is the unsatisfactory state of the coastguards as records show that coastguard staff were "overwhelmed" as the numbers of operators on shift in the Dover control room fell below internal targets.

A former coastguard said that Junior officers tackle record numbers of distress calls with "very little apparent leadership and direction."

It's the same story everywhere you turn. And of course if we had safe and legal routes for all asylum seekers none of this would be happening.

****

The vultures are now circling closer and closer to that other inadequate MP, Boris Johnson. The resignation of **Richard Sharp** has re-ignited the interest in the £800,000 loan. Who actually gave it to him? What was it for? Where did it go?

I think he has said it was from a British bank. And that actually he won't comment further on what is a private matter.

I beg your pardon. You might have forgotten but we certainly haven't. You were actually the Prime Minister at the time mate. But good to know it was a **British** bank. As opposed to what exactly?

****

So we finish the month of April with more Brexit statistics.

The Office for National Statistics states that there are currently 142,000 unfilled jobs in the accommodation and food services sector.

This represents a 6.5 % job vacancy rate, which is almost 50 per cent above pre-Brexit levels, and is the highest rate across all of the UK's business sectors.

Almost 4.600 pubs, clubs, hotels and restaurants have closed in the year to 31st March 2023. Many owners have cited persistent staff shortages since leaving the EU as the main reason they had to close.

Lord Heseltine, the former Deputy Prime Minister who campaigned for the UK to remain in the EU, said "The quicker Britain wakes up to the interdependence of this country with Europe and finds a way of accessing the single market again, the better our economy will be."

Oh my goodness, I say Amen to that and so do well over 60% of the British people today. What a note on which to end the month of April. The month which starts with a fool's day but seems to have persisted throughout the month this year. We had the jumble of January, the futility of February and the madness of March, so I wonder what May will bring.

Well, hold on to your hats, fasten your seat belts; we will soon find out.

****

THE MERRY MONTH OF MAY

1ST MAY

Well the first stories continue with the sheer nastiness, the lies and the avarice of this Conservative party.

Liz Truss is facing a bill of £12,000 for expenses incurred whilst entertaining at Chevening House as Foreign Secretary. Apparently bath robes each costing £120 are missing plus slippers, but she is also accused of not paying for personal entertaining.

A source told *The Daily Mail* that 'Ms Truss used the residence as a "mini-No 10", holding meetings with her inner circle which often turned into parties in the evening.'

Well we know how much Tory MPs like their parties.

She is disputing these costs but has said she will pay up.

****

Ministers are really worried.

Are they worried about the NHS and the strikes today by nurses, or the fact that the UK economy will shrink and perform worse than other advanced economies, including Russia, or the fact that more than one million children in the UK are now growing up in poverty due to the two-child benefit system, or the fact that more than 1,500 police officers have been accused of violent offences against women and girls over a period of six months, and less than 1% have been sacked?

Er no. They are very concerned that their Illegal Migration Bill will be blocked or significantly watered down by the House of Lords.

Gosh they do not like that. So what to do? Well what any Tory MP will do when thwarted which is to dredge up an old law which has only ever been used seven times before. **This is the Parliament Act which could literally force this bill on to the statute book.**

****

But this is really frightening.

National Conservatism. Remember these two words and be very afraid.

There is a long article in *The Guardian* today by John Harris, a political columnist, and it makes very disturbing reading.

He talks about this new Conservative group called **National Conservatism.**

So what does this group stand for? Well it wants "a world (a world?) of independent nations", centred on the traditional family. In other words a man and a woman together for ever with no sex outside marriage and absolutely no homosexual partnerships. Plus a hugely more important role for Christianity ("which should be honoured by the state and other institutions both public and private").

Well I say good luck with all of that. They really are on another planet.

But they also have views on what constitutes national communities. They say they are not racist which in my experience nearly always predicates a racist view. Its main advocates claim that modern immigration "has become a source of weakness and instability", and that countries may need to go as far as imposing complete moratoriums.

Does this all sound a long way from the UK? Well John Harris states that "the intersection between national conservatism and the Tory mainstream is actually well advanced..... It is a mixture of authoritarianism, nostalgia and an insistence that immigration somehow threatens to corrode countries' very idea of themselves."

Indeed Robert Jenrick, recently said Conservatives, "should not shy away from their belief that the nation has a right to preserve itself", nor from the insistence that "excessive, uncontrolled migration threatens to cannibalise the compassion of the British public". This is unbelievable rhetoric until you realise that he is a Conservative Immigration Minister.

Then of course there is no show without Braverman stepping in who says the attitudes and behaviour of those crossing the Channel are "at odds" with British values. What? Quite apart from the fact that she herself is an immigrant, there are doctors, nurses, lawyers, plumbers, electricians, farm workers, hospitality workers and builders fleeing war and trauma and desperate to work in this country.

I say we need more immigration not less.

In a fortnight's time, there is going to be a two-day political conference of National Conservatism happening in central London and guess who is going to be there. Yes, the Home Secretary, Suella Braverman, her cabinet colleague Michael Gove, and a host of voices from the right wing media outlets such as the *Daily Telegraph* and GB News.

Jacob Rees-Mogg and David Frost (a leading Brexiteer) are also very happy to be seen to be associated with this lot.

John Harris writes that, "thirteen years of Conservative government have created no end of insecurity, poverty and powerlessness – but those things have also sown exactly the kind of resentments that national conservatism trades on."

I find this very chilling but it is actually just an extension of what has happened to the present so-called Conservative government.

****

2ND MAY

Teachers strike today.

And at a meeting between the government and 14 health unions representing all NHS staff apart from doctors and dentists a pay deal was signed off. It is for a 5 % pay deal and a one off payment of at least £1,655. Ministers said it was time to bring the strikes to an end - but three unions are threatening to continue action. However, only one - Unite - currently has a strike mandate and that is for local strikes in some ambulance services and a few hospitals. But the RCN said it would be balloting members to see whether strikes will continue.

It is being questioned as to why this was not offered 6 months ago. Anyone would think there was an election coming up shortly. And it is not clear where the extra money is coming from.

****

3RD MAY

So three days before the coronation we hear that the Public Order Bill has been given Royal Assent.

Well this is interesting because democracy campaigners had expected the new laws to be finalised on June 15 and were surprised that they had been brought forward. I wonder............could it possibly have anything to do with the coronation and the fact that republicans are planning to hold up banners saying "Not My King"?

You do need to know about this draconian bill because it is saying that the police can arrest you if they even think that you look suspicious. It follows hard on the heels of the **Police, Crime, Sentencing and Courts Act 2022**. As Amnesty International says, they have 'long held the view that police already have sufficient powers to manage protest safely and to prevent violence or other serious criminal activity. These measures are neither proportionate nor necessary and place the UK government in breach of its international obligations.

Existing international human rights standards require governments not to introduce any measures that place undue restrictions on people's freedom of expression and assembly. Under international standards, it is accepted that protest by its very nature can be disruptive, and governments should not introduce laws that create a "chilling effect" on people's ability to exercise those rights.'

In fact the campaign group 'Republic' and others have been sent "intimidatory letters" from the Home Office's Police Power Unit to say that new laws could be used to stop "disruption at major sporting and cultural events".

It is all very confusing and completely unnecessary and Tory MP Tom Tugendhat could not say whether banner holding would be permitted or not on Saturday when asked the question on the 'Today' programme this morning.

Ahh, we have just heard this afternoon from the Deputy Assistant Commissioner of the Met, Ade Adelekan say at a press conference that, "Protest is lawful". Officers would not intervene over someone merely "holding a placard" in London.

However he goes on to say that "If at any point any protest, either during the coronation or afterwards, moves from being a protest that is lawful into criminal intent then you will see extremely swift action from us."

So I hope that has cleared that up for everyone. But I am sure that Suella Braverman will be watching very closely.

****

4TH MAY LOCAL ELECTION DAY

Well we are hearing some very disturbing cases of people being turned away from the polling booths because they haven't got the correct documents. This ID law has been rushed in at great expense to the tax payer by the Tories in an effort to address a problem which wasn't there. As someone said on Twitter more Conservative MPs have been accused of sexual assault than people being accused of electoral fraud.

I think the Tories thought that the elderly would definitely have the correct ID and are more likely than the young to vote Tory. And many young people actually do not possess a passport or driving license. But it seems to be backfiring as many elderly people are in tears because they have been told that they do not have the correct documents. Anger too from immunosuppressant people who were told to remove their masks.

An Electoral Commission spokesman said: "We already know from our research that the ID requirement posed a greater challenge for some groups in society, and that some people were regrettably unable to vote today as a result. It will be essential to understand the extent of this impact, and the reasons behind it, before a final view can be taken on how the policy has worked in practice and what can be learned for future elections."

Many democratic groups have called it a "dark day for democracy."

One person turned away because of this rule is one person too many. It is being referred to as voter suppression.

So we wait to see what tomorrow brings when we discover what the general population thinks about everything.

This is our one chance to shout and be heard.

****

5TH MAY

Conservatives said it would be a bad day if they were to lose 1,000 seats. This was seen as expectation management because then of they lost say 300 seats they could say well there you go, not nearly as bad as expected.

Well they lost over 1,000 seats. So it was worse than the worst case scenario.

There was a lot of tactical voting so Lib Dems did well as well as Labour.

It certainly looks as though Labour is on course to win the next general election.

Many Conservative MPs are looking extremely worried.

They can talk all they like about how well they are doing and Sunak says he doesn't see a real movement towards Labour but the people have spoken loud and clear through the ballot box.

So many Tory bastions lost overall control including Hertsmere where Oliver Dowdon is MP. Also Windsor and Maidenhead of Theresa May. Then the so-called 'red-wall' is collapsing as they wait for their 'levelling –up' which has never happened.

Many areas which voted for Brexit and the Tories are still waiting for all of that money we were due to get back for the NHS and so they have drifted back to Labour.

Sir Keir is jubilant but not complacent. And we are all cautiously optimistic.

Rishi Sunak? Well the **Conservative Democratic Organisation** (CDO) is ramping up pressure on the PM following these dismal results. This is yet another Conservative think tank. Johnson-supporter Lord Peter Cruddas will hold a conference for this grassroots campaign in

Bournemouth on May 13.

So Sunak has that to look forward to as well as the NatCon one from the 15th -17th May.

But tomorrow the focus is on the coronation of King Charles III.

****

CORONATION DAY 6TH MAY

There is loads of coverage in the press of course so I don't need to write much here.

It was a damp day, as we were expecting, but that never deters crowds in the UK.

Some members of the Republic group were arrested under the new laws which I and others found disturbing. Yesterday I heard an interview with their leader, Graham Smith, who said that he had been talking to the police for four months telling them what they were planning and where they would be and they were told that there would be no arrests so long as they just held up banners. Well maybe they were threatening to do more than that and obviously possibly infringing on other people's enjoyment but I was shocked to hear of 6 arrests before they had done anything and that the banners were removed as soon as they were unloaded from a van. Was this due to the new Public Order Bill?

Well yes it was. The Met detained them for 16 hours and then released them with no charge. They say that luggage straps which were going to be used to hold up the banners could have been used to 'lock on' which is something that the new bill says is now against the law. Well the Met have apologised to Graham Smith and have expressed 'regret' over the arrests. Mr. Smith is not accepting this apology and is taking legal action and calling for an inquiry.

This is what happens of course, when new laws are rushed through without due diligence.

The coronation all went superbly though with the service full of the most magnificent music. Wonderful orchestra, wonderful singing, both solo and choral and as the conductor Sir John Gardiner said, at last we have a beacon of light in the King who is a massive supporter of the arts. Sir John was interviewed by the BBC when he slated the BBC for its cuts to its orchestras and singers. Well done that man.

'Zadok the Priest' was the highlight for me. As someone said, if your heart doesn't swell with emotion when you hear that magnificent music you are either an algorithm or a robot.

Of course we hear a lot from antimonarchists about an unelected head of state but I worry about what we would replace it with because we are not doing too well with those we elect at the moment. In fact we have a prime minister who was not elected directly by many of us; who is twice as wealthy as the King if you just compare it with Charles's personal wealth, and who has no interest in the environment or the arts, unlike King Charles.

In fact Charles has done more for the arts and music, for highlighting the natural world and the planet and for helping the vulnerable through the big volunteering day in just three days than the government has done in 13 years.

The monarchy also demonstrates the value of soft power. I cannot think of any other head of state who could command such interest in all corners of the world as the British monarchy. I think the only country not represented at the coronation today was Russia.

The crowd stretched as far as the eye could see down the Mall when they all surged forwards for the balcony appearance and in spite of the weather we got the Red Arrows.

Yes I am a bit conflicted about the rights and wrongs of a monarchy but I just say be careful what you wish for.

****

MONDAY 8TH MAY

So after a brilliant concert at Windsor Castle last night and a big 'Help Out' day today the coronation celebrations are almost at an end. What a shame we can't say that about the government's crazy announcements because we hear today that they have got an interesting idea about pharmacies. Over 160 pharmacies have closed over the last two years but nevertheless the government is announcing a new primary care plan which will include an expanded role for pharmacists. Hmm, not sure how that is going to work.

Sanjeev Panesar, who owns Pan Pharmacy in Birmingham, told the BBC that he fears services might have to be cut back and staff numbers may have to be reviewed. He has said the situation faced by pharmacists are in "serious jeopardy" and the business has had its "worst ever" year. He has invited the PM to come and see his pharmacy for himself. He wants him to see first-hand the pressures faced by staff to meet the demands. He says that "the sector is crumbling, and is going to fall down like a stack of dominoes, if there's no intervention urgently."

Community pharmacies in England are in the middle of a damaging five-year funding freeze, under their national contract with the NHS but nevertheless we now hear that Stephen Barclay our Health Secretary and our Prime Minister have found some money. £645 million over two years to be precise. Well doctors and nurses must be excited about that.

Oh wait a minute. This is just part of a new primary care plan from the Prime Minister to reduce the pressure on GPs. Receptionists are now to be called 'care navigators' as they will decide whether you need to see a GP or a pharmacist. No longer will you be stuck on hold listening to music when you phone at 8 am on a Monday morning apparently and if they decide you do need to see a GP you will be fast–tracked for an appointment.

It all sounds very dangerous to me and on Radio 4 this morning Neil O'Brien, who is Parliamentary Under-Secretary of State for Primary Care and Public Health, was asked what do you do about back-ache. You might be told to self-refer to a physio but it might be something very serious such as cancer. It could be missed.

He kept dodging the question and all we could hear through his convoluted spiel was the poor interviewer saying 'back-ache?' 'back-ache?'

And it hasn't gone down well with others either.

Shadow health secretary Wes Streeting said: "Expecting the Conservatives to fix this is like expecting an arsonist to put out the fire they started."

The King's Fund health think tank warned some pharmacies will not be able to offer the services because they may not have access to diagnostic tools, or sufficient staff and consultation rooms. Senior fellow Beccy Baird said that "not all pharmacies will be able to offer these services and it will be really frustrating for patients to be bumped from pillar to post, only to end up back at the GP".

Lib Dem Health spokeswoman Daisy Cooper added: "Accessing faster care is critical for patients but ministers just don't seem to grasp the scale of the problem. Without a serious plan to recruit the pharmacists and GPs that our NHS needs, this could be yet another Conservative health pledge not worth the paper it's written on."

And yes that is the problem isn't it?

According to the Health Foundation, GP shortages now top 4,200 and will double to 8,800 by 2031. To put it even more succinctly Mr. Sunak and Mr. Barclay:-

THERE ARE NOT ENOUGH GPs.

What part of that sentence don't you understand?

****

Oh wait a minute here are two solutions from the government which they say will solve all of their problems.

1. The first one is they are going to send SAS hospital doctors into to GP surgeries.

2. The second one is that they are going to allow students to start working on wards after their A-levels, while being trained to become doctors and nurses. There will be no need to go to university.

I do not need to say any more. I leave you to analyse those options and maybe give them a score from 1 to 10. A minus score is acceptable.

****

10TH MAY

But let us not forget Boris.

We are still waiting for the results of the Partygate investigation and it would appear that we are still paying for it all as well.

We, the tax-payers, are being billed up to £245,000 to cover the cost of his lawyers.

The bill for his defence team increased this week for a second time. According to the BBC, the Treasury did not sign off the decision to use public money to pay the bill. Ministers and civil servants are expected to follow Treasury guidance when making decisions about spending public money. He is earning shed loads of money from his speaking engagements but he never wants to spend it himself and of course he will never follow guidance from places such as the Treasury because he considers himself to be above the law.

And where is Boris Johnson? I know you are asking. Well he's just been giving a speech in Seoul. That **is** a long way from his constituency.

And he has just bought a £3.8 million, nine bedroom, Grade II listed mansion with a three sided moat in the Cotswolds, paying in cash. Hmm then, remind me. Why are we still paying his legal fees?

****

11TH MAY

The Bank of England has raised interest rates to 4.5% from 4.25% - the highest level since 2008. The rise comes amid soaring inflation, which is currently at 10.1%

****

But this is very disturbing and well done to Rebecca Thomas, health correspondent of *The Independent*. **Apparently children's waiting lists for outpatient care and inpatient surgery are "increasing at double the rate of adults."** Leaked documents show that the backlog has hit 400,000 for the first time. So we are back to this government's total disregard for the health of our children. Young people have been "deprioritised" in order to cut adult lists. One NHS leader warned the long waits were likely to affect some children's "ability to lead full and active lives" and will worsen existing inequalities between adult and children's care.

The leaked documents show that :-

70% more adults were seen for scans and diagnostic tests in 2022 compared to children.

The rate of children's surgery is 15% lower compared to adults in the worst performing area – the east of England.

Between September 2021 and March 2022, the number of children waiting more than 78 weeks for hospital care increased by 43% compared to 21% for adults.

Ronny Cheung, officer for health services at the Royal College of Paediatrics said that, "fundamentally we need urgent action and investment from the government to help close these gaps between adult and children's services."

I do not know why this is not front page news. It is despicable.

This government is not fit to govern.

****

Here we go again! A headline in *The Express*.

"Rebel Tory MPs plotting to overthrow Sunak with no confidence vote after Brexit U-turn"

Can we believe this? Well yes sadly we can. They do not like the U-turn which is watering down the EU Retained Law Bill. Kemi Badenoch was forcefully told off by the Speaker today in parliament which is unheard of. I have never heard him so cross as he reprimanded her for announcing this in *The Telegraph* before the Commons. When she said she was sorry he didn't like it, he exploded again and nearly expelled her there and then. "Who do you think you are talking to?" he said.

Anyway she kept saying that "I have decided" about the scrapping of the bonfire of EU laws which annoyed MPs even more. One MP said: "There is no way this could not have happened without the blessing of the Prime Minister. In the end the buck stops with him."

But Downing St is distancing itself from this decision and trying to put all the blame on to Ms. Badenoch. But of course. When does it take the blame for anything?

Well I don't think we are quite at the letters stage yet but there is anger, division, confusion and the ongoing chaos and incompetence at the heart of government.

****

14TH MAY

People are still looking for those **40 new hospitals** promised by Johnson 4 years ago.

So many hospitals are in disrepair to a dangerous level with lifts not working and wards being shut due to severe flooding and sinking foundations.

30 projects have yet to receive planning permission and the original estimated cost has doubled to £32billion due to delays and inflation, incompetence and neglect. Some hospital buildings pre-date the NHS itself. But we knew this wouldn't happen from the very first moment we heard Johnson announcing it in the cabinet room with the cabinet behind him. It was like a pantomime act. "How many hospitals?" he asked. "40" they all shouted. It looked stupid then. And of course some will not be new hospitals at all just a new wing. But actually competent repairs and general maintenance would be a good start.

****

And as people registered with the Winton Health Centre in Bournemouth are told they will have to register with another surgery as they are closing at the end of July we also hear that a survey by the Royal College of General Practitioners showed that more than **470 GP surgeries have closed across England, within the last decade** - with 39% of GPs "seriously considering leaving the profession" within five years.

****

Hospital consultants are balloting for strike action for the first time in their history. And our Deputy Prime Minister said in PMQs that the NHS is in good hands. .

****

18TH MAY

Then some good news as we hear that Sunak's plan to persuade fellow leaders to change European Court of Human Rights rules blocking Rwanda deportation flights was dealt a blow as summit leaders dismissed the idea of reform. Hooray.

Iceland's foreign minister, Thordis Gylfadottir, said that this week's Council of Europe summit in Reykjavik would not be used to reform the rules covering the kind of orders that prevented the first deportation flight from taking off last year.

It is complete madness to even think that this could be done or even is a good idea.

****

Talking about specific MPs there is always the name **Suella Braverman** of course.

She is a qualified barrister and has been accused of breaching the Bar Standards Board's code of conduct. Nine organisations including the 'Society of Asian Lawyers', the 'Association of Muslim Lawyers' and the 'Joint Council for the Welfare of Immigrants' have written to the Bar Standards Board urging it to investigate and take action against what they claim is racist and inflammatory language used by Suella Braverman about British men of Pakistani heritage and asylum seekers. "These comments are not only highly inaccurate and offensive, but they also perpetuate harmful stereotypes and contribute to a climate of hate and prejudice," the complaint letter states.

The letter cites three specific Bar Council code of conduct rules it claims have been breached, including behaving in a way which is likely to diminish trust and confidence, conduct which the public may reasonably perceive as undermining honesty, integrity or independence, and a breach of the instruction not to discriminate against any other person on the grounds of race, colour, ethnic or national origin or other grounds.

Although not a practising as a barrister she is still bound by their code of practice.

****

16TH MAY

Today Sunak had a meeting with farmers, food producers and some of Britain's largest supermarkets and called it a 'Downing Street Food Summit' and a 'From Farm to Fork' Summit.

But it seems that he might just as well not have bothered.

Those attending said it amounted to no more than a PR stunt and it completely failed to tackle key issues. One representative of a trade body that attended the summit described it as an "empty meeting" with no action on price or inflation discussed. "It was there for the Tories to show they are supporting farmers," they said

The summit had been expected to tackle topics such as food price inflation, fairness within the supply chain and helping farmers to invest in domestic production, but there was no subsequent announcement on those issues.

But, "if you are not doing something about the cost of living, cost of production, access to labour and affordability of food then you are never going to fix the overall problem," the attender said.

And ministers offered no commitments in response to a call by the National Farmers' Union to stop Britain's self-sufficiency in food slipping below its current level of 60%.

So, like everything else at the moment, it would appear to be just a lot of hot air with no action.

****

17TH MAY

The two conferences connected to the Tory Party have come to an end and my blood runs cold.

The **Conservative Democratic Organisation** met in Bournemouth on the 13th. Priti Patel was there as so was Jacob Rees-Mogg and Nadine Dorrries. They all insisted it was not a 'Bring Back Boris' campaign and actually Johnson did not attend. But it was certainly a 'Watch Your Back Rishi' event. But Rees-Mogg said that the party would "be toast" if it tried to change leaders again. "It would make us look ridiculous," he said.

Hmm, I think the ship has already sailed on that one mate.

Priti Patel obviously didn't know whether she was coming or going because in her speech, which she read out, she said "Socialism is trying to force Britain back into the UK." No I have no idea what that means either. We presume she meant the EU but that is not what she said.

But she received a standing ovation as she warned the party was in decline – and called on those present to defend Johnson's 2019 manifesto, which she warned was being torn up by the current leader.

So it was all about how good things were under Boris and completely re-enforces how out of touch they all are.

But this is nothing compared with the **Nationalist Conservatism** conference in Westminster over the following three days. It is being called NatCon for short or even just Nat-C. You will understand the significance of that one when you have read the following and if you say it out loud.

Suella Braverman, Michael Gove, Jacob Rees-Mogg, Lee Anderson, Douglas Murray and David Starky were some of the key speakers which should give you a clue.

Left wing media outlets were banned from the event although openDemocracy managed to sneak in.

It was all about nationalism obviously. **Suella Braverman** said in her speech that we need to train up our own workers such as HGV truck drivers, butchers and fruit pickers rather than relying on foreign workers. Otherwise she said "**Britons will forget how to work.**"

She continued: "The unexamined drive towards multiculturalism as an end in itself, combined with identity politics, is a recipe for communal disaster. Brexit enables us to build a high-skilled, high wage economy that is less dependent on low-skilled foreign labour."

Then we have **David Starkey** who says "Movements like critical race theory and 'Black Lives Matter' are not what they pretend to be. They are attempts at destroying the entire legitimacy of the Western political and cultural tradition." There was wild applause for this.

Douglas Murray said "There was nothing wrong with nationalism in Britain. It's just that there was something wrong with nationalism in Germany. **I don't see why no one should be allowed to love their country because the Germans mucked up twice in a century.**"

I am trying not to comment on all of this because they speak for themselves but this is the most disgusting sentence in this book.

Then Jacob Rees-Mogg said "Parties that try and gerrymander end up finding their clever scheme comes back to bite them, as dare I say we found by insisting on voter ID for elections. We found the people who didn't have ID were elderly and they by and large voted Conservative, so we made it hard for our own voters and we upset a system that worked perfectly well."

And it has just been reported that nearly 10,000 voters were unable to vote because they didn't have their correct ID.

But leaving the conference for a fraction of a second just to illustrate the bizarre things he says this is what he said on Sky News' 'Sophy Ridge On Sunday' programme about what had been the main benefits of leaving the EU.

"We were able to show global leadership over Ukraine. Putin would probably have invaded Ukraine successfully if the UK had been bound in by the requirement of sincere cooperation and had had to follow a Franco-German line in dealing with Russia, which is what we did in 2014."

Then we have an ex-headmistress speaking at the conference. **Her name is Katherine Burbalsing and calls herself the strictest head-teacher in Britain.** She has urged Tory parents to take their children out of schools if they are "too woke". "If we don't get on top of the culture that these schools are propagating, we will lose our country," she said.

It is all about controlling our borders and keeping our country free of foreigners.

And when she was a head-teacher she used to isolate children who were unable to pay for their meals. They had to sit in detention with some fruit to eat until the debts had been paid off by their parents. I have just watched her speech. She needs to be avoided at all costs.

Then women were told to have more babies and that it is basically better to stay at home to look after them. Oh I thought we had to go out and pick fruit.

But yes, MP Danny Kruger, said that heteronormative families should be "at the heart of our fiscal system. The normative family, the mother and father sticking together for the sake of the children, is the basis for a safe and functional society. Marriage is not only about you, it's a public act to live for the sake of someone else." Single parent? Single from choice? Childless? Divorced? Homosexual? Sorry you should all be cast out into the wilderness. National Conservatism does not want you.

These people are very frightening. They don't just make my blood run cold they chill me to the bone.

Read these words which we think were said by Churchill although not absolutely sure. But be very afraid:-

"There will come a time when Fascism would take over this great nation of ours and destroy the peaceful and economic ties we enjoy with our neighbours in Europe. They will come with their silver tongues and promising the earth. Be extremely vigilant."

They are already here.

****

18TH MAY

Brexit raises its ugly head once more as we hear that one of the world's biggest carmakers has warned it may have to close UK factories if the government does not renegotiate the Brexit deal.

Stellantis, which owns Vauxhall, Peugeot, Citroen and Fiat, had committed to making electric cars in the UK, but says that is under threat. It warned it could face tariffs of 10% on exports to the EU due to rules on where parts are sourced from.

The stance has been supported by Jaguar Land Rover, Britain's largest car manufacturer, which branded the Brexit deal "unrealistic and counterproductive" for the electric vehicle industry and demanded it be changed.

It is the first time a car firm has openly called for a renegotiation of the terms of the Brexit trade deal, and the BBC understands all major manufacturers in the UK have raised similar concerns with government.

Stellantis warned the current rules meant manufacturers could relocate abroad, pointing to BMW's decision to make its new electric Mini in **Germany** and Honda's closure of its plant in Swindon.

Earlier this week, French President Emmanuel Macron hosted Tesla's Elon Musk, who hinted he might invest in a battery plant - or gigafactory - **in France**.

Meanwhile, the Spanish government is currently trying to woo the UK's biggest car manufacturer, Jaguar Land Rover, into building a gigafactory **in Spain**.

With the rules due to tighten again in 2027 experts believe UK exporters will find it impossible to sell cars overseas tariff free unless they can source batteries domestically. And 90,000 jobs could be lost.

Well Mr. Sunak I have to say that we told you so. Sadly you and your mates are blind to reality.

****

Oh wait a minute everyone. Our Chancellor, Jeremy Hunt, has just found £500 million down the back of his sofa to give to Jaguar-Land Rover to keep the factory in the UK. He didn't even have to think twice. Strange that there is no money where that has come from to give to teachers or doctors or nurses.

****

19TH MAY

Oh my word I cannot believe this, except that after writing about this government nearly every day since July 2019 of course, sadly, I can.

The National Symphony of Ukraine is due to come to Britain this autumn to tour 17 different venues. But....... they have to have visas. In order to get visas all 90 of them will have to travel from Kyiv to Warsaw and then back to Kyiv. But........this is a war zone. It is a 12 hour journey each way. Surely the answer is to waive the need for a visa completely. Our culture secretary said at the Eurovision song contest last week that we will "be assisting the National Symphony Orchestra of Ukraine to share their music as they tour the UK this year". Not if they can't get here because of your incompetence you won't.

As Richard Morrison writes so accurately in *The Times* today the words of Lucy Frazer "suggest she either doesn't have a clue what's going on or is being flagrantly hypocritical."

He goes on to say that, "Neither is a sacking offence in this particular government, I know but it's not a good look either."

****

Then it is back to the way this government treats our children and my burning sense of anger that makes this book slightly longer than anticipated.

I have just discovered a new charity called 'Children Heard and Seen' which was set up in 2014, by Sarah Burrows, for children who are left on their own when their parents go to prison.

What? How is it that I haven't heard of this before or even thought about this problem? I, who have been a member of the Howard League for Penal Reform for 30 years. I am ashamed of myself.

Sarah Burrows says "this is the 21st century, how is it possible that there are children living alone?"

The answer is because there is no statutory duty for any government body – whether it's the care system, the criminal justice system or the Department for Education – to identify or support children impacted by parental imprisonment. Absolutely no-one in any official capacity, appears to care.

Ms. Burrows says that when she set up CHAS, she was struck by the "shame, stigma, isolation and loneliness" that children were dealing with. Some were bullied at school, others faced violent attacks on their home. One story that particular resonated was that of a five-year-old boy who was the only one not invited to a classmate's birthday.

Often, Ms. Burrows discovered, parents failed to inform social services that there was a child at home after their arrests for fear of losing their child altogether.

Her attention was drawn to the following cases.

One was a 15-year-old boy, who had been alone for months – with no gas or electricity – after his mother had been jailed. Another time, a victim support officer visited the home of a teenage girl, only to find she had been alone since her father's arrest. A third time, a criminologist visiting a house for research purposes found just children living there.

Then there was Layla, who when she was eight – along with her six siblings – lived for several weeks without any parent or carer after her mother was arrested. "No one cared enough about who was going to look after us, we just got left," Layla, now 21, says. Her ten-year old sister was the eldest and "took on the whole clan". It was only when they took their malnourished six-month-old sister to the hospital that anyone realised their situation. "I received little to no support during the process of my mum being arrested and going to jail,' says Layla. "This impacted me hugely and I still struggle with attachment issues, poor mental health and poor physical health."

Ms. Burrows says that "The biggest challenge has been identifying who the children and families are because there is no Government database that these children are on.

Current figures for children in England and Wales with a parent in prison range from 96,000 children to 310,000 every year – but these are estimates, there is no official data about the children of prisoners.

This lack of robust research is a key barrier to offering such children the support they need, according to James Ottley, family and project operational manager at CHAS. "There isn't the data, there isn't the funding and it seems like there isn't the interest," says Mr. Ottley, adding that this feels like purposeful avoidance by the government. "By identifying how many children of prisoners there are, then you'd have to do something about it. By not identifying it, it's not a problem." He believes that children of prisoners should be eligible for the government's 'pupil premium' – a grant to improve educational outcomes for disadvantaged children, including those in the military. With the extra funding the premium provides, schools would have the capacity to offer individualised, expert support, such as educational psychologists and therapists.

But I hear about a new "child impact assessment toolkit" which sounds really helpful. This is a project led by Sarah Beresford in collaboration with the Prison Reform Trust. "The trauma that children go through when their parent goes to prison is huge," says Ms. Beresford, "particularly if they witness the arrest."

This could be avoided if the systems and agencies that such children came into contact with – police and probation staff, social workers, teachers at school – had specialised training and adequate support to help them. Currently, this is completely lacking.

This toolkit aims to combat this, providing a framework that practitioners from a range of fields can use to understand how a child impacted by parental imprisonment is feeling, and determine what kind of support is needed. The toolkit, which was published in December, is already used by some practitioners, including social workers, teachers and mentors in England and Wales, and is helping support pilot projects within criminal justice processes, such as in sentencing.

And they say what I, and others, have been saying for years which is that short sentences should be abolished entirely, particularly for mothers.

Dr Shona Minson from the Centre for Criminology at Oxford University says that,

"Some 70% of prison sentences handed to women are for less than 12 months, but spending just a few months in prison is enough for a mother to lose her home and often her children, says Minson, and I would add her job and her partner.

"The mother is in a catch-22 situation where she is recorded as 'intentionally homeless', meaning she doesn't get housing priority, meaning she's placed in a single room in a hostel, and she's not eligible to have her children back."

"The impact on children, who often bounce from one care arrangement to another, is severe," she adds. The sheer cruelty and negligence is beyond belief.

But this is hopeful I think. There is a women's problem-solving court (PSC) in Greater Manchester, where community orders are combined with progress reviews. "It's a fantastic model," says Ms. Minson, "because it actually treats people as people, allowing them to continue with their community ties, their children, their jobs, while helping them to address the issues that have led to their offending." Oh goodness, this sounds amazing. Actually treating people as people. (Suella Braverman are you listening?) Three more PSC pilots – for women and men – are to be rolled out in Birmingham, Liverpool and Teeside. Community sentences and prevention schemes would be implemented as alternatives to custodial sentences. Again, this has been advocated for decades. These are initiatives of the Ministry of Justice but for the moment it is up to small charities like CHAS to stand up for these children.

****

21ST MAY

And this is still about children. If you have children of school age you need to read this and then you need to take to the streets.

Funding in schools is so low that head teachers are now saying that by next term classes will have to double up and so there will be 60 in a class. The school day might have to be shortened and they might be forced into a 4 day week.

The DfE said "Since this government took office there are now 24,000 more teachers in our schools, and our secondary schools have an average of 22 pupils per class". So as you see they will never solve the problem because they do not admit to their being a problem.

The DfE keeps saying that there is enough funding in their budgets to cover the 4.5% pay rise which has been overwhelmingly rejected.

But the independent pay award body has recommended that teachers should be given a 6.5% increase in spite of warnings from the Treasury that it could contribute to inflation. I've never worked that one out actually. But if that is not forthcoming we have been warned. The education of our children will go down the pan.

****

23RD MAY

The Conservative Party or the Brexit and UKIP Party?

I have been following this government's decline for the past four years and the downward spiral is, in my opinion, complete.

This government cannot govern, it cannot make decisions, it is profligate with tax payers money for its own use rather than for the good of the tax-payer and it lies with impunity as the following stories show. In fact it is not the once well-respected Conservative party anymore.

For today we hear that the junior doctors' pay negotiations have broken down and so they have announced a 72 hour strike from the 14th June until the 17th.

It really is unbelievable that a government can let this happen as we hear about further possible NHS strikes.

The Royal College of Nursing's second ballot of its members, seeking a legal mandate for another six months of stoppages, opens today and the BMA is also balloting hospital consultants to see if they want to join the junior doctors in striking in pursuit of better pay.

The doctors said that the government would simply not accept the fundamental reality of the pay cuts junior doctors have faced. "This was made clear when they finally made their pay offer of 5%. Not only is that nowhere near addressing pay erosion over the last 15 years, it would not even have matched inflation this year."

****

And then we hear about our foreign secretary **James Cleverly**. Never was a name more inappropriate. He is on a 4 countries tour of Latin America and the Caribbean to "cement partnerships on climate, people and peace." That is the blurb.

Well "climate, people and peace|" is not breaking out back home he may be interested to learn, as we discover he is using a private jet to fly around which costs £10,000 an hour of tax-payer's money.

It is an Embraer Lineage 1000E – lauded as "the crème de la crème of private business jets."

It has been called "one of the best luxury private jets money can buy" and "the ultimate statement of wealth"

Well it includes a lounge area with big-screen TV and a master suite for its main VIP, complete with queen-size bed, private bathroom and shower.

Labour attacked the hire of the jet from a German aviation company as a "ludicrous extravagance", which showed how Rishi Sunak's government was out of touch with the public. Absolutely.

****

Then I see, in the House of Commons, an MP getting visibly upset as she rebukes the Home Secretary. As I delve further I, too, get more and more upset.

In 2015 Theresa May founded an independent inquiry into child sexual abuse. Now, seven years later the report has concluded and she has asked the government to take immediate action on its many recommendations. I have just watched the concluding speech by its chairman Baroness Jay and I am shocked. I am shocked at their findings and I am shocked by the response of the Home Secretary.

In a long and detailed speech she asks for a Cabinet Level Minister for children, a public awareness campaign, specialist therapeutic support for victims of child abuse and mandatory reporting. This, she says, is not a historical problem, it is a national epidemic and is an ever increasing problem. Just one horrifying statistic: Out of a year group of 200 children, 10 boys and nearly 30 girls will have experienced sexual abuse before the age of 16. We all have a "moral, ethical and social responsibility to make safety and the protection of children an absolute priority."

So why was Sarah Champion (a very appropriate name this time) so upset in parliament?

Because the Home Secretary was saying, yes we will look into this further, no we don't need a special minister we have the education secretary, there will be further assessments, consultations and reviews and of course no further funding for anything.

Ms. Champion told parliament that "accepting the need to act isn't the same as acting. We have had seven years of victims and survivors laying their stories out there," she added.

The NSPCC called the government's response "disappointing" and lacked "concrete commitments".

Head of policy at the NSPCC, Anna Edmundson added: "Children at risk of sexual abuse today need government to commit to and follow through with a step change in preventing abuse through reforming child protection and investing in support services. This and future generations deserve nothing less to protect them from the devastating harm of child sexual abuse."

So yet another appalling lack of responsibility and accountability by this government.

****

So where is Boris? I know you're asking! Well he is not in his constituency that's for sure. He is actually in Texas on a 'whirlwind' tour of America. Then he goes on to Las Vegas where he will get a six figure sum for a speech.

To date, the ex-PM has earned a staggering £4.23m just through public speaking arrangements alone, according to his register of interests. This comes on top of the £510,000 he was given as an advance on his memoirs during his time in Downing Street, bringing his total earnings to just shy of £5m since leaving office. But the globe-trotting comes at a cost to his constituents. He has voted just three times since he was forced to resign as PM, so missing 187 Commons votes.

But I actually think that perhaps he should be here because he'll never believe what is happening now.

He has just been referred to the police over more possible breaches of lockdown rules.

Apparently the Cabinet Office was obliged by the Civil Service Code to hand over certain documents to the public inquiry on the pandemic. These are now in the hands of the Thames Valley Police and they show that there were visits to Chequers by family and friends between June 2020 and May 2021.

Oh hang on. They have also gone to the Met as there were reports of similar breaches at Downing Street. And they have been sent to the Privileges Committee.

Oh but wait a minute. We are hearing from Johnson's spokesman. He is saying it was all "totally untrue" that rules had been broken. They were all official meetings and held outdoors "or came within another lawful exception" and he concludes by saying that "many will conclude that this has all the hallmarks of yet another politically motivated stitch-up."

Oh of course. Never, ever, let it be said that Johnson takes any responsibility for his own actions. Anyway he is so busy talking to Republicans in America that he really doesn't care. .

****

2pm

Oh my word I think I am wrong. He does care.

He has just sacked his government appointed lawyers because they handed over this information to the police and so he will now appoint new lawyers to represent him at the Covid inquiry which will be funded by the tax payer at a cost of over £1m. We have already paid a huge sum to his original lawyers who were given a budget of £7 million to defend him and other cabinet office ministers at the Covid 19 public inquiry, and this is on top of the £240,000 in fees for lawyers to defend him in the investigation by the Commons Privileges Committee.

But we are hearing from the Chairperson of the inquiry, Lady Hallet, who is demanding the release of Johnson's phone exchanges that he had with his senior ministers, senior civil servants and advisers during the pandemic– insisting they were of "potential relevance" to the inquiry. She has also said that his diary entries, notebooks, WhatsApp messages and emails should have been handed over by the Cabinet Office. She is threatening legal action if they don't comply.

In a series of letters released on Wednesday, the Covid inquiry revealed a legal notice on 28 April 2023 requesting un-redacted communications from the phones of Mr. Johnson and his ex-adviser Henry Cook – a friend of Carrie Johnson. They include their messages with former strategy advisor Dominic Cummings, then health secretary Matt Hancock, cabinet secretary Simon Case, chief medical officer Sir Chris Whitty and then-chief scientific adviser Sir Patrick Vallance. The inquiry also asked for Mr. Johnson's diaries and notebooks. But on 15th May the Cabinet Office denied the request, arguing it was unlawful.

Baroness Hallett said the request was made under section 21 of the Inquiries Act 2005 – pointing out that failure to comply could be a criminal offence and punishable with a fine of up to £1,000 or even imprisonment for a maximum of 51 weeks.

It sounds as though the Cabinet Office has been picking and choosing which contents could be redacted.

But she said "entire contents of the documents" were of "potential relevance to the lines of investigation that I am pursuing" and urged the Cabinet Office to provide them by the end of 30 May.

Oh goodness. Just as I think I can close this book something else almost unbelievable is reported.

It seems to be turning into a macabre soap opera. I really hope you are all keeping up.

****

25TH MAY

But we are hearing about another potential breach of the code by Suella Braverman over Rwanda.

Straight from *The Independent* I read that she was a co-founder with Cherie Blair of a charity called the 'Africa Justice Foundation', which trained Rwandan government lawyers between 2010 and 2015. Several people the charity worked with are now key members of President Paul Kagame's government and are involved in the UK's £140m deal to send asylum seekers to Rwanda.

Oh my word this does not look at all good for her, for Rishi or for the government in general. ,

I always wondered why Rwanda? Well now we know. This story has not been leaked by anyone. It is not a 'witch hunt'. It is down to excellent investigative journalism by Lizzie Dearden, who is Home Affairs Editor of *The Independent*. As she says on Twitter "it is the result of a six month investigation by me and only me."

Sir Alistair Graham, former head of the Committee of Standards on Public Life, told *The Independent*: "If the Rwanda policy was there when she produced a declaration of interest, and did not include it, then I would have thought that could be a breach of the ministerial code. It would be a personal failure that the Prime Minister should address, and may want to consult his ethics adviser on."

Sir Alex Allan, the former adviser on ministerial standards, said the Home Secretary's past work should have been declared after she became responsible for the Rwanda deal. "I would have thought that it would be an issue that she would have had to discuss with the Home Office Permanent Secretary," he added. "There would have been an internal discussion."

He went on to say that Ms. Braverman should have referenced any previous work with the Rwandan government to colleagues: "It absolutely has to be flagged - this is all part of the ministerial code."

I would have thought that this would have been absolutely obvious.

The code states that ministers "must ensure that no conflict arises, or could reasonably be perceived to arise, between their public duties and their private interests".

This is not yet on the main news but of course is on Twitter. A question has just been asked about it during the debate on the urgent question but the Minister said he has only seen the tweet and doesn't have enough information to comment.

****

But on delving further it looks as though no code has been broken over her links with Rwanda after all. She was not Home Secretary until 5 months **after** Johnson mentioned Rwanda as a possible location for deported refugees. However I still think that we should all be aware of her links with Rwanda as she pursues this policy with such vigour.

And she has just announced visa restrictions for international students' dependants and reductions in their post-study work visa rights. This, she thinks, will reduce the immigrant figures, but for goodness sake what an own goal. (What another one?) This will obviously act as a deterrent to many potential overseas students and will destroy what is, in actual fact, a boost to the economy. The economic benefit that foreign students bring to the UK has jumped by a third in three years, **boosting the economy by an estimated £42bn in 2021/2, according to by analysts 'London Economic'.**

Does she not read these reports?

In fact SHE is becoming the story which never ends well. Despite migration figures, announced today, showing a record high she appears to have "gone to ground". As Yvette Cooper says "Despite migration being one of the Home Secretary's key policy areas, Ms. Braverman did not comment on the figures or attend an urgent question on immigration in the House of Commons."

She then went on to say "What is the point of her?"

Well we have all been asking that question for a long time.

****

26TH MAY

There is much more about immigration today of course and it will go on and on.

But we are hearing from those who are telling the other side of the story.

As James Moore of *The Independent* says, the real scandal is that there is not enough immigration. (I agree!) He takes the one example of the food rotting in our fields as there is no-one to pick it.

As he says, "If there are people willing to do this work – and there are – we should welcome them. The benefit would be a wider availability of cheaper food. We should therefore make it easier for them. They're doing us and our economy a favour, not the other way around."

And Tom Peck also of *The Independent* writes positively about immigration and that actually the British public "can see that it is good for the economy, the NHS, and every other facet of British public life. They can see that migrants pay more in tax than they claim in benefits; and also – and this is the big one – unlike actual born-and-bred Brits, once they've stopped working, they tend to go home again. They don't retire here, racking up massive healthcare bills for the younger and much poorer generation to cover. And nor do they commit, more or less en-masse, other huge acts of economic vandalism like, say, voting for Brexit."

And everyone is still looking for Suella Braverman.

****

Ah, but wait a minute, we are hearing about something that the Conservative party **is** world- beating at. **A secret plot**. Senior Conservative MPs are said to have gathered at the Carlton Club – the party's spiritual home in London – to talk about how to get rid of the outspoken Home Secretary. There's a lot of unhappiness among Tory MPs, with the harder right members of the Government very angry with her and the members on the left just wanting her to go. A recent survey finds that the public think she is not trusted, not likable and not competent.

But senior MP Alicia Kearns said: **'There is absolutely, categorically no plot.'**

Well I think we all know what that means.

****

But Boris? Just as you think he can't go any lower we hear that he had dinner last night with Donald Trump.

****

And back to Sunak and his government and in particular the Department of Education. Foreign teachers from places such as India and Nigeria are being offered £10,000 to work in English schools in an overseas recruitment drive to fill teacher vacancies. I must be missing something here. They are trying to stop all immigration, they say they want British workers for British jobs, they refuse to pay teachers a decent salary so teachers are leaving in droves, but they are going to spend thousands of pounds on recruiting teachers from overseas.

****

28TH MAY

The Tory party conference will take place in Manchester this autumn. However, as at last year's conference, all media outlets, journalists and reporters have been asked to pay an attendance fee once more. Well there is fury at this as you might imagine and a boycott by the media is being threatened.

****

29TH MAY

Just more news about the failings of our education system. The wonderful focus on vocational training which has been seen as so important by this government is failing due mainly to lack of funding. 40% of apprentices have dropped out of the scheme costing training providers £1.9 billion in lost earnings between 2018 and last year. Lizzie Crowley, senior policy adviser for skills at the CIPD, a professional body for human resources, said "Apprenticeship achievement rates are a national disgrace. If almost half of A-level students dropped out before completing there would be uproar. We need a similar level of urgency in tackling this critical failure."

Yes, well, the only time we see any urgency from this government is when they think they will lose the next election. Then they spout complete rubbish and make us all despair even more.

An article by Jenni Russell in *The Times* compels me to write yet another letter.

Sir, Jenni Russell has written a very important and perceptive article this morning (29th May) about our education system. Last year Rachel Sylvester chaired The Times Education Commission which produced some excellent resolutions. But our politicians do not appear to be listening and our schools continue to be underfunded and under-resourced. To stifle the natural enthusiasm and joy for learning which is to be found in most young children is shameful. Socrates said **"Education is the kindling of a flame, not the filling of a vessel."** *And here we are, still teaching to the test.*

All very depressing.

****

And also another frightening statistic about our failing maternity services. To quote from *The Times* today, "Last month *The Times* commission found that the NHS was spending more than twice as much on the cost of harm caused by maternity services as on maternity care itself."

****

But at last...............the comedians have finally taken over. The real ones that is.

Lee Mack, Steve Coogan and Paul Whitehouse have joined protesters at Lake Windermere to highlight the 'national scandal' of the sheer volume of raw sewage being pumped into our largest and most beautiful fresh-water lake.

So it takes footballers and comedians to do the politicians jobs for them.

Mind you I am a bit worried that we might hear from the Environmental Secretary now. Would really spoil my cup of coffee.

****

30TH MAY

My letter is in *The Times* this morning. There are also three other letters about the last few issues I have written about. One about the lack of safety in our maternity services, one about the lack of action by the government in the sexual abuse inquiry and one about the lack of promised funding for the apprenticeship scheme.

****

We also hear, yet again, about an appalling waste of tax-payers' money in the building of a hi-tech control border post in Portsmouth. It has cost the tax-payer £25m to build this structure to government specifications and has sat empty for almost a year.

The government announced in April last year that the introduction of post-Brexit import checks would be delayed for a fourth time.

If the government had outlined its latest border strategy straight after Brexit, the port would have been able to build a considerably smaller facility, costing about a fifth of what it actually spent. Worse still, it faces spending more to adapt the facility to the new requirements – or even build a second one.

****

And here is another appalling waste of money and education. On October 9th 2017 Justine Greening, the then Education Secretary opened the new National College for High Speed Rail in Doncaster.

At the launch she said the following: "It has been great to attend the official launch of the NCHSR. It is part of how we are steadily transforming technical education in this country, training up a new generation of skilled young people and the existing workforce so that British business has the skills it needs and people have the opportunities they want – a win-win for everyone."

And the government spiel about it said: "This college is the largest of five new national colleges created by the government to ensure young people can learn world-class technical skills, including, engineering, design, planning, manufacturing and construction."

It is certainly a very impressive looking building of steel and glass.

And now? Six years after this exciting and important initiative it is closing down forcing students to go elsewhere.

It was basically aimed at training some of the 2,000 apprentices it was thought would be needed to build the HS2 rail network.

For some reason it was renamed the National College for Advanced Transport and Infrastructure but obviously the change of a name didn't do the trick. It has been the victim of the atrocious mismanagement of HS2 with U-turns, dither, delay and ever-increasing costs.

Just to a remind you: the original projected costs of HS2 in 2009 were £37 billion whereas now the final bill is expected to top £100 billion.

HS2 has scarred the country-side, destroyed ancient forests, ruined people's lives who have been forced to move house, has had major cuts to original promised projects and is now an expensive failed government white elephant.

They say they want a high skilled, high waged economy. We say we want a highly intelligent, highly competent government.

Neither anywhere on the radar as yet.

****

But we are all waiting for the 4pm deadline today which will decide whether or not there is going to be a court case between the chair of the Covid inquiry and Boris Johnson. Watch this space.

12 mid-day: BREAKING NEWS.

The dead-line has been extended to 4pm on Thursday 1st June.

The Cabinet office is now saying that it does not currently have the WhatsApp messages or notebooks in its possession.

But I thought they had given some heavily redacted material already. And they have said that some of it is irrelevant. And Cabinet Office sources would not confirm what material they do not currently have. So they don't even know what they haven't got.

Baroness Hallet, the chair, has asked them for a SWORN statement to this effect if documents are not forthcoming on Thursday.

****

I'm sure we will be back to this very soon but meanwhile another interesting story has come to light.

Civil servants in the Home Office are saying they will go on strike if forced to implement measures that they believe are unlawful. They are extremely critical of the new bill which will endeavour to detain and deport asylum seekers and are not prepared to support deportations to Rwanda. This is reported in *The Independent* and as one asylum official previously told them. "You can't do this kind of s*** and still pretend that you are legal,"

"Being elected doesn't give you the right to break the law."

Head of bargaining, Paul O'Connor of the Public and Commercial Services (PCS) union, said "staff were also sick of being used as a political football", amid frequent accusations from senior Tories that they are part of a politically motivated blob obstructing government policy. Civil servants are not the type of people who go around plotting in dark corners to bring down administrations,"

I say, upset the civil servants who work for you at your peril. If you can't keep them on board then your days are numbered and rightly so.

****

31ST MAY

4.45pm. Breaking news. Boris Johnson gives all notes and diaries in un-redacted form to the Cabinet Office. He actually says they have had access to them for months. They can give them to the inquiry. Do we understand all of this? No we don't. Well we wait with baited breath to see what the 4pm deadline brings tomorrow. But as everyone on Twitter is saying, remember Boris never does anything unless it is absolutely in his own interest to do so.

****

And of course it is important not to ignore what else is going on today.

The post-Brexit Australian trade deal comes into force today and we are hearing about a scandalous story which involves,.......well you won't believe this, ... Boris Johnson.

It reads like a 'Faulty Towers' script.

The Guardian reports that apparently Johnson and the Australian high commissioner George Brandis, were having dinner in No 10 in early 2021 and were discussing the trade deal. This was when Liz Truss was International Trade Secretary and so actually all negotiations should have been through her.

Well this dinner event has been described as "chaotic", "farcical" and an "embarrassment". So no surprise there then.

Johnson allegedly blundered into a £10 billion trade deal concession with Australia and he agreed to measure beef imports by the weight of only cuts of meat, rather than the entire cow, which is much heavier – effectively signing off a massive increase in how much meat Australia can send to Britain. When questioned about it later he said that he had agreed to the deal because he wanted to apologise to Australia for Britain's decision to join the EU 50 years ago.

No I don't understand either. What on earth is he talking about?

One former adviser to Ms Truss told *The Guardian* he did not think Mr Johnson was across the detail, adding that the dinner "was very slapdash."

No surprise there then. The Australian Prime Minister was also there and this, would you believe, is how the deal was finalised.

Apparently realising that the deal was too good to be true, George Brandis scrawled down the unexpected bonus and fled to the loo. On the way, he gave the piece of paper to an aide to hurriedly scan and turn into a trade document – before it was returned to the dinner table for Mr. Johnson to sign.

People are saying it was scribbled down on loo paper but I absolutely can't verify this detail.

When Liz Truss later tried to unpick the deal she is said to have been told, **"Your boss has conceded the whole kingdom."** Advisers said that if she tried to reopen the talks the Australian PM Scott Morrison had threatened to "tell the media the UK was going back on its first post-Brexit trade deal".

Darren Jones, the chair of the Commons business and trade committee, said the events would "make our professional trade negotiators weep ... this is just an embarrassment".

The Brexit trade deal with Australia has always been controversial and was condemned as a sell-out by British farmers, while even the former environment secretary George Eustice said the government "gave away far too much for far too little in return".

A furious Ms. Truss was reportedly told by the gleeful Australians that her boss, Mr. Johnson, had already "given away the kingdom", according to a former minister involved in the talks.

Minette Batters, President of the National Farmers' Union said the concessions were "a real breach of trust and confidence for farmers", adding: "The anger is still visceral."

So May ends in complete and utter turmoil. Failure at every level.

****

FLAMING JUNE

1ST JUNE

Well the 4pm dead-line has been and gone.

4.45pm and nothing seems to have happened.

Everyone is waiting for some news. Have they handed over the documents or haven't they? I'm guessing they haven't. Will let you know!

5.30pm. I was right. They haven't.

The government are launching a judicial review where a judge will decide whether the inquiry has overreached its legal powers to demand evidence. The government says much of the information the inquiry requires is irrelevant or personal and would prejudice future confidential discussions.

The Covid inquiry says they will be the judge of that.

There is no love lost between Mr. Sunak and Mr. Johnson and at the moment Sunak is making Johnson look like the good guy which is an unheard-of achievement. But Boris gave him his documents and said he was quite happy for them all to go to the inquiry and Sunak is refusing to pass them on.

Sunak is looking like the big loser here. As Chancellor at the time he obviously has something to hide.

Oh hang on what is this we are hearing? Johnson got a new phone at some point and has only given in one phone. That's right. I remember. He had a phone with a public number so anyone could get in touch with him. This was thought to be a security risk as the number was available online! So he had to get a new one. In fact I wrote about his phone on page 233 of *Beneath the Bluster* on April 23rd 2021. Yes, I say, his phone has a story all of its own. He has apparently given in his new phone but not the one he had before May 2021 which covered most of the lockdowns. I hope you can keep up with all of this.

So just to recap, this is the inquiry into the handling of the pandemic initiated by the government in order that we can see what was done well and what wasn't and what lessons we can all learn from it. Baroness Hallett was chosen by Johnson to be the Chair.

Everyone who lost a loved one due to the pandemic is really anxious to know all the details. I think we all need to walk along the memorial wall opposite Westminster to look at the hearts drawn there, each one representing a dearly loved person no longer here. It is overwhelming.

As Rivka Gottlieb, spokesperson for 'Covid-19 Bereaved Families for Justice', said it is "absolutely obscene that the Cabinet Office is going to spend hundreds of thousands of pounds of taxpayers' money on suing its own public inquiry into being unable to access critical evidence".

Asked how long a judicial review could take, Lord Saville, who conducted the inquiry into Bloody Sunday, said: "It needn't necessarily be slow – but it probably would be rather expensive."

He and many other top lawyers including Michel Mansfield KC, are saying the government will not win and the "cards are stacked" against them. And everyone is saying what on earth have they got to hide?

I say where is Lady Hallett? Oh goodness this could go on and on. It is unprecedented.

Oh here she is. I have just seen a statement from her team which says that a further statement would be made at a scheduled inquiry hearing on Tuesday morning at 10.30am. That is the 6th June.

World–beating? Yes. This government is world beating at deceitfulness, corruption, greed, incompetence, cruelty, self-entitlement, lies and hypocrisy. We have been down the rabbit hole for a long time and now we're being taken through the looking glass. They deserve to fail.

****

2ND JUNE

Well I've slept on it and it still all feels completely bizarre.

But I need to look at some other snippets of news that might get over-looked.

Do you remember **Alexander Lebedev**, former KGB intelligence officer, who bought *The Evening Standard* and who was a friend with Boris Johnson who made him a peer? I have written about him before and about his connections with Johnson.

Well Canada has imposed sanctions on him and Ukraine has just imposed sanctions on him but surprise, surprise Britain has not yet done so. A year ago Canada named him as being on a list of 14 people who had "directly enabled Putin's senseless war in Ukraine and bear responsibility for the pain and suffering."

Well in an article in *The Times* this morning it quotes the Cabinet Office as saying that Lebedev is a "man of good standing", that no complaint has been made about his conduct and that he has been a critic of Putin.

They say that attempts to contact Lebedev were unsuccessful. It really does beggar belief.

****

Morale in the armed forces has dipped to a five-year low. The defence of our country is the first duty of every government and this really does not look good. Incomes have taken a real-terms cut, and the state of military housing is substandard with repairs taking too long and being of poor quality. Five in ten are dissatisfied with their earnings.

I suppose the Ministry of Defence is being very careful with their, oh sorry, our money? Well Chris Smyth of *The Times* reports that the National Audit Office identified more than a £1billion in losses and errors due to many cancelled projects which had already had a significant amount of money spent on them.

And can you explain this? The MOD said that it actually benefited from cancelled projects because "it regularly reviews our programmes and assets to determine how best to meet future threats. This helps avoid future support and maintenance costs on programmes and assets that are no longer required."

I think I just need to give my head a wobble.

****

Before lockdown roughly 10% of children were persistently absent from school. It is now 22% or 1.6 million children missing at least a tenth of their schooling. Dame Rachel de Souza, the children's commissioner for England, says something that we are all aware of which is "The value placed on their education is not where it should be."

She goes on to say that "When we look at what works, we see groups of schools with their local authorities using the systems to identify the children [then find] out what is really going on and getting them back to school. It costs time, it costs money and it's got to be a national priority."

It won't happen with this government.

****

It looks as though Steve Barclay, our health secretary has been misleading Parliament. Remember 40 new hospitals? Well he told MPs that work had started on temporary wards at Charing Cross hospital so that the rest of the building could be refurbished and also that a rehabilitation cardiac hub was being built at Hammersmith hospital. Well, apart from the fact that these plans do not constitute new hospitals, this is news to Imperial College Healthcare NHS Trust, which manages these hospitals. They told the BBC that work had not started on either hospital.

How on earth does he get away with these lies? Why is he not being held to account?

****

10.56am BREAKING NEWS

Boris Johnson has said he will hand over all un-redacted messages straight to the Covid inquiry, so by-passing the Cabinet Office.

This will make him look such a good guy doing the right thing whilst leaving Sunak to drown in his own lies and confutation.

What about the old phone Mr. Johnson?

Oh here it is! He says in his letter to Lady Hallett that "I would like to do the same with any material that may be on an old phone which I have previously been told I cannot access safely." Oh goodness. He has asked the Cabinet Office for their help to turn on the device safely in order to be able to hand over the material. He has forgotten the password!

People are saying give it to me and I'll give it to my young grand-children and they will have it open in five minutes.

And if the Cabinet Office refuses to hand over his note books, which they have, he will go and demand their return in order to deliver **them** personally as well.

Oh my word he is saying loud and clear:-

"I AM THE GOOD GUY. SUNAK YOU ARE TOAST"

****

3RD JUNE

Well we will no doubt be returning to this story but it was interesting to watch BBC *Question Time* last night.

Chris Patten was on the panel and absolutely tore Brexit apart. Now Chris Patten, was chairman of the Tory Party from 1990 to 1992 and was made a life peer in 2005 so when people say oh he's a 'leftie' or he's 'woke' they couldn't be further from the truth. He's a Conservative politician from the Thatcherite era. People need to realise just how far to the right the current government has lurched.

He said that until politicians started telling the truth about our situation we will never be able to put things right. "The truth is we're in one hell of a mess." he, said. "Our GDP per capita now is less than not only France, Germany, the Netherlands, it's lower than Ireland. It's lower for heaven's sake than Lithuania. **The poorest 20% in Britain are poorer than the poorest 20% in Poland. That is not the sign of a country which has things going for it."**

He went on to say that, "It's because of what Brexit did to the value of the pound. It's because of what Brexit has done to make it more difficult for us to import goods and for us to import labour and for us to import food.

Now it's costing us, (according to the London School of Economics), £7 billion more a year because we're outside the European Union."

Unanimous applause.

In a recent poll only 9% of Britons think Brexit more of a success than a failure.

Goodness, who on earth are they?

****

Divide and Rule.

In a brilliant article by Andrew Fisher of *the i,* we hear how the right wing media exploit and emphasise our prejudices. We see this with asylum seekers all the time of course and we also are seeing it with the unemployed and the disabled. It is so much easier for the government to blame others than to take responsibility of their own abysmal failings. So *The Telegraph* has a piece about benefit scroungers and how there are so many people not at work at the moment. This, they say is because your hard working and well deserved earnings are going on their benefits, now how do you like that? they screech.

Actually a vast proportion of the welfare money goes on pensions. This is more than twice as much as is spent on sickness and disability benefits. And yes there are more people claiming sickness benefits today but could that be because there are a record 7.3 million people on NHS waiting lists due to the under-investing of the NHS by this government? Also of course, because of the number of people suffering from long Covid.

As Mr. Fisher says "It is so much easier to find scapegoats than solutions."

****

4TH JUNE

Our children.

Barnardo's, the children's charity, has issued a stark warning about the fact that a record number of children will be at risk of sexual and criminal exploitation over the summer holidays. Because so many families are facing abject poverty children will lack adult supervision as parents struggle to keep going. Children then become increasingly vulnerable to criminal gangs. Many young children are not aware when they are being targeted as approaches can seem innocent and many say that they have no-where safe to go anymore.

Since 2010, 760 youth centres have closed. And real terms expenditure by councils on youth services has fallen by 70%. In some areas there was no funding at all as seven councils admitted that no money had been allocated to youth services in 2020-2021.

Government data shows that more than 19,000 children face sexual exploitation every year with at least 27,000 at risk of being exploited by criminal gangs. Because exploitation is generally hidden, experts agree that such data is the tip of the iceberg.

Well it is certainly kept hidden from the general public because I at any rate have not seen this in the main stream media.

However it is in *The Observer* today written by their Home Affairs editor Mark Townsend so I look forward to an outbreak of headlines, shock and anger tomorrow.

****

5TH JUNE

Well there is concern about the children missing school but nothing about the above.

****

The Covid inquiry debacle rumbles on.

There seems to be a problem with Johnson's notebooks and phone. A spokesperson for Mr Johnson has said: "As Mr Johnson has repeatedly made clear, including directly to the inquiry, he has no objection whatsoever to the inquiry inspecting the notebooks in un-redacted form." Johnson has said he would get them back from the Office and deliver them directly himself if needs be. But he has been warned that he could lose public funding for legal advice if he tries to "frustrate or undermine" the government's position on the Covid-19 inquiry.

And Hugo Keith, lead KC for the inquiry, and Lady Hallett reacted with astonishment as the Cabinet Office's legal team doubled down on its position.

And they were rather bemused when the government's lawyer, Nicholas Chapman, said: **"The position is, the Cabinet Office is working out its position." Yes he really said that.**

Mr Keith said of Mr Chapman: "I'm afraid in our respectful submission, his position will not do."

Lady Hallett has given the Cabinet Office until the end of the week to set out formally what access it will grant to Mr Johnson's material, including the notebooks and the old phone.

****

6TH JUNE

The big story today is Prince Harry arriving at the High Court in London to give evidence in his phone hacking case against the Mirror Group Newspapers.

But something far more important is going on which we all need to be concerned about.

The Illegal Migration Bill is going through the House of Lords at the moment but the opposition peers have called for it to be stopped from progressing until an impact assessment is published. A junior migration and borders minister has said that they will be published "in due course". But Lord Vernon Coaker says it is of the "upmost importance" that the House has the facts available to them, and a debate cannot happen if "one hand is tied behind their back". He adds that the impact assessment is "crucial" for the Lords to discuss the matter properly. "Nobody has a clue what in due course means." he says.

They are particularly concerned about specific parts of the bill that refer to children.

"I think it's an awful bill," Lord Dubs said. And Baroness Ruth Lister says, "The government should remove children from the scope of the Illegal Migration Bill entirely. These are children who are scared, traumatised, needing security, support and the opportunity to experience their childhoods,"

Crossbencher Lord John Kerr adds that it is "not in keeping with British tradition" to remove migrant children from the UK.

Well no that is true but we have seen time and time again that cruelty to children is the norm under this government.

And we hear that the debate in the Lords went on till 4am which is almost unprecedented. The government has insisted that the bill has to be rushed through at top speed and the Lords are angry and frustrated. As Lord Bach said "What we are trying to do is our job of sensibly and calmly dealing with a Bill that has huge potential for the liberty and lives of some of the most vulnerable people in the world." He went on say "Can I for my own part say how disgraceful I think it is we are debating these really important and serious matters at this hour in the morning."

****

But this sounds even worse. It is about the Public Order Bill.

Baroness Jenny Jones, who is a member of the Green Party, has tabled a 'Fatal Motion' for 13 June to stop the government from using a 'Ministerial decree' to overturn a vote in the Lords.

This is the first time ever that the government has tried to use secondary legislation to directly overturn the will of Parliament.

The Government lost a vote in the Lords on the Public Order Bill to change the interpretation of 'serious disruption' of other people's day-to-day activities to mean 'anything more than minor'. In other words they basically don't want any of us to be able to protest in any way at all. But this bill received Royal Assent on the 2nd May and just today a woman was arrested for walking down a street on her own carrying a banner.

Baroness Jones said: "This is a make-or-break moment for parliamentary democracy. The Lords defeated the government on this issue and the Minister is now acting like a seventeenth-century monarch by using a decree to reverse that vote. What is the point of Parliament if a Minister can just ignore the outcome of debates and votes by imposing draconian laws on the public?

This is not a one-off, but part of a trend of legislation that undermines parliamentary democracy by giving Ministers increasing powers to make, delete or change laws. In the last four years, we have seen a series of skeleton bills pass through parliament that hand over powers and discretion to Ministers to make decisions with minimal parliamentary scrutiny."

We wait to see what happens on the 13th June.

****

But here is some good news at last. Michelle Mone is under criminal investigation. You will remember that her company acquired VIP contracts for the supply of PPE worth over 200 million pounds. She has been evading the powers that be for years but is now, at last, being investigated for fraud.

****

Sunak is being told that if he loses the rural vote he will lose the election. As Alice Thomson writes in *The Times* today "The government post-Brexit subsidy system remains chaotic. The EU's basic payment scheme is on the way out but its replacement (Elms) is in flux. The old Countryside Stewardship Scheme to protect the landscape was nearly scrapped and is still underfunded, over-complicated and inadequate."

Apparently Sir James Dyson (the largest farm owner in England) wrote to the agriculture secretary last year to ask how the government could help farmers to produce food profitably while protecting nature. They have not replied. They absolutely do not govern and don't care. Ah wait a minute. We must remind ourselves of the name of the said secretary. Here we go: **Therese Coffey.**

****

Well, well perhaps this is one of the reasons that Sunak does not wish the Covid inquiry to see his WhatsApp messages . There was a significant rise in fraud cases when he was Chancellor apparently. Government fraud quadrupled after he approved £97 billion to be spent on the pandemic furlough scheme, the bounce back loan scheme, and his 'Eat Out to Help Out' scheme.

A report from the Public Accounts Committee states that while HMRC implemented its Covid-19 employment support schemes quickly to businesses and individuals, the tax body nonetheless had to reduce 'its compliance staffing to support Covid schemes, and the level of fraud and error is high'. The report also goes on to highlight that the government does not expect to recoup nearly £1 billion, mostly lost to errors in local authority administered grant payments.

But this is exactly what the inquiry is for. We did all appreciate the help these schemes gave to everyone but obviously the team which has to implement them needs more training and help. These are the things we need to learn.

****

8TH JUNE

5:21PM BREAKING NEWS
The Privileges Committee has reached its verdict on whether Boris Johnson knowingly mislead Parliament.

At last.

However we mustn't get too excited. Johnson now has two weeks to scrutinise their findings and if they have decided to criticise him they will take into account any further submissions from him. They will then report back to the House of Commons. That is when it will be published.

A spokesperson for the Committee said, "The Committee will then report to the House in the usual way, and it will be for the House - not the Committee - to decide on this matter. MPs will vote on whether to approve whatever sanction the Committee recommends."

Absolutely. We understand that.

****

The latest figures by the NHS show that there are now 220,000 more people waiting for treatment than when Sunak made cutting waiting lists one of his five priorities.

Ben Zaranko of the Institute for Fiscal Studies says: "There's no putting a positive spin on today's figures. It is getting hard to see how the numbers can be turned round in any meaningful way before people get to vote on this Prime Minister's future."

****

FRIDAY 9TH JUNE

Well this is interesting. Nadine Dorries has just said she is stepping down as an MP "with immediate effect." What is that all about? I think it might be something to do with the Honours list. She is expecting a peerage (yes I know) but has to resign her seat first. Well she won't be missed. The worst culture secretary in living memory.

****

And Boris Johnson has just released his honours list and I am in shock. Jacob Rees-Mogg is to be knighted and Priti Patel is to be a dame. There are others of course, in fact 44 altogether but these are the two which first catch my eye. I have written about these two at length and consider them both long over-due for dismissal. They are a disgrace.

Then there are these which are also inexplicable, at least to me.

Michael Fabricant is to be knighted, Andrea Jenkins, she of the middle finger, is to be a dame and Martin Reynolds is to be a knight. He was PPS to Johnson and it was he who issued the invitation to a party which said BYOB.

Shelley Williams-Walker has been awarded a damehood and she is Johnsons' head of operations in No 10. She was at the party on the evening of the Duke of Edinburgh's funeral and allegedly arranged the music for the event.

Dan Rosenfield, Johnson's former chief of staff, is to be given a peerage. He was among senior officials who attended a Christmas quiz in Downing Street when we were all in lockdown. So this disgraceful list goes on.

But what do you make of this one?

Charlotte Owen, 29, will become the youngest serving member of the House of Lords as she is given a peerage after serving less than two years in the No 10 policy unit. She worked as a special adviser to both prime ministers, Johnson and Liz Truss. She has served in parliament for approximately five years and eight months, meaning she has transitioned from parliamentary intern to Baroness in just six years. She is attractive and has long blond hair. You can probably imagine what is being said about this. I say no more.

Hang on, I say I am in shock but I think I am not in as much shock as Nadine Dorries. She is not on the list at all. Absolutely no peerage.

****

8pm. BREAKING NEWS! WHAT?

What is this I am hearing?

Boris Johnson has announced that he is stepping down as an MP with immediate effect.

But this is the sentence I have been waiting and wanting to write for three years. Oh my goodness I have to stop and take a deep breath and give a cheer at the top of my voice.

I am with family and everyone is grinning and some have gone to open a bottle to celebrate. Oh happy day.

And the chairman on Radio 4s 'Any Questions' has just interrupted the programme to make this announcement and the audience have gone wild. **They have erupted with cheers and applause.**

But this is amazing. I actually do not understand. What on earth is going on? He has two weeks to study the report and surely he hasn't read it all already. I actually think he was given it last night and perhaps he just looked at the conclusion. Perhaps it was really bad.

This is turning out to be an amazing day and maybe more will be explained tomorrow.

Did you get that though? I have to say it again.

Boris Johnson has announced that he is stepping down as an MP with immediate effect.

Oh happy day! Or have I already said that too?

****

SATURDAY 10TH JUNE

'The party's over now' is the headline in *The Times* today.

And so it is but if you expected Johnson to go quietly you haven't been paying attention. He has written the most vituperative and vitriolic attack on the Privileges Committee that you could ever, ever read. It is appalling. They have obviously found against him and we are hearing that they recommend a 20 day suspension. He is apoplectic with rage. He said that he was "bewildered and appalled" to be "forced out, anti-democratically" by a committee that was guilty of "egregious bias." He starts off by saying, "I have received a letter from the Privileges Committee making it clear – much to my amazement – that they are determined to use the proceedings against me to drive me out of parliament. They have still not produced a shred of evidence that I knowingly or recklessly misled the Commons." He goes on to accuse it of being a "witch- hunt" and a "kangaroo court". He continues in that vein and the accusations he makes are actually scandalous.

What on earth will happen now?

****

SUNDAY 11TH JUNE

Well what happens now is that the Privileges Committee is said to be considering adding further sanctions against Boris Johnson for his disgraceful accusations, plus those others who have spoken out against the process, over concerns that their comments could amount to contempt of Parliament. They are ready to publish the report probably as soon as Wednesday.

We also hear that Johnson was on a flight to Cairo (to Cairo?) when he received the information that the Committee had found against him.

When told that the government would not whip Tory MPs to vote against the sanctions he said "I'm f***ed". So rather than face the music he decides to go and in doing so he blames everyone else but himself.

So to those who are supporting Johnson and accusing the Committee of bias there are some important facts for them to get their heads around.

The committee comprises of 7 people, 4 of whom are Conservatives. Two of those, Sir Charles Walker and Sir Bernard Jenkin are staunchly Conservative and are experienced and absolutely sticklers for due process. The Labour Chair, Harriet Harman, only has a deciding vote and as the result was agreed unanimously she didn't need to use it. Johnson has not been "forced out". It is for his fellow MPs to vote on whether to accept the findings or not.

The members of the Committee have been given extra security due to the nature of the threats they have received.

****

And the honours list debacle drags on. Not only had Johnson promised a peerage to Nadine Dorries, but also to Alok Sharma, and Nigel Adams. It all sounds very messy but apparently they thought initially that they would not have to stand down as MPs, but then as these last two have also been left off the list they too are standing down 'with immediate effect'. So that is the final present to Sunak from Johnson: three by-elections. No time to waste either. Labour and the Lib-Dems are flooding their constituencies as we are told everything will be put in place to start proceedings tomorrow so they will hopefully take place before the summer recess.

****

MONDAY 12TH JUNE

Did I say that was the final present from Johnson? When will I ever learn?

It sounds as though Johnson asked Sunak to overturn the vetting process in order to award these three peerages. Sunak has said at a public event that actually yes, Johnson asked him to do something which he thought was not right and so he was not prepared to do it. Boris Johnson has replied "Rishi Sunak is talking rubbish. To honour these peerages it was not necessary to overrule Holac (House of Lords Appointment Commission) but simply to ask them to renew their vetting, which was a mere formality."

So this war of words continues in public as the rest of us watch the Conservative government descend even further into chaos and degradation.

Some senior Tories have called for Johnson to be blocked from standing ever again as an MP. Well we are hoping that this could be a final punishment by the Privileges Committee. Hoping? Desperately waiting with baited breath.

****

TUESDAY 13TH JUNE

Whilst this has been going on it is important to see what else is happening out here in the real world. Well this is good news. Sunak has stopped the boats!

Oh hang on a minute. I don't think it was these boats he wanted to stop.

The port operator in Liverpool has said there is no way they could support up to 1,500 asylum seekers on a vessel berthed in the vicinity of Wirral Waters. And London's Royal Docks confirmed it had rejected permission for the Government to use one of its east London waterways for refugee accommodation.

And later we hear that a boat due in Edinburgh could find no-where to dock and so had to turn back. So that plan has been scrapped.

But it is also revealed that there was no previous discussion between the Home Office and the ports about the possibility of mooring boats full of asylum seekers in their waters. So they just turned up and then had to return back to their owners. How much tax-payers money was involved is as yet un-known.

****

Whilst talking about refugees we hear that the charity ECPAT is launching a legal challenge against the Kent County Council and the Home Secretary on the accommodation of unaccompanied children in Home Office hotels. ECPAT stands for End Child Prostitution and Trafficking and is concerned about sexual crimes against refugee children. As we already know, many children have gone missing and there are 154 still not yet found. Some have certainly believed to have been trafficked.

Patricia Durr, the chief executive of ECPAT UK, said: "This is a national child protection scandal that we cannot allow to continue." The move comes after a family court ruled late on Friday that unaccompanied children should not be looked after by the Home Office and should be considered "children in need."

****

And Rishi Sunak is planning a multimillion-pound publicity campaign to promote his five pledges. Well fair enough you might say but as he mentions them all in answer to every single question he is ever asked I think we know them all by now and he is not succeeding with any of them.

And you might not be so happy when you hear that he will be charging it to us, the tax- payer.

Some within the civil service have questioned whether it is too political.

The rules state: "It is possible that a well-founded publicity campaign can create political credit for the party in government. But this must not be the primary or a significant purpose of government information or publicity activities paid for from public fund"

Well I think that is clear enough.

****

And of course there is the Covid-19 inquiry going on and hearings from individuals have just begun. There will be mountains of information about this for years to come.

****

WEDNESDAY 14TH JUNE

We are still awaiting the Privileges Committee Report. Johnson continues to play his disgusting and corrupt games. At 11.57pm on Monday evening he delivered a letter to the Committee making "further representations." He has been working with his lawyers and is saying get on and publish it so I can refute every accusation. There is not a shred of evidence. So this is causing a delay plus also the logistics of printing hundreds of bound hard copies. We hope to see it tomorrow.

And Nadine Dorries still hasn't formally resigned her seat. She is still looking for her peerage. She is demanding an investigation into where it has gone and says she won't resign till she has found it.

I say she could look in the House of Commons because she hasn't been there very often. She has only voted 6 times since November. Ah no, she is demanding to see WhatsApp messages and emails and is going to get to the bottom of this. Not making life easier for Sunak who would like to get the three by-elections done before the summer.

Just been announced that the by-elections will be on the 20th July.

****

The Privileges Committee report is going to be published tomorrow morning.

****

15TH JUNE

IT'S HERE! 9am and the Privileges Committee publishes its long-awaited report.

Oh my word, no wonder he jumped before he was pushed. It is damning.

They recommend **a 90 day suspension** the second longest suspension ever proposed, which is obviously now not possible as he has already gone BUT they also recommend **no future parliament pass.**

Oh happy day!

So this is far worse than any of us could have hoped for. In fact it was made worse because of the way in which Johnson criticised the committee calling it a "kangaroo court."

He was found to have committed five serious offences:

1. Deliberately misleading the Commons
2. Deliberately misleading the Privileges Committee
3. Breaching confidence (by leaking part of the report in advance)
4. "Impugning" the committee, and thus parliamentary processes
5. Complicity in a "campaign of abuse and attempted intimidation of the committee".

So just one tiny part:-

The evidence submission, which was sent to the Committee on 7th February this year, says the notorious "Wine Time Fridays" drinking events in the press office continued "throughout" the pandemic with no social distancing. The drinking sessions were "calendared weekly events in our Outlook diaries starting at 4pm" on Fridays and staff who questioned whether masks should be worn were told there was "no point".

And one No.10 official said the building's security team sent around operational notes telling staff to be "mindful of the cameras outside".

It is all over the news and I have just heard Max Hastings say again what he always says which is that the people he is appalled by are the people who put him there knowing very well what sort of character he was.

Then, surprise, surprise, we see that his team is now circulating a 6-point analysis purportedly explaining why the Privileges Committee report is flawed.

And then there is this. Johnson has issued a 1,700 word reply to the committee.

Basically he still does not know what he has done. "He is bored with the truth" was a comment this morning by someone who knows him well. And yes, "he is a serial liar."

Here are just a few of his words.

"That is a load of complete tripe."

"This report is a charade."

"I was wrong to believe in the Committee or its good faith."

"The terrible truth is that it is not I who has twisted the truth to suit my purposes. It is Harriet Harman and her Committee. The only exception is the June 19 2020 event, the so-called birthday party, when I and the then Chancellor Rishi Sunak were fined in circumstances that I still find puzzling (so the police also got it wrong!) I had lunch at my desk with people I worked with every day. I didn't think for one minute that a committee of MPs could find against me on the facts, and I didn't see how any reasonable person could fail to understand what had happened."

Penny Mordaunt, Leader of the House, has just announced the debate will take place on Monday and it will be a free vote. (No whip but apparently it also means that MPs don't have to turn up.) She urged MPs to take it all seriously and to vote with their conscience. Not that there were many there.

The leader of the SNP has said that our money which was spent on this investigation should be recouped from Johnson, his honours list should be shredded and his PM's retirement salary should be scrapped.

So this will be written about all over the next few days. But as Deborah Ross points out in *The Times* today we are all suffering from BFS. **Boris Fatigue Syndrome. Please, please make this man go away.**

****

17TH JUNE

But here he is again.

He has broken the law **again,** as photographs show him driving a car without his seatbelt on.

He has broken the ministerial code **again,** by accepting a job as a columnist on the Daily Mail.

And he is actually urging all Tories to **vote in favour** of the recommendations from the Privileges Committee. Now why is that I wonder? Apparently it is because he wants to avoid further humiliation when we see how few MPs will actually support him.

****

18TH JUNE

Today we see the most damning video of an illegal party during lockdown which is said to have taken place at Conservative Campaign Headquarters on December 14th 2020. At least 24 people were reportedly at the party and we see some of them dancing together, laughing, drinking, chatting, and we hear them say "As long as we don't stream that we're like, bending the rules," before laughing . Oh it was a 'jingle and mingle' party apparently and 30 were invited. London was in a tier 2 lockdown which banned indoor socialising, and was about to go to a tier 4 with the strictest lockdown rules over Christmas.

This has gone viral on Twitter and is actually on the main stream news.

At the same time we hear thousands of stories from people who were not allowed to visit their dying children or parents or attend funerals of loved ones.

It is disgusting.

****

Another Conservative MP has resigned. David Warburton is standing down saying that allegations about him have made his life a misery. So that is a fourth by-election coming up.

****

19TH JUNE (MONDAY)

So today is the day when we will be watching all Tory MPs to see who, if any, display a shred of honesty, accountability or integrity. We already know that our PM will not be there as he continues to demonstrate his complete lack of any sort of leadership. But I do give a muted thumbs-up to Tobias Ellwood Conservative MP who changed his mind on air at LBC yesterday. Initially when questioned he said: "I am actually taking the defence committee on an important visit to Portsmouth, if I'm back in time I'll support the report but I'm not going out of my way." But after hearing messages from people who had stuck to the rules in spite of dreadful situations he actually changed his mind and said that he would get there and vote for it. But he, I'm afraid, is a dying breed.

****

The junior doctor's 72 hour strike finished on Saturday and teachers have announced two more days of strikes on the 5th and 7th July. Education secretary Gill Keegan and Health secretary Steve Barclay are accused yet again of sitting on their hands and doing nothing. And very little reporting of this going on.

****

And because of strikes by university lecturers, students who have just completed their courses have not had their degrees marked. This is the year of students who also do not have any A level grades because of the pandemic. They will owe tens of thousands of pounds in loans but have no degree. My heart goes out to them.

****

Breaking news: 12.45pm. The Met police has launched a NEW investigation into breeches of Covid laws at No.10, Chequers, inside Parliament and at CCHQ. (Conservative Campaign Head- Quarters). Well in fact, everywhere connected with government.

****

THE FINAL BETRAYAL

19TH JUNE

This will be a short chapter thankfully but such an important one.

Today saw the debate and vote in the House of Commons about the report on Boris Johnson by the Privileges Committee.

The debate began just after 4pm and it has been amazing. It has been like a lancing of the boil. For the first time MPs have been able to stand up in parliament and say exactly what they think of Boris Johnson. And, my word, they haven't held back.

One of the highlights for me (and there were many) was when Dawn Butler (Labour) stood up and called Johnson a liar. She, you might remember, told the Commons in July 2021 that Mr Johnson had "lied to the House and the country over and over again". For this remark she was temporarily suspended from parliament. But today? She let it rip and was able to speak the truth without fear or favour.

But the debate started with the Leader of the House, Penny Mordaunt, giving a statement and declaring that although it is difficult to speak critically about friends and colleagues it is important that everyone follows their conscience. She praised the Committee for their hard work and said she would be voting in favour of their findings. She impressed me with her seriousness and good sense.

But what on earth was this? The rest of the front bench was virtually empty. Penny Mordaunt spent the entire debate sitting in isolation.

So where was the PM? Nowhere to be seen.

So the first seven speeches were given by very passionate articulate women. Penny Mordaunt, Thangham Debbonaire, shadow leader of the House, Shona Robinson SNP, Theresa May, Harriet Harman, Andrea Leadsom, and Angela Eagle. They were all on fire in their damnation of Johnson.

Many too many to comment on but later we had Iain Blackford, Chris Bryant, Caroline Lucas and Pete Wishart. Many called out the PM for not being there and the other Conservatives for supporting Johnson and putting him there in the first place when they knew exactly what sort of person he was.

Obviously we also had to endure Rees-Mogg and someone called Lia Nici, and Jake Berry but they were the only ones in the 'against' tribe.

9pm. Keir Starmer has just arrived in the House having travelled back from Scotland to be in time for the vote.

The PM is still hosting the Swedish PM in No 10 just across the road.

Ah 9.30pm and they are voting! Penny Mordaunt has given a summing up and it has not been nodded through because there was a loud shout of "**no**" when the Speaker called it out. So we will see exactly who votes for what and who abstains.

Here it comes.........

The Ayes 354...... the Noes 7

Oh my goodness his support was even smaller than we thought. As someone has just said on Twitter he has more children than this.

****

20TH JUNE

Well this morning I hear where many Tory MPs were last night. Can you guess? Yes, at a party.

Well strictly speaking it was a sort of conference for the International Democratic Union. But we saw them all walking into this event all dressed up and for some reason unable to talk and reply to journalist's questions. And who was the speaker? None other than the person whose lack of democratic skills was being discussed in the House of Commons. Boris Johnson. Unbelievable.

But I think we need to look more carefully at the IDU.

Its headquarters are in Munich and it is an international alliance of centre-right political parties. However it has been increasingly seen as further right on the political spectrum and so to me anyway, it is no surprise that many of our Conservative MPs were there last night rather than representing us, their constituents, in the House of Commons in an important and unprecedented vote on democracy.

So is that the end of Johnson? He has lost his parliamentary pass. But I think he will keep surfacing somewhere like the bad penny that he is.

****

29TH JUNE

Oh my word as we come to the end of June we hear three amazing pieces of good news.

- Dominic Raab's controversial Bill of Rights has been quietly scrapped.
- Seven MPs and one peer have been accused of trying to interfere with the Johnson inquiry by the Privileges Committee. They are Nadine Dorries, Jacob Rees-Mogg, Mark Jenkinson, Brendan Clarke–Smith, Andrea Jenkins, Priti Patel

and the peer, Zac Goldsmith. They are all in contempt of parliament. We wait for the Prime Minister to admonish them in some way. And we keep waiting.

But just wait till you hear this one:-

* The Court of Appeal has just pronounced on Suella Braverman's plan to deport asylum seekers to Rwanda and declared it to be unlawful.

Well we have all known this to be the case but whilst Braverman can argue with the likes of us she can't argue with a court of law. She will try mind you and she will be issuing a statement at the end of parliament procedure this evening.

****

30TH JUNE

Surprise, surprise, indeed both Braverman and Sunak fundamentally disagree with the findings of the Appeal Court and will now send it up to the Supreme Court at great expense to the tax-payer.

But here's a thing. On the BBC's programme 'Question Time' last night the mainly Conservative voting audience were asked how many of them approved of the Rwanda programme for asylum seekers. Not one single hand went up.

Ms. Braverman keeps saying that she speaks for the British people.

No, Ms. Braverman, I don't think you do.

****

THE END GAME

Well this month, July, the last in this book, is proving to be absolutely bizarre.

****

Zac Goldsmith has just announced that he is stepping down as a minister. His reason is that he was working on the environment brief at the foreign office, and has resigned in disgust at the government's apathy and complete disinterest on climate change issues. Well that is certainly true as we hear from the government's own advisors that the Tories have "missed climate targets on almost every front" but interesting that he chooses the day after he is accused of contempt of parliament by the Privileges Committee. So there we go. Another Tory MP bites the dust. Oh wait a minute he is still a Lord so he can still keep all the money and privilege.

****

Today begins a two day hearing at the High Court of the government's legal challenge over the UK Covid Inquiry's demand for the un-redacted messages of Boris Johnson's phones, WhatsApp messages and diaries.

So many court cases it really is difficult to keep up.

****

3RD JULY

Oh my goodness what is this I am hearing?

About 12 Conservative MPs have launched **another** group within the Tory party. It is called **The New Conservatives** not to be confused with **Nationalism Conservatism (NatCon)** or the **Conservative Democratic Organisation (CDO)**.

This one was launched in May. Well I might have missed it then but I've got it now. The New Conservatives are made up of 25 Tory MPs elected since the Brexit referendum. Their three founders are Miriam Cates, Danny Kruger and '30p' Lee Anderson. That is really all you need to know but I will just say what their main project is about in case you are unfamiliar with the names. Immigration is their concern. Basically they're against it.

This is what Miriam Cates stated after the launch: "Yesterday I spoke at the launch of the New Conservatives' Plan to Cut Migration, explaining how high levels of low-skilled migration into the UK has had a negative impact on wages, productivity, and living standards." She went on to say that "swift action" is needed for the Conservatives to "keep our word" on immigration.

I'm not sure what Sunak has to say about this but I discovered it when I heard Lee Anderson saying that he wants to block overseas workers from UK care homes.

At the moment social care workers, care assistants and home care worker roles are currently included on the Shortage Occupation List. This means staff are eligible for the Health and Care Worker visa, lasting either three or five years.

I believe that what these people are thinking is that if we stop all foreigners from entering the UK and doing these jobs then there will be jobs available for 'British' workers. However at the moment there are 165,000 vacancies in adult social care so there doesn't seem to be a flood of interest. And to suggest that we stop those who **do** want to look after elderly people, just because they are coming from abroad, is insane.

****

The government has suffered what is thought to be a record 20 defeats in the House of Lords over its controversial Illegal Migration Bill. Tory peer Baroness Stroud called for more safe and legal routes for refugees. "The moral credibility of the entire bill depends on the existence of the creation of more safe and legal routes," she said.

But Mr Sunak has said he "fundamentally disagrees" with the Court of Appeal's ruling and will appeal it at the Supreme Court. So it drags on.

£169,000 is what it will cost to send each and every refugee to Rwanda. Is that really a good use of tax-payer's money?

And just to be clear, as *The Observer* editorial states, the UK is home to a tiny fraction of the world's refugees and receives far fewer asylum applications per head than the EU average. More than three-quarters of displaced people live in low and middle income countries. We are fed lies and mis-information in order to promote divisiveness and a 'culture war'.

And ask yourself this question: How is it that there are no refugees from Ukraine or Hong Kong on those small boats?

****

The cruelty towards asylum seekers, especially children, continues unabated. The government published its Child's Rights impact assessment for the Illegal Migration Bill yesterday, on 4 July 2023. **This is part of what it says about the use of reasonable force on refugee children:**

"We are also reviewing our existing policy position in respect of use of reasonable force, or physical intervention, to enable the Home Office to facilitate removals of families with children under this Bill ... Use of force is not currently used against minors for compliance/removal purposes. We do not envisage the use of reasonable force being used for such purposes under the auspices of the new Bill unless it is necessary as a last resort where other methods to ensure compliance have failed."

I call this child abuse. What do you call it?

****

For then we must turn to Robert Jenrick who is an Immigration Minister.

You might have to read this twice because it is unbelievable.

In a centre for unaccompanied refugee children in Kent there is a colourful mural of Disney characters and other cartoons together with large welcome notices in different languages.

Mr. Jenrick has ordered the staff to paint over this mural and to take down the welcome notices.

He says this is a law enforcement centre not a welcoming committee.

I find it difficult to process this. How can anyone even think of doing something like this? How?

And it is not long before Twitter goes into meltdown about it. The backlash is enormous and this is why I love Twitter. The kindness and support and offers of help for anyone in trouble is amazing and is what gives me hope for the future. Cartoonists and artists are all saying they are going to Kent to paint another mural. Those who say they can't paint for toffee have offered to buy the brushes and the paint and others have offered tea and biscuits.

But it really does get worse.

Apparently the staff refused to paint over the mural so, listen to this, the government got contractors in to do it, presumably at our expense.

Keep going tweeters.

But then I hear about 8 and 9 year olds at a primary school in Birmingham who were so ashamed at this action by Robert Jenrick that they have painted pictures especially for refugee children. Listen to the young. Kind, compassionate and clear-sighted. They should rule the world.

****

6TH JULY

Well this is a red-letter day for the Tories. We are going to hear from the standards watchdog about the Chris Pincher affair this morning and we will hear the result of the High Court hearing about the Covid WhatsApp messages this afternoon. Ha, and I bet the one person we **won't** be hearing from will be the Prime Minister. He never seems to be very visible these days.

10.07am Here it comes. Wow. **The watchdog recommends that Chris Pincher is suspended for eight weeks.** Eight weeks? That is massive. I'm sure you will remember that it was his actions which were the final straw in getting rid of Johnson last June. He was deputy chief whip and was accused of drunkenly groping two men at the Carlton Club in central London. The Committee said his behaviour was "especially grave" as his senior position in government meant his actions were "an abuse of power". They said he was guilty of "an egregious case of sexual misconduct". Well this has to be voted on in the House of Commons but it could be yet another by-election for Sunak to cope with.

2.30pm. And here is the next one.

The government have lost their judicial review against the government Covid inquiry. I know.....you really couldn't make it up. So this means that Lady Hallett can see all un-redacted phone messages, diaries and notes which she thinks are relevant to the inquiry. The' Bereaved Families for Justice' have praised this decision but called the whole episode a waste of time and money. Yes well, how often do we hear that one?

****

So where is Sunak?

Well it would seem that he really does not like being questioned, he does not like being criticized and he definitely does not like anyone who won't vote for him. Revealing plans to crack down on degrees with poor career outcomes, it has emerged that he told Tory supporters in Bury, Greater Manchester, last August: "We've got to get far tougher on those university courses that are simply not paying their way, because we are spending your money to subsidise these courses, which are not producing the goods for people, right? **So it's great news for the universities largely full of, you know, people who don't vote for us anyway."**

So is this correct? He is basically saying that the people who enter higher education are generally not Conservatives. Well that does explain a lot.

Justine Greening who ran the Department for Education from 2016 to 2018, warned that the proposal would disproportionately affect more disadvantaged people from the poorest communities. "No 10 plans are bad for disadvantaged young people and bad for universities working hard to give access to higher education in less privileged areas. This will be anti-levelling up in action," she tweeted.

And students will now have to pay off their loans from when they earn £25,000 a year instead of £27,295, and repay for a maximum of 40 years, instead of 30.

****

Then he had to attend a Liaison Committee. The whole idea of these hearings is for a detailed cross-examination of a PM on his or her policies away from the pressured atmosphere of Prime Minister's Questions. But the very first comment he made was that he had a pressing engagement at 3.30pm so they mustn't go over time.

This made them all inclined to rush a bit which was probably his intention, and he talked over everyone as much as he could without answering the questions, until they got to Sir Chris Bryant, a future Labour PM. (That is purely my subjective wish).

Chris Bryant exploded at Sunak in furious disbelief. He slammed Sunak's decision not to attend the Privileges Committee vote on Johnson and he also commented on his poor record of attendance at PMQs, the worst attendance record since 1979. And then, when questioning him on the second report by the Privileges Committee about the seven Tory MPs denouncing the Boris Johnson Partygate inquiry as a "whitewash" and "kangaroo court", Mr Sunak said: "I haven't read every page of the report." Chris Bryant was scathing. **"You.....haven't...read...the...report?"**

"Er well not cover to cover" the PM said.

"It's three pages long," says Bryant. I think the PM eventually realised there were two reports being discussed but it took a bit of time.

****

So we ask again? Where is Sunak? Not at PMQs this week not at PMQs next week and then it is the summer recess.

OK I'll tell you. **He is watching the cricket.**

Yes, yes we all know how important cricket is and this is the Ashes test match with our Aussie friends and the weather is perfect and we are playing really well. But I would have thought that with the country in crisis it would be important to read reports, answer questions and attend Parliament. He gives absolutely no comment whatever on any of the problems of today which, as you know, are huge and effecting nearly everyone.

Oh but wait a minute. **Here is a comment on the rules of cricket**. And it is a very suspect comment in my opinion. Rishi Sunak has accused Australia of breaking the spirit of cricket over the controversial dismissal of England's Jonny Bairstow last Sunday (2nd July).

Trust me this just shows, either that he does **not** understand the rules of cricket or that he is very happy to support those accusing the Australians of cheating when they did no such thing.

I do not know all the ins and outs of cricket but I do come from a family of dedicated cricketers and I know the importance of **staying behind your crease**. The issue is that Bairstow had ducked a bouncer and the ball had been caught behind his wicket. Mistakenly thinking that the ball was out of play he moved forward to bash down a bit of grass with his bat. So he was stumped out as he was away from the crease. Well the English did not like that because we were doing quite well up to this point so they started to accuse the Australians of cheating. This is disgraceful behaviour.

And I am now hearing that three members of the MCC have been suspended from Lords. They were accused of 'aggressive and abusive' behaviour in the Long Room against the Australians.

So Mr. Sunak where are your principles please? Indeed do you have any?

****

Oh but wait a minute I've just discovered him somewhere else. Of course. He had to be at the 75th anniversary service in Westminster Abbey for the NHS. And it just happened to coincide with PMQs.

So we had to listen to the deputy chairman Oliver Dowden giving questionable statistics at PMQs and we also listened to Mr. Sunak reading the lesson in Westminster Abbey. It was taken from Matthew chapter 25, vs. 35 to 39. You know it. It goes like this:

"For I was hungry and you gave me something to eat, I was thirsty and you gave me something to drink, I was a stranger and you invited me in, I needed clothes and you clothed me, I was sick and you looked after me, I was in prison and you came to visit me."

Hmm, I think someone was being a bit mischievous here. But the fact that he could stand there and read this out indicates an appalling lack of self-awareness. As someone said all it missed out was "I needed to travel and you gave me a helicopter."

****

And here we go again. The talk in Westminster, behind closed doors, is that the back-benches are out for Sunak. They are all concerned that the five pledges are not cutting through with the public. Well of course they aren't. See above.

Conservative MPs have already begun discussing who will replace Rishi Sunak if the party loses the next election and if Keir Starmer does become Prime Minister – a fate for which many in the parliamentary party are increasingly resigned. Despondent and braced for defeat, speaking to *PoliticsHome* this week, one former secretary of state said that the level of unrest within the Conservative party might become unmanageable for Sunak between now and the end of the year, and force him into calling an early general election.

Please, please roll on that day.

****

10TH JULY

This afternoon there is to be a debate in the Commons about the second report by the Privileges Committee which found that seven MPs, allies of Johnson, had undertaken a 'sustained' and 'co-ordinated campaign' to undermine its investigations. We know the names. There will again be a free vote and if approved then I think sanctions will apply. It won't surprise you to hear that the accused are trying to table an opposing amendment to water it down a bit.

But the main question is, "Will Sunak be there to vote if it goes to a vote?"

Actually Biden is in town. Tea at Windsor Castle with him and the King and all that. A perfect excuse.

****

We also look ahead to tomorrow when Sunak will decide whether or not we will rejoin the Horizon programme. At the moment he is still dithering about whether to rejoin it or force our scientists to go it alone with an alternative scientific programme called Pioneer which will have UK funding only. It really is concerning that he is dithering about this decision. Sir Paul Nurse, the Nobel laureate and head of the Francis Crick Institute in London, says that: "Everywhere where science and technology matter will be damaged if we don't associate with Europe's Horizon programme."

****

12TH JULY

Michael Gove has handed back £1.9billion to the Treasury saying that he was struggling to find anything to spend it on. This money, budgeted for 2022-23, included £255m for new affordable housing and £245m for improving building safety. It really is unbelievable. The number of homes suffering from mould alone would benefit from this money. It should have been distributed to local authorities who could have used it for social housing.

And what about the target of 300,000 new homes a year? In the same article in *The Independent* written by Archie Mitchell, one spokesman says "Our target of delivering 300,000 homes per year remains" whilst they also go on to talk about Mr Sunak's decision to **abandon** mandatory targets to build 300,000 new houses.

Shadow housing secretary Lisa Nandy accused the government of "giving up trying to solve the housing crisis that they helped create."

****

13TH JULY

Still no decision about Horizon. More dither and delay.

****

BREAKING NEWS 11.13am

The High Court has just ruled that the draconian anti-strike laws are illegal. This is a huge victory for more than 10 unions who took legal action against the government for a law which would allow bosses to bring in agency staff to cover for striking workers.

This legislation was pushed through at speed by former Business Secretary Kwasi Kwarteng last year, after he ignored the advice of civil servants. So the High Court has ruled that the 2022 Conduct of Employment Agencies and Employment Businesses (Amendment) Regulations -which lifted a ban on agency staff standing in for striking workers - were unlawful.

TUC General Secretary Paul Nowak said: "This defeat is a badge of shame for the Conservatives, who have been found guilty of breaching the law.

"Bringing in less-qualified agency staff to deliver important services risks endangering public safety, worsening disputes and poisoning industrial relations."

Meanwhile the **Illegal Migration Bill** continues its journey backwards and forwards between the Commons and the Lords. Another disgraceful and probably illegal Bill. Braverman still wants to defy the courts.

****

And Mr. Sunak has just announced that all pay review recommendations will be paid in full. Goodness anyone would think there were elections coming up. Ah yes. A week today.

However if we look carefully we see that nearly all the funding will have to be found from existing budgets.

But the Government is also planning to increase the NHS surcharge charged to migrants in the UK from £624 to £1,035 per year in order to fund the increases. This will cause a lot of distress and Unison warned that this would push more people into poverty. As Christina McAna, Unison's general secretary said "Migrant workers should be welcomed, not punished for the government's failure to fund public services properly."

Teachers look as though they will accept the offer. Strange U-turn here as Sunak has always said it is completely unaffordable.

But he really does set himself up to fail. The doctors are still not happy and are on strike this week and are saying that strike action will continue throughout the coming winter unless a better offer is forthcoming. But Sunak is insisting that there will be no further pay talks for anyone this year. Senior NHS figures are saying that this entrenched attitude could poison relations with consultants for years to come leading to a crisis in morale and many further disputes.

And I now hear that actually teachers are **not** happy and that GPs are threatening to strike for a whole week.

****

Of course we could always ask Boris for a sub. He is making **£21,800** for his work outside parliament. Er, that is per hour. Oh and then there is Liz Truss. Not quite so lucrative at **£15,000** an hour for speaking engagements.

Commons Health Committee chairman Steve Brine, who worked 497 hours in second jobs during this Parliament on an average of £200 per hour, warned against "smearing MPs".

He said "Be very careful before you run our profession into the ground."

Oh my word. You really don't need any help from us, but yes, blame us for your own greed and duplicity.

****

14TH JULY

This is rather worrying. The Intelligence and Security Committee have just produced a 207 page report which concluded that Britain was being subjected to a "whole state assault" by China, which had targeted politicians, sensitive infrastructure, the military, private companies and the academic sector. They say that successive governments have readily accepted Chinese money with "few questions asked, so placing national security at serious risk." They concluded that Britain faces a "nightmare scenario" of China controlling sensitive national infrastructure including nuclear power stations, universities and the technology sector.

****

So we go in to the last week. Well maybe I should define what I mean by this. It's not the last week of the planet although that appears to be getting ever closer. It is the last week of this parliamentary session.

The Sunday papers are having a field day.

****

16TH JULY

Temperatures are soaring all across Europe and are edging upwards of 40 degrees centigrade. Scientists are saying that globally heatwaves are becoming more frequent, more intense and are lasting longer due to global warming.

Governments however, are still not doing enough to combat this threat. UN secretary general Antonio Guterres says that "climate change is out of control." He warns that we must limit fossil fuel emissions without delay.

But what are the Tories doing? They decide to pursue a new round of North Sea licences. This comes as we see a report by the Office for Budget Responsibility which warns of catastrophic effects on the economy of continued over reliance on gas and fossil fuel. More onshore wind farms are essential they say.

I wonder if the government's plans have anything at all to do with the fact that the the Conservative party appear to be a bit close to energy companies, having received more than a million pounds in donations from the energy sector since the last election. These figures are from openDemocracy. Who knows?

****

And buses might not be your first interest but I think this is worth noting. It sounds like a typical Boris promise. You might not remember but he introduced a 'flagship' policy to roll out 4,000 "green" buses that run on electricity or hydrogen by 2025.This would drastically reduce emissions. So how is it going?

Well local councils have spent at least £45million since 2016 trying to retrofit the buses but the retrofitted buses are not reducing emissions as expected. And Transport Secretary Mark Harper was forced to admit last May that only 87 green buses are currently on the road outside London.

Abdul Jabbar, a Labour councillor in Oldham, said: "To say that retrofittting doesn't work in the real world after spending millions pounds of public money, it's just unbelievable." Trouble is I **can** believe it.

****

17TH JULY

And of course no week would be complete without hearing from Suella Braverman, She is embroiled in a row with Ben Wallace the defence secretary. It is said that she had demanded that 750 armed forces personnel be made available to cover immigration posts in the event of wider strikes at airports and sea ports, warning of major travel disruption. However Mr. Wallace has refused this request and said that the Home Office should have made contingency plans. A source told *The Mail on Sunday* newspaper: "The Home Secretary must not be allowed to always rely on our hard-working armed forces to be there to mop up for Home Office incompetence. If she was so worried, she should have planned ahead."

Ben Wallace, one of the few reasonably competent Tory ministers, has said that he will step down from defence in the next reshuffle which is expected in September. He will leave politics at the next election.

****

18TH JULY

It continues to be a story-a-day.

openDemocracy has uncovered this. Volga-Dnepr Airlines which is a controversial Russian cargo airline, was handed 8,700 free credits under Britain's Emissions Trading scheme in 2022, one day after the Russian invasion of Ukraine. Not only did this absolve them from having to pay an estimated £690,000 bill but the ETS is supposed to penalise big polluters, including airlines, for their carbon dioxide emissions.

Alexey Isaikin who owned the airline at the time of this payment was on sanctions lists around the world and is now sanctioned by Britain. But the government has been criticised for not acting more quickly.

****

19TH JULY

Barges. The compassionate face of modern Conservatism

Having thought that all barges and cruise ships for asylum seekers had been stopped we see one that has sneaked in to the Port of Portland in Dorset. I say sneaked in but actually it is enormous and was towed in by two tugs having come all the way from Falmouth. It will hold 500 men instead of the 250 it was designed for. And there was a huge crowd of protesters on the quay-side watching it arrive. There were two groups. One saying they welcomed all refugees and the other saying we don't want them here. Police had to be called in to separate them. So the government's aim to promote division and hatred amongst the population is succeeding. However looking more closely, both groups deplored the use of the barge.

So why is it that when the local councils at all other ports have refused permission for barges or cruise ships to dock in their waters Portland Port has agreed?

It is because it is privately owned by Langham Industries who took over control of Portland Harbour from the Royal Navy in 1997. Conservative run Dorset Council voted in favour of a motion demanding housing the men on the barge to be stopped. But actually there is nothing they can do. Did a significant amount of money exchange hands?

I honestly do not know. What are your thoughts on the matter?

****

And the first module of the Covoid-19 inquiry has just concluded. The report is due to be published next year but we have sight of some of the general findings now.

Module 1. Preparedness.

It would appear that the nation was caught badly off guard and as 'Covid-19 Bereaved Families for Justice' group said the evidence showed the UK was "catastrophically unprepared". We were prepared for a flu pandemic but not for this one. So there was little if any consideration given to the measures such as shielding, employment support, managing disruption to schools, borders and lockdowns.

And Prof Dame Sally Davies, chief medical officer from 2010 to 2019 said that compared with similar countries, the UK was bottom of the table on numbers of doctors, nurses, beds, intensive care units, respirators and ventilators. "We didn't have the resilience," she said. The BMA said the state of the system was "brutally exposed" by the pandemic.

The UK entered the pandemic with its public services depleted, health improvements stalled, health inequalities increased and health among the poorest people in a state of decline," said the epidemiologist Sir Michael Marmot and Clare Bambra, a professor of public health.

The NHS was not given the resources it needed. In the decade preceding the pandemic it had £40 billion a year less than France, and £70 billion less than Germany. The TUC union provided evidence that public service spending was cut by 24% per capita in the decade leading up to the pandemic.

And why, they want to know, was power taken away from local control. The government took central control which was not the recommended approach and was not happening anywhere else.

Also, the testing regime was not very sensible as, instead of the 44 NHS labs coming online, the tests were outsourced to the private sector. Patients were directed to 111 and then to a test station with no clinical contact whatever.

The findings I read about today make very worrying reading. But it is the government who need to be really worried. This inquiry will take years to complete but we will understand the general incompetence before then.

****

The illegal 'Illegal Migration Bill' becomes law as the House of Lords decides to "respect the will of the elected House."

The UNHCR (United Nations Refugee Agency) is appalled and urges the government to reverse this decision. In just one small paragraph from a very long press release it says, "All those who leave their country of origin to seek safety and protection elsewhere are entitled to the full respect of their human rights and dignity, regardless of their legal status, mode of arrival or any other distinction."

The international respect that we used to have has now completely dissipated.

****

It would appear that Sunak will make no decision about **re-joining the Horizon** programme until after the summer recess. Totally dysfunctional.

****

20TH JULY

By-election day!.......and

21ST JULY...THE RESULTS AND IT IS A VICTORY FOR ...... THE CONSERVATIVE PARTY!

Hang on a minute. What is this? As with all things mentioned by the Conservatives we need to look at all of this a little more closely.

Yes indeed the Tories held on to Uxbridge, Johnson's old seat, having initially thought they could win it. But his majority of over 7,000 was cut to 495. The main stumbling block was extending the reach of ULEZ which the Labour mayor of London was advocating in order to decrease air pollution but it came at a cost. However it should have been emphasised that many people would not have to pay it and there was financial help available. Labour seems to have been caught on the back foot by this and really should not try to roll back on what is an important health policy. The Tories are saying what a dreadful Labour policy this is but again we do need to remind everyone that it was Boris Johnson who introduced it when he was mayor of London and it was just a pity that he never got round to implementing it.

But in Somertone and Frome the Lib Dems turned a Tory majority of 19,213 into an 11,008 majority for them which is a 29% swing and this was the result of tactical voting.

And in Selby and Ainsty, North Yorkshire, there was a swing of 23. 7% as the Conservative majority of 20,000 became a Labour majority of 4,161. This marks the first time since 2010 that the constituency will not be represented by the Tories and it was the highest majority the party had ever overturned in a by-election. A similar swing across the country would result in Labour winning more seats than in Tony Blair's 1997 landslide.

If this looks like a Tory victory, the Tories need to be more worried than I thought.

But we have the Chair of the Tory party, Greg Hands, on Radio 4's *Today* programme this morning saying that: "I think the standout result was the one in Uxbridge. That's the one that people weren't expecting." We then heard people laughing in the background! The presenter, Nick Robinson interrupted Greg Hands and he said: "We are joined, I should explain, by Sir John Curtice and [BBC political editor] Chris Mason. I wouldn't be disrespectful enough to laugh at your answer, but they just did."

Sir John Curtice, is a leading pollster and professor of politics at Strathclyde University, and he said the Conservatives were in a "difficult position" after losing two out of three by-elections. I think that as Sunak keeps talking up their win in Uxbridge, he is looking at the wrong election results.

So no...........definitely not a victory for you Mr. Sunak.

****

4pm Breaking news. The phone! Technical experts have recovered all relevant messages from Boris Johnson's old mobile phone so they can be handed to the Covid-19 Inquiry, a spokesperson for the former PM has said. At last and not before time. How has it taken so long?

And so now all MPs leave parliament for their summer recess. A brief respite from this on-going psycho-drama.

****

But just before we leave you Mr. Sunak, as indeed I am afraid we must, is there any explanation for this?

When you were Chancellor in March last year you said: "I am urging firms to think very carefully about their investments in Russia and how they may aid the Putin regime."

But now I read that Rowena Mason and Peter Walker of *The Guardian* have reported that on the 9th June Labour urged the Conservatives to hand back a £5m donation from the party's senior treasurer, Mohamed Mansour, as it questioned why it had taken so long for one of his companies to wind down its business in Russia.

Labour drew particular attention to Mansour's co-ownership of 'Mantrac', which earlier this week still appeared to have a Russian-language website advertising its services as an authorised dealer of Caterpillar hardware and equipment, with 14 offices in the country. Anneliese Dodds, Chair of the Labour Party, said it had been brought to her attention that "the Conservative party senior treasurer Mohamed Mansour's firm is operating a Russian-language website" and questioned his previous financial ties to Russia "at a time when the UK is rightly imposing sanctions on the Putin regime and the Prime Minister has repeatedly called on British companies to pull out of Russia in order to 'inflict maximum economic pain' on Putin's regime".

Mansour revealed last month that he was giving £5million to the Conservatives, the largest donation to the party since Sir Paul Getty in 2001. 'Mantrac' said it was winding down its business in Russia at about the same time.

When questioned about this by Chris Bryant at the Liaison committee Sunak said he knew of no company with that name. A bit strange as he received such a large donation from them.

****

The unlawful activities of the Ministers in this government continue un-abated and won't stop until there is a general election. So let me finish by summing up the legacy of this Conservative government.

****

THE LEGACY OF 13 YEARS OF TORY RULE IT IS NOT LOOKING GOOD

We have the **highest taxation** since the second world war coupled with the **highest inflation** in 40 years.

We have the **biggest drop in living standards** since records began with wages falling at their fastest rate for two decades.

Food prices increased by 19.1 per cent in the 12 months to March 2023, which is the sharpest jump since August 1977.

The Trussell Trust saw record numbers of people seeking help between April 2022 and March 2023, with more than **760,000 people forced to turn to the charity's food banks** for the first time. In fact food banks are becoming multi-banks with bedding, furnishings, toiletries, clothes and baby needs and so are becoming replacements for benefits which would imply that the welfare state is failing. Corporate donors such as Amazon and Tesco are being asked to donate goods to these banks and so are doing more than the government.

59.9% (so almost 3/5) of people in poverty are in a household where someone works.

Mortgage rates have risen to 6.6%, the highest level since 2008.

But Rishi Sunak says "The record is clear. The number of people in poverty is lower." As Gordon Brown writes in *The Observer*, "**The most generous way to explain his interpretation of the data is that he is looking at the data upside down.**"

And openDemocracy can reveal that every senior official at the bank of England – except for the governor, Andrew Bailey – has had their salary increased, averaging more than £4,300 each. His deputies each now earn between £348,000 and £378,000.The comments from bosses at the bank telling ordinary workers not to request big pay rises has sparked anger among trade union leaders. I think we are all angry actually.

Our education system is in crisis as 67% of teachers now claim that their workload has become unmanageable – a rise of 45% since the 2020 survey.

97% of them attested that the job has adversely affected their mental health in the last 12 months. Teachers are leaving the profession. Classes could rise to 60. Many children are still out of school after the pandemic and suffering with mental health problems.

It was the 75th anniversary of the NHS on the 5th July and we have NHS England saying that more than 27,000 medical staff, including consultants, GPs and surgeons, quit between July and September – around 2% of the entire workforce. The mass exodus is the largest since records began in 2011. Almost 7,000 said they left because they could no longer live a normal life. Nurses and doctors and midwives are leaving the profession in droves. Junior doctors and consultants have voted to strike. The Social Care system is in crisis.

A study by 'The Kings Fund' health think tank reports that Britons die sooner than patients in other countries from cancer and heart disease partly because of lack of beds, staff and scanners but also due to years of under-investment. The recent 15 year workforce plan report for the future of the NHS is just more words and is too little too late. Neuro-surgeon Henry Marsh says these plans for cheap instant doctors are terrible. And an inquiry into the maternity unit at Nottingham University Trust hospital to be led by Donna Ockenden, is expected to uncover the largest maternity scandal in the history of the NHS with more than 1,700 families involved. Already the NHS has had to pay £90 million in compensation to traumatised families.

And almost 11,000 people in England were admitted to hospital with malnutrition last year. Doctors warn that the rise in Victorian illnesses such as rickets and scurvy, especially prevalent in children, is due to the cost of living crisis.

Rishi Sunak says waiting lists are coming down and he is confidant of reaching his target by the end of the year as we hear that waiting lists reach a record high.

Lack of funding for NHS dentists means people are so desperate they are pulling out their own teeth.

4,600 pubs, clubs, hotels and restaurants have closed in the year up to the 31st March due in the main to Brexit but also due to the cost of living crisis. Britain now has 13,793 fewer pubs, bars, hotels and restaurants, nightclubs and other licensed premises than it had three years ago. There are currently 142,000 unfilled jobs in the accommodation and food services sector, according to the Office for National Statistics. This represents a 6.5% job vacancy rate, which is almost 50% above pre-Brexit levels, and is the highest rate across all of the UK's business sectors.

Our criminal justice system is broken and collapsing, quite literally in many cases, as courts are not maintained and so are crumbling before our eyes. There continues to be a huge backlog of criminal cases. Judges and barristers are leaving the profession.

The asylum seekers system is broken with all refugees being treated as criminals. It is also a distinctly racist approach by this government as the only safe and legal routes are for the Ukrainians and those from Hong Kong. There are none being set up for Sudanese refugees, there have been very few Afghan refugees and there are none for anyone else. Out of the 22,000 places promised for Afghan refugees just 22 have now been placed.

If you are black or brown you haven't got a hope. All refugees are to be locked up and then deported. The Home Secretary admits that the government's target of clearing the asylum backlog by the end of the year will not now be met. Home Office staff who are assessing claims are being retrained as 'detention decision makers.' The illegal 'Illegal Migration Bill has been passed into law although the decision on Rwanda will be decided by the Supreme Court in the autumn.

All our rivers and many coastal resorts are full of raw sewage. As Andrew Rawnsley says "we have gone from the affluent society to the effluent society."

The Carbon Budget Delivery Plan continues to be too slow and the statuary progress report for 2023 has raised new concerns. They report that "despite new detail from Government, our confidence in the UK meeting its medium-term targets has decreased in the past year. The increased transparency embodied in the CBDP is welcome, but a key opportunity to raise the overall pace of delivery has been missed.

Farmers and fisherman are struggling with the food supply chain amid a complete lack of help or understanding from the government.

Red tape destroys musicians trying to tour the EU, as the scale of the slump in British performers in Europe is revealed. But it is also becoming increasingly difficult for foreign orchestras or bands to enter the UK. Cuts in funding for the arts are catastrophc.

Then we come to the most vulnerable of all and to those who affect me the most: our children. The way in which this government has treated our children is despicable. The government have been, and still are, negligent, incompetent, mean and cruel. I don't use those adjectives lightly. They simply don't care.

At the time of writing (June 2023) there are **4.2 million children living in poverty** in the UK which is one in three children. Work does not provide a guaranteed route out of poverty in the UK. 71% of children growing up in poverty live in a household where at least one person works.

Many children **did not receive computers for home learning** during the pandemic and so are still behind in their education. **Children are going to school hungry** and so are unable to concentrate on their work. For the first time ever Unicef are helping hungry children in the UK. They estimate that there are children going hungry in a fifth of all UK households.

Many Primary schools do not have a library and many children move to secondary school without appropriate literary skills.

Many schools are structurally unsafe and staff are concerned about the likelihood of accidents to children and teachers whilst at school.

Children are still being abused both physically and emotionally in privately run residential homes. I have written about this since 2019 and nothing improves.

And the waiting lists for children's surgery is double that of adults, as a definite choice is made to prioritise those over the age of 18.

Young people in Young Offender Institutes, already vulnerable, suffer abuse and neglect due to underfunding, cuts in prison staff, cuts in education and no books or exercise or rehabilitation. We don't need new prisons, we need more help for vulnerable families and teenagers and to follow the example of Norway and the Netherlands who send fewer people to jail but spend more money on their general care and rehabilitation outside prison and who have found that their crime rates have plummeted.

Recent reports describe the over-crowding of our prisons and say it is a powder-keg waiting to explode.

And the children of prisoners are left to fend for themselves.

And children are being handcuffed when transported from one privately run children's home to another.

And then there is just one word, but one which has destroyed Britain as we knew it. **BREXIT**

Any future government needs to reverse as much of the Brexit debacle as they possibly can. I actually think that Keir Starmer needs to be bolder on many issues but on this subject in particular. Caution is sensible but not where Brexit is concerned.

The 23rd June is the 7th anniversary of Brexit and all I can do now is to quote some final words of an article by that brilliant writer John Crace of *The Guardian*. He is talking about Rishi Sunak and how he still seems intimidated by Johnson.

"Everyone knows his integrity is shot" he writes of Sunak. "Sooner or later he will have to call Johnson out. The longer he leaves it, the worse he looks. **For a politician, Sunak isn't even very good at politics." The polls are looking terrible for Sunak.**

And they continue to be so as we see in the Selby and Ainsty by-election.

Many Tory MPs are saying they are resigned to a complete wipe-out.

We have a government which takes its own inquiry to court and we listen to Matt Hancock giving evidence to the Covid inquiry and saying that we were completely unprepared and caused many more unnecessary deaths by not following scientific advice. Also that he didn't know how many care homes there were.

And we hear about a previous prime minister who is found guilty of lying to Parliament which is unprecedented.

We also hear more about Johnson's connections with the Russians from a brilliant Dispatches programme on Channel 4.

****

I cannot believe that anyone is happy with this legacy. Every single Conservative politician should hang their head in shame. But as people struggle to pay their mortgages and feed their children all our Prime Minister can say is "I have a plan. I'm 100% on it. **Hold Your Nerve**." This does not go down at all well with anyone.

And he repeats this message about climate change policies. "I am 100% on it" he says. But as Gaia Vince writes in *The Observer* (9th June) these are the questions you should be asking him:-

- How many reservoirs are you planning for the chronically drought-affected south-east?
- What plans have you got for the future influx of climate migrants who will arrive from the tropics?
- What strategy have you got in place to deal with the ever-increasing deaths of fish and insects?
- When are you going to make it mandatary for all new housing stock to have solar roof panels and adequate insulation?
- When will you be massively increasing investment in electrification with renewables, heat pumps, onshore wind and grid infrastructure?
- Why are you still backing the fossil fuel industry?
- What exactly is your 100% plan?

****

But I now have to bring this book to a close. I know there will be more negligence, more incompetence and more cruelty before this government is kicked out of office.

But I first started writing these books in July 2019 and enough is enough.

I can assure you that this period of governance will be seen as the most shameful in our history. The last Conservative prime minister who had any vision at all was Sir John Major. Every Tory prime minster since then has failed this once great country of ours. They want the power but not the responsibility or the accountability. All of the men have come from Eton or Winchester which doesn't say much for the education of our public schools. The two women, I'm afraid, were just completely out of their depth and totally unsuited for the job.

To be prime minister of the UK you need to be passionate about what you want to do to make it a better place for everyone. You must have a clear vision of how you want the UK to look both at home and abroad and you need to devise a road map which will show you and others how that goal will be achieved.

You need to surround yourself with good people who know what they are talking about and you need to realise that it is not about you. It is about the integrity and compassion and hard work of those around you. And it is about the people of this country who are trying hard to survive when all the odds have been stacked against them. So you need to show leadership and talk to the people of the UK.

We need a general election and we need one soon. I hope with all my heart that we will then be on the long road to recovery. Politicians need to remember they are only there because we put them there. So we need to be very careful about the choices we make. Discard all prejudice, open your eyes and see clearly what your options are.

To quote Kenan Malik of *The Observer* "**Those who try to limit democracy don't begin by scrapping elections.** They begin rather by allowing people to put a cross on a ballot paper every four or five years, but placing restrictions on the right to protest, to take collective action, to speak freely. From Russia to Belarus to Saudi Arabia that is the playbook of authoritarians."

He ends his article by saying that when Lee Anderson MP was questioned about the arrests during the coronation Anderson said so many people had supported this and he dismissed the protesters as 'trouble causers'. "That may be true," says Mr. Malik. "**But what is also true is that it's trouble causers who help keep democracy alive.**"

****

And then there are these words written by another eminent journalist Sean O'Grady of *The Independent*. He has been writing for *The Independent's* titles since 1998 and before that was working in parliament, in the City and for the BBC. Believe me he knows what he is talking about.

He begins his article by saying that the Tory party as we know it will be extinct in two years.

It is indeed true that the Conservative party of old was the most successful party in the history of democratic politics and has in fact governed Britain for the great majority of the last century and more. But today? Well it is obvious to me and I hope to you after reading these books that it is no longer a reputable party of economic stability and infinite wisdom.

As Mr. O'Grady says "it has a terrible whiff of decay about it right now. The next two or three years will bring existential threats – crushing defeat followed by disarray, and then a schism."

"The party," he says, "is moving away from the mood and instincts of the British people; and there are forces at work that will make that alienation more permanent."

Then he goes on to write the most incredible paragraph ever.

"Whatever the polls show, the effect of widespread tactical voting will be to turbocharge them into oblivion. It will make Blair's landslide in 1997 look like a rehearsal. It will in fact be the worst showing for the Tories since the dawn of modern politics in 1832. Let that sink in, as they say." Oh it has sunk in Mr. O'Grady, it has!

472

He says that the party is actually loathed, which is very true, and he thinks they will split four ways.

If, as we are all thinking, Suella Braverman gets the leadership when Sunak is dumped as he surely will be, the party will go headlong further to the right. "The agenda," says Mr. O'Grady, "would be **to renegotiate Brexit, but make it even harder, even purer and even worse than the present deal – a terrifying prospect**. The Braverman party will be demanding "more Brexit", not less,

"As if banging on about Europe wasn't enough, we know what else she'll be obsessed by. Migration, the European Court of Human Rights, abortion, divorce, race, trans-rights, the BBC, hanging, multiculturalism, risible and unfunny Johnson tribute act attacks on some mythical tofu-eating elite. Plus wanting a rehash of the disastrous Truss-Kwarteng economic experiment of huge unfunded tax cuts. Or else turning the NHS and the welfare state into a pauper's "safety net". Protectionism. More limits on protest and the right to strike.

Suellaland is a hostile environment for the rest of us."

So you have been warned.

"Meanwhile, to borrow a phrase, Labour and Starmer will be "getting on with the job". Without any effort whatsoever, the Labour front bench – Rayner, Reeves, Streeting, Ashworth – will look responsible and conscientious next to the Tory front bench."

To which I will add, Yvette Cooper, Bridget Phillipson, David Lammy, Anneliese Dodds, Emily Thornberry and Jim McMahon.

This government is in an ever increasing downward spiral and everyone seems to be aware of this except themselves.

And as I complete my trilogy I just say to you, all of you, protect our children. Stand up for them, write to your MP about them, be angry, be active and maybe I will meet you outside parliament with our placards! It will take a long time to repair the damage this government has done to our country but with honest sensible people at the top it can be done. And as I write these words I have just seen Sir Keir Starmer give the speech of his life and so I can finish with the two main causes closest to my heart: the NHS and our children. As someone has said, he spoke more sense about the NHS in one hour than the Tories have in 13 years. The NHS is certainly safe in his hands. And he said that our children's health is important to him. There will be breakfast clubs for every primary school child, they will ban advertisements for sugar, fats and vaping and they will target misogyny and threats to women and children on social media.

Labour won't be perfect and I am sure I will be critical of some of their plans but we desperately need them to take over and stop the ongoing destruction of the UK.

****

But I leave you with these words which are a fitting finale to this book.

On the 3rd June there was an astonishing article by David Maddox, Political Editor of *The Daily Express*.

He was writing about the summer recess.

He was saying that many MPs think they will have nearly 3 months away from Westminster this summer. They start the summer recess on the 20th July and would normally return 2 weeks before the Conservative Party Conference which this year is at the beginning of October. But a Conservative former cabinet minister told *The Express* that: "I know they have set the dates, but **I really would not be surprised if we are not back in September and wait until after the party conferences.**" One Conservative backbencher said: "I've stopped telling my whip if I am going to come in or not. **Very little is happening and we are really doing the minimum.** At the moment, I can be more productive by just staying in my constituency, doing casework and surveys. There's very little to come in for. I don't even see why we would come back in September. There's nothing to do here."

A Labour former minister said: "It has the feel of the end of the Gordon Brown government when we seemed to have run out of ideas and steam. People talk about zombie governments and this definitely is one."

So there we have it. A nonfunctioning government. A vacuum. Inadequate, ignorant and incredibly stupid. It is unbelievable. And in the future people won't believe it. But it is all written down in my books. Month by month, week by week, day by day and sometimes hour by hour and minute by minute. It is all here in black and white. I acknowledge that it is a despairing scenario but it is important to record it all as we must never allow this to happen again.

Be alert. Be concerned. Be involved. We all deserve better than this and these people must never be allowed anywhere near government again. Listen to the philosophers of old and take note.

Plato said:-

"If you do not take an interest in the affairs of your government, then you are doomed to live under the rule of fools."

****

But wait. I hear two items of news which warm my heart. In the first I listen to Sir Keir Starmer talking about how important music was to him as a child. He played the recorder, the piano the violin and the flute. He was a junior scholar at the London Guildhall School of Music. **Mozart** was his favourite composer then and now he listens to **Beethoven** and **Brahms** in order to unwind. He strongly supports music and the arts generally in schools.

This is unprecedented. It has actually been written about in the 'Thunderer' column in *The Times*. I have never heard these words spoken by an MP, let alone a future PM, before. Classical music? Music in schools? The well-being of children?

And before I get over my shock and excitement I then hear this.

It is a message from that unfailingly polite and courteous man Michel Barnier, the French diplomat.

He writes that "As long as the United Kingdom, as it has chosen to be, remains out of the single market and the customs union, there will be barriers in our trade and economic relationship."

But he goes on to say that, **"Progress is possible"**.

He writes that, "Brexit treaties can be completed by other agreements in key sectors where Mr. Johnson refused to negotiate. I am thinking of security, defence or cooperation over development matters.

"Despite being separated by Brexit and the Channel, we will be more efficient and stronger if we find in these areas and in others, including research, good cooperation between the European Union and the United Kingdom.

"The United Kingdom is a great country I have always admired and for which I have a lot of respect. While I still believe Brexit is negative, I think it is now time to move forward."

So more welcome news.

****

And whilst it is good to end on a slightly positive note I bring this trilogy to a close and say to all who will ask, why did this Conservative government collapse so drastically, the reasons are all here with its massive swerve to the right.

I do believe that there is hope for a better future. Our children and our grand-children depend on it. But it is going to take time. The destruction to every aspect of our lives by an un-caring and inadequate government has been unprecedented.

The previous Conservative prime ministers have been dangerous in their unsuitability for the highest office in the land. We have had Cameron the betrayer, May the robot, Johnson the clown, Truss the lettuce and Sunak the puppet.

It is more important than ever before to make your voices heard.

I leave it, all of it, with you.

****

ACKNOWLEDGEMENTS

I want to say a huge thank you once again to all journalists and columnists everywhere. The accurate and fearless reporting of news is more important than ever before.

My thanks go to;

The Times
Sky News
The Sunday Times
LBC
The Financial Times
Channel 4
The Sun
The Good Law Project
The Guardian
The i
The Observer
Care4Calais

The Independent
Politics home
The Evening Standard
Twitter
The Mirror
HuffPost
The Daily Mail
openDemocracy
The Daily Telegraph
Left Foot Forward
The Express
The Canary

Many, many people, charities and protest groups have been credited throughout this text and if I have left anyone out I apologise. But without all of you this book could never have been written.

ABOUT THE AUTHOR

Sue Wood was born and brought up in a medical family in Coventry. She was educated in Leamington Spa and Maria Grey Froebel College in Twickenham. She worked as a Primary school teacher in Coventry and Cambridge and then took a break from teaching and worked as Director of Public Relations at Coventry Cathedral. After her wedding there she moved with her husband first to Abu Dhabi and then to Aberdeen. She is now settled in Hertfordshire with her husband and has two children and two grand-children.

She returned to teaching, first in Bushey and then in Elstree. On retiring she became a volunteer Speaker for Save the Children. She has always been concerned about those whom she feels are being treated unjustly and has been a member of the Howard league for Penal Reform for nearly 30 years.

She started writing at the age of 10 when her American aunt gave her a 5 year diary, and she has written many books for family and friends. Her first two published books for the general public are:-

Beneath the Bluster. A Diary of Despair. Ignorance, Incompetence, Confusion and Lies. The Conservative Government 2019-2021" and

Behind the Headlines. A Parallel Universe. Arrogance, Corruption, Dither and Delay. The Conservative Government 2021-2022".

She has always been interested in news and politics, and these three books together cover the most shameful period in the history of the UK.

BV - #0007 - 140923 - C0 - 229/152/27 - PB - 9781916572256 - Gloss Lamination